**DO NOT REMOVE
CARDS FROM POCKET**

Baudelaire in Russia

BAUDELAIRE IN RUSSIA

Adrian Wanner

UNIVERSITY PRESS OF FLORIDA

GAINESVILLE

TALLAHASSEE

TAMPA

BOCA RATON

PENSACOLA

ORLANDO

MIAMI

JACKSONVILLE

01   00   99   98   97   96   6   5   4   3   2   1

Library of Congress Cataloging-in-Publication Data

Wanner, Adrian, 1960–
    Baudelaire in Russia / Adrian Wanner.
        p.   cm.
    Includes bibliographical references and index.
    ISBN 0–8130–1423–9 (cloth: alk. paper)
    1. Baudelaire, Charles, 1821–1867—Appreciation—Russia.
    2. Russia—Intellectual life—1801–1917. I. Title.
    PQ2191.Z5W26   1996   95-32663
    841'.8—dc20   CIP

The University Press of Florida is the scholarly publishing agency for the
State University System of Florida, comprised of Florida A & M University,
Florida Atlantic University, Florida International University, Florida State
University, University of Central Florida, University of Florida, University of
North Florida, University of South Florida, and University of West Florida.

University Press of Florida
15 Northwest 15th Street
Gainesville, FL 32611

To my parents, Rosette and Oscar Wanner

CONTENTS

Charles Baudelaire (1821–67) has become a legendary presence in many parts of the world as a seminal provider of poetic inspiration and charismatic icon of a peculiar personality cult. As the title of this book suggests, I explore the variegated and idiosyncratic reaction to Baudelaire in Russia, which began earlier than anywhere else in Europe and reached its culmination at the beginning of the twentieth century during the so-called Silver Age of Russian culture. While several book-length studies in the past have dealt with Baudelaire's reception in other countries,[1] no comprehensive investigation of the Russian response has ever been undertaken before, in spite of its amazingly early inception and unusual intensity. The only aspect of Baudelaire's Russian legacy that has received some scholarly attention is the impact, real or imaginary, that he exerted on Russian symbolism.[2] The symbolists certainly counted some devoted "Baudelaireans" among their ranks, and the notion of "correspondences," inspired by Baudelaire's sonnet, became an omnipresent slogan and catchword in the first decade of the twentieth century. As a consequence, Baudelaire's name is mentioned frequently in the critical literature on Russian symbolism. Yet in many cases these references amount to hardly more than name-dropping, perhaps in an unconscious imitation of the Russian symbolists' habit of dropping Baudelaire's name. There is a general *impression* of Baudelaire's importance, although this impression has more the status of a rumor than of an established fact. The Baudelaire scholars Robert Kopp and Claude Pichois, for example, wrote in their literature survey on the occasion of the one-hundredth anniversary of the poet's death in 1967 "Baudelaire's reception in the Slavic world is a practically unexplored topic, although of an amazing richness: up to 1917, Baudelaire's influence *seems* to have prevailed over that of all other French poets."[3] A puzzlingly different claim was made seven years later by Pierre Trahard, who asserted that "Baudelaire's poetry is so contrary to the Slavic spirit, so disruptive to the Russian ideal, his satanism mixed with eroticism so offensive to the simple and pious souls in the country of icons with their little light burning from time immemorial, that it has no effect and is only of interest to specialists."[4]

More than anything else, it was the desire to find out "what really happened" and to cut through the tangled web of stereotypes, superficial impressions, and unsubstantiated claims that prompted my research for this book. Not surprisingly, I found some of the received truisms to be in need of revision (after all, Baudelaire himself would have been amazed to learn that he was a "symbolist poet"). I hope that my investigation will yield new insights into the cultural interrelation of Russia with the West at a crucial stage of its intellectual history. Methodologically, my study belongs to the field of reader-response criticism, which, after the reign of author-centered positivism and text-centered formalism, has become a central focus of literary theory. However, it is not my aim here to prove, or disprove, a specific theory of reception but to document a concrete case history and to analyze and expose some of the myths it bore. Because of its interdisciplinary character, I believe this study will have relevance for literary historians of Russia and France alike. It should also interest comparatists, literary theorists and critics, translators of poetry, and, last but not least I hope, aficionados of Baudelaire.

My own interest in Baudelaire goes back to my school days in Switzerland when, in an experience similar to the one decribed by the Russian translator P. F. Yakubovich, *Les Fleurs du Mal* "immediately captured me with its strange and powerful mood."[5] In an embryonic form, my book began as a *Lizentiatsarbeit* (master's thesis) under the direction of Professor Peter Brang at the Slavisches Seminar of Zurich University. A Swiss-Soviet exchange scholarship enabled me to spend a year in the Soviet Union, where I conducted research in various libraries and archives. I am especially grateful to my Soviet adviser, Professor A. B. Muratov of what was then Leningrad State University, for helping me gain access to the manuscript division of Pushkinskii Dom, the Russian Literature Institute of the Academy of Sciences (IRLI) in St. Petersburg. The "Kartoteka Bakhtina" kept at this institution, a rather chaotic-looking file of jumbled handwritten notes, proved an invaluable bibliographical tool for Baudelaire's reception up to the 1920s. Useful help was provided also by the "Kartoteka Umikian" in the Russian National Library (formerly the Saltykov-Shchedrin Library) in St. Petersburg. In Moscow, the intervention of the Swiss Embassy's cultural attaché, Dr. Pircher, was crucial in securing access to the Russian State Archive of Literature and Art (RGALI, formerly TsGALI) and to the manuscript division of the Russian State Library (the former Lenin Library), where I was able to consult Valery Bryusov's unpublished translations of Baudelaire, which are presented in the appendix of this book.

Having moved to the United States, I later developed my research into a Ph.D. thesis at Columbia University. I am grateful to my advisers, Richard Gustafson, Robert Belknap, and Robert Maguire, and the two French department readers, Antoine Compagnon and Serge Gavronsky, for their competent help and advice. In addition, I owe a particular debt to Bernice Rosenthal, who read the entire manuscript and offered numerous comments and helpful suggestions. Many others have read parts or all of my manuscript and provided useful advice. For words of wisdom and encouragement, I thank Rosamund Bartlett, Natalya Bochkaryova, Pamela Davidson, Roman Doubrovkine, Boris Gasparov, Claude Pichois, Irina Reyfman, Carol Ueland, Leonid Vaintraub, Michael Wachtel, and my colleagues Bill Hemminger and David Gugin. Most of all I thank my wife, Cathy, for her unflinching support, patience, and love. For financial support of my research, I am indebted to Columbia University, the Swiss Benevolent Society of New York, the S. Giles Whiting Foundation, and the University of Evansville. A previous version of the portion of chapter 1 on P. F. Yakubovich has appeared under the title "Populism and Romantic Agony: A Russian Terrorist's Discovery of Baudelaire" in *Slavic Review* 52, no. 2 (Summer 1993). I thank the American Association for the Advancement of Slavic Studies for permission to use it here.

NOTE ON THE SPELLING OF RUSSIAN NAMES

I am using the Library of Congress System of transliteration with certain modifications to make the text more accessible to non-Slavist readers (e.g., "Gorky" rather than "Gor'kii," "Gumilyov" rather than "Gumilev," "Mandelstam" rather than "Mandel'shtam," "Yakubovich" rather than "Iakubovich"). However, in all bibliographical entries, I adhere to the Library of Congress system without modifications. Russian titles and texts published before 1917 are quoted in modernized orthography.

Introduction

The reputation of Charles Baudelaire as a revolutionary figure in the history of European literature, if not as the father of modern poetry *tout court*, has become firmly ingrained in the mythology of twentieth-century culture. In his landmark essay "Situation de Baudelaire" (1924), Paul Valéry pointed out, not without a whiff of French chauvinism, that "with Baudelaire, French poetry finally steps out of its national borders. It is read in the world, it imposes itself as the poetry of modernity itself, it generates imitation, it fertilizes numerous minds."[1] Valéry considered Baudelaire, if not the greatest or most gifted, certainly the most *important* French poet. T. S. Eliot, who promoted Baudelaire in the English-speaking world as enthusiastically as Baudelaire himself had promoted Edgar Allan Poe, concurred with this opinion, hailing his French idol as "the greatest exemplar in *modern* poetry in any language, for his verse and language is the nearest thing to a complete renovation that we have experienced."[2]

In probing the nature and impact of Baudelaire's proclaimed revolutionary modernity, the reaction of the readers of Russia deserves particular attention. Having experienced both political and aesthetic convulsions of considerable magnitude, Russia has replaced France as the revolutionary country par excellence in the twentieth century. In Russia, dithyrambic praise of Baudelaire could be heard and read two decades before Valéry and Eliot. Andrey Bely celebrated the French poet together with Nietzsche in 1909 as a "patriarch of symbolism";[3] Valery Bryusov, the *chef d'école* of the Russian symbolists, wrote in the same year: "Is it possible to question the importance of Baudelaire's *Fleurs du Mal* for the formation of the whole worldview of modernity?"[4] Ellis (L. L. Kobylinsky), the most zealous of all Russian symbolist "Baudelaireans," even tried to convince the Menshevik Social Democrat N. V. Volsky that Baudelaire was "the greatest revolutionary of the nineteenth century, in comparison with whom all Marxes, Engelses, Bakunins, and the rest of the brotherhood which they created, are simply nothing."[5]

However, the symbolist enthusiasm for Baudelaire should not mislead one about the character of his first discoverers in Russia. What has been largely overlooked so far is the fact that the symbolists had by no means a "monopoly" on Baudelaire. The poet was discovered in Russia before the awakening of symbolism in the 1890s. In fact, the earliest Russian Baudelaireans were members of the radical intelligentsia of the 1860s and 1870s who had little in common with discoverers of Baudelaire such as Verlaine and Rimbaud in France, Swinburne in England, or Stefan George in Germany. Remarkably, the first Russian edition of Baudelaire's poetry was prepared by a convicted terrorist of the People's Will Party, P. F. Yakubovich, while he was in a Siberian labor camp. If some of Baudelaire's earliest followers in Russia were rather anti-symbolists than symbolists, the same holds true for his later admirers among the acmeist and futurist avant-garde. Russian "Baudelairism" is a phenomenon that exceeds the boundaries of symbolism. In fact, perhaps the most striking feature in the Russian response to Baudelaire is the surprisingly various images of the French poet. Baudelaire was seen in turn as a social critic, decadent, symbolist, revolutionary, reactionary, aestheticist, pornographer, nihilist, and religious prophet. Like Nietzsche, with whom he has much in common, Baudelaire appealed to members of both the "progressive" and the "decadent" camp. As do the changing colors of litmus paper, Baudelaire's metamorphoses indicate the character of the milieu in which he was immersed.

Of course, the contradictory, mutually exclusive character of many Russian judgments should be less of a surprise if we keep in mind that no *unité de doctrine* has emerged from the ever increasing Western flood of Baudelaire criticism either. All attempts, Russian or Western, to detect in Baudelaire's poetry and thought a unifying "figure in the carpet" (such as "Baudelaire the Catholic" or "Baudelaire the social critic") seem eternally frustrated by an inconsistency perhaps fatally inherent in a character who once claimed self-contradiction as a human right: "Among the rights which have been talked about in recent times, there is one which has been forgotten, the demonstration of which is in everybody's interest—the right to contradict oneself."[6]

Not surprisingly in light of this statement, no unanimity has ever been reached as to the exact nature of the Baudelairean "revolution." In his influential study on the structure of the modern lyric, which was later translated into twelve languages, the German scholar Hugo Friedrich defined Baudelaire's seminal modernity in mostly negative terms such as "depersonalization," "aesthetics of ugliness," "ruinous Christianity," "empty ideality," "decomposition and deformation," and "abstraction and arabesque." This emphasis on the "destructive" potential of Baudelaire's poetics is also shared by critics with a keener interest in the social implications of literature. Walter Benjamin has pointed to Baudelaire's "shock value" as a lyric poet in the era of high capitalism with his particular use of allegory, where the objects of the world have become commodities that can be invested only with contingent meaning. The American Marxist Fredric Jameson, in terms that seem yet another variation of Friedrich's influential paradigm, has approached Baudelaire's modernity in terms of the "dissolution of the referent" and the production of an "artificial sublime."[7]

While these may all be valid descriptions of Baudelaire's modernity, they still do not explain why someone would venture to call him a more potent revolutionary than Marx, Engels, or Bakunin. Despite claims to the contrary, poetical and political radicalism seem more often to be mutually exclusive than to work in tandem. It is well known that some of the most important Russian revolutionaries, including V. I. Lenin, tended to be aesthetically conservative philistines, whereas the aesthetic revolutionary Baudelaire at times expressed reactionary political views. Some Russian radicals such as G. V. Plekhanov, the founder of Marxism in Russia, in fact rejected Baudelaire for his conservative political stand. Amazingly enough, however, the revolutionary populist P. F. Yakubovich, despite his hostility toward modernist poetry and his knowledge of Baudelaire's contempt for progressive values, still embraced him as his favorite poet and role model.

Baudelaire's revolutionary significance must have meant very different things to different readers. It becomes clear that, rather than being a quality inherent in specific texts, the Baudelairean revolution is a phenomenon of reader response. In this sense, a study about Russian readings of Baudelaire is an investigation of a chapter of Russian literary history rather than a contribution to Baudelaire criticism. This is not to say, of course, that it cannot be illuminating also for our understanding of Baudelaire's texts, especially if we share the hermeneutic assumption of the Constance School that the potential meaning (*Sinnpotential*) of a text is only accessible through the unfolding of its infinite succession of readings, or even more if we agree with Stanley Fish that it is essentially the reader who "writes" the text.[8] To be sure, whomever Baudelaire had in mind with his famous "Hypocrite lecteur,-mon semblable,-mon frère!," he was hardly thinking of a Russian reader. Trying to give a definitive answer to the question of how "adequate" are the Russian readings of Baudelaire raises difficult issues of validity in interpretation.

The "meaning" of Baudelaire's texts is understood in this study neither as the author's intention nor as an abstract significance emanating from the text per se, but as the effect of a text on an interpretive community. My concern is what Baudelaire meant to Russian readers in a specific historic context. The reader's response was conditioned by a complicated conglomerate of both extra- and intraliterary factors, from government intervention (censorship!) and political prejudices to genre expectations based on the internal evolution of Russian literature. Yet it would be naive to believe that they can be disentangled entirely and the process of reception rendered transparent and predictable. We must keep in mind that each reader is a reservoir full of experience, knowledge, feelings, and expectations. We have to reckon with the possibility of idiosyncratic, possibly irrational, reactions.

For obvious reasons, this study can be concerned only with a subgroup of Baudelaire's Russian readers: those who not only read him but *produced texts* in reaction to their reading (some people, incidentally, seem to have produced texts on Baudelaire without having read him). These texts belong to various genres: letters, diaries, censorship reports, book reviews, encyclopedia entries, psychiatric studies, critical essays, monographs, translations, imitations, parodies, and so on. A rigorous classification of these documents poses certain problems. Some theoreticians have tried to establish a distinction between "reproductive" and "productive" reception, with the latter category reserved for writers or poets, who use their reading as an inspiration for their own creative endeavor.[9] However, it seems often difficult to distinguish between reproduction and production. Balmont's and Annensky's "impressionist" literary criticism, to name just one example, would have to be characterized as a productive mode of reception within a reproductive genre. The distinction becomes even more illusory if we believe, as Harold Bloom does, that "all criticism is prose poetry."[10]

Another traditional dichotomy in comparatist reception studies has been the opposition of "fortune" and "influence." The most authoritative French introduction to comparative literature defines *succès* (fortune) as a quantitative phenomenon that implies a passive reader and *influence* as a qualitative phenomenon that implies an active reader.[11] This distinction also raises certain problems. Besides the fact that a "passive reader," in the light of current reader response theory, seems to be a *contradictio in adiecto,* it is impossible to keep track of one even if such a party exists, since a passive reader is by definition a mute reader. It is possible, to be sure, to make statements about the availability of texts to a certain public. The spate of Baudelaire editions in Russia in the first decade of our century and their complete absence from Soviet bookstores up to 1966 certainly had a bearing on Baudelaire's "fortune." Since Russia had more or less a market economy before 1917, we can infer that his frequent publication responded to a genuine interest of the Russian reading public. The lack of publications in the Soviet Union, conversely, does not necessarily indicate a diminished interest, since the production of books in this country did not follow the law of supply and demand. It is interesting to note that the first Soviet edition of Baudelaire's poetry, 50,000 copies published in 1966, was sold out within *hours.*

A prominent role in comparative reception studies is usually given to the analysis of translations, since it is through them that an author becomes accessible to a foreign audience. Translations often shape the reception in a decisive fashion (a case in point would be the Schlegel/Tieck translation of Shakespeare in Germany). The situation is somewhat different in our case. Since a knowledge of French was widespread in educated nineteenth-century Russian society, virtually all Russian readers of Baudelaire discussed here were able to read him in the original. This cultural "openness" had certain consequences: the Russian public was familiar not only with French primary literature but also with literary criticism. The essays of Théophile Gautier and Paul Bourget, for example, influential documents for Baudelaire's reception in France, also had an impact on his Russian reception. It is impossible to study the Russian readings of Baudelaire without taking into account his French reception and status as a legend. The situation changed in the Soviet period, when a knowledge of French could no longer be taken for granted even among educated members of society and Baudelaire was accessible to most readers only through the screen of translations. Marina Tsvetayeva's rendering of "Le Voyage," written in 1940 after the poet returned to the Soviet Union, has made this poem perhaps Baudelaire's most popular work in Russia today.[12]

Most Russian poets who translated Baudelaire did not do it with the intention of rendering a service to readers who did not know French. They saw the translation of poetry as a challenge *sui generis* and as a worthy task for its own sake, as Valery Bryusov made clear:

Pushkin, Tyutchev, Fet, of course, did not engage in translations out of philanthropic desire (*iz zhelaniia "posluzhit' men'shei bratii"*), out of indulgence for insufficiently educated people who did not study or did not study enough German, English, or Latin. Poets are attracted to the translation of verses by a purely artistic problem: to render in their own language what captivated them in a foreign tongue; they are attracted by the wish to "feel what is foreign as one's own for a moment," the wish to possess this foreign treasure. Beautiful verses are like a challenge to the poets of other nations: to show that their language too is capable of accommodating the same creative idea.[13]

Any translation of a poem is a "reading," and its analysis can give us insights into the underlying values and assumptions of the reader. To study the Russian translations of Baudelaire is all the more rewarding as there are several major poets who engaged in this endeavor. It is particularly interesting to confront various translations of a single text, since in such a confrontation, as in a phonological minimal pair, the distinctive features of the translators emerge more clearly. My goal is not an analysis of these translations in their totality—a task that would include the systematic survey of all their semantic and formal features—but rather to show their typicality in the context of a larger pattern of reception. Although I will not shy away from value judgments—some translations clearly *are* better than others—I am less interested in the question how, or if, the meaning of the original is preserved than how it is *transformed* through the process of translation. Harold Bloom contended that every strong reading is a misreading; one could also argue that every strong translation of a poem is a mistranslation. In this sense, the process of translation would be better described as a form of creative writing than the attempt to create an ever elusive "equivalence." As Douglas Robinson has argued in his recent book *The Translator's Turn*, translation is ultimately more a "somatic" than a cerebral activity.

Phenomenological parallels between Baudelaire and Russian writers, if they are not based on direct reception, are beyond the scope of my investigation. A case in point is Dostoyevsky, who was born in the same year as Baudelaire and shares many features with him.[14] However, it seems Dostoyevsky never read Baudelaire, except for his translations of Poe.[15] Quite a different problem, of course, is the fact that the comparison of Baudelaire with Dostoyevsky became a topos of Russian Baudelaire criticism in the 1890s. If Dostoyevsky as a reader is not an object of this study, the overlapping of his reception with Baudelaire's certainly is. The legacy of Dostoyevsky, or rather the symbolist reading of his work by D. S. Merezhkovsky and others, was a conditioning factor for the Russian reception of Baudelaire at the end of the nineteenth century.

Is there any pattern to the way the Russians read Baudelaire? I will try to impose some order to the seeming chaos of Russian Baudelairism by identifying four principal modes of reading that were operative in Russia: social, decadent, symbolist, and formalist. Chronologically, these approaches follow each other, although they can also coexist and in some cases overlap. In fact, there are dialectical relationships among them: decadence was a reaction against, and antithesis to, the social mode of reading propagated by the radical critics. The symbolist mode, although stylistically an outgrowth of decadence, rejected decadence in the name of a higher "truth," returning with the notion of *sobornost'* to some of the concerns of the social readers. Formalism in its turn was a rejection of both religious mysticism and social propaganda and, ultimately, of any "content-oriented" reading.

The four chapters of this book follow these four modes of reading. Chapter 1, "Searching for Social Relevance," deals with Baudelaire's discovery by the Russian *narodniki* (populists) and, in particular, with P. F. Yakubovich (1860–1911), the most devoted populist Baudelairean. It also addresses the Marxist approach, both pre- and post-1917, and discusses the convolutions and contortions of Soviet Baudelaire criticism, which can be characterized as a perverted outgrowth of the nineteenth-century social approach. Chapter 2, "The Decadent Response," analyzes Baudelaire's impact on the genesis of Russian decadence in the 1880s and 1890s as well as some later decadents such as Innokenty Annensky. It also includes a discussion of the violent anti-decadent backlash triggered by the psychiatrist Max Nordau and sustained by a heterogeneous alliance of such various figures as Konstantin Pobedonostsev, Lev Tolstoy, and many critics of the political left. Chapter 3, "The 'Younger Symbolists,'" is devoted to Vyacheslav Ivanov and Ellis (L. L. Kobylinsky, 1870–1947), probably the most fanatic Baudelairean of all time. Although Ivanov and Ellis had some common concerns (both of them converted to Catholicism), it will be shown that their approach to Baudelaire differed considerably, which perhaps demonstrates that a unified religious reading of Baudelaire remains a problematic endeavor. Chapter 4, "Toward Modernity," addresses the incipient formalist approach to Baudelaire in the critical writings of Andrey Bely (who, although frequently classified as a mystic, is here seen as a demystifier) as well as in the essays and translations of the acmeist Nikolay Gumilyov and the cubo-futurist Benedikt Livshits. The conclusion tries to give a general assessment of Baudelaire's influence on Russian literature.

While there is nothing exclusively Russian about any of the four modes of reading discussed here (all of them can be found at various periods in Western Europe), the timing of their appearance deserves attention. The Russian reception of Baudelaire is distinguished by its amazing precocity. Baudelaire was translated earlier into Russian than into any other language. He was discussed in the Russian press at a time when he was not yet well known even in his own country. Frequently, the Russians seem to have anticipated trends that became productive in the West only much later. For example, the social concerns of the narodniki and early Russian Marxists became a focus of Western Baudelaire criticism only in the wake of Walter Benjamin. N. Valentinov claims that he learned nothing from Marcel Ruff (the most distinguished French Catholic interpreter of Baudelaire) that Ellis had not already explained to him half a century before.[16] Vyacheslav Ivanov, in his essay "Two Elements in Modern Symbolism" (1908), postulated a fundamental dichotomy between two opposed kinds of "correspondences" that anticipates Jean Pommier's *La Mystique de Baudelaire* (1932) by twenty-four years. Sometimes, Western Baudelaire critics seem to reinvent wheels that were invented in Russia long before but, because of the widespread ignorance of things Russian, remained unknown in the West. Surely it is no accident that the Russian discovery of Baudelaire coincided with one of the most dynamic periods of Russian culture, a time of ferment and experimentation and of artistic and political upheaval, culminating in the overthrow of all received standards of artistic expression. It is not astonishing that the Russians of this period were attracted by, and capable of responding to, a creative mind who in many ways was himself ahead of his time.

CHAPTER 1

Searching for Social Relevance

In his magisterial history of Russian literature, Victor Terras has identified the "persistent claim to a social function" as the "one trait of Russian literature that distinguishes it from the major literatures of the West."[1] With a few notable exceptions, Russia has never proved fertile ground for doctrines of pure art. A pronounced sense of the social relevance of poetry and fiction has long been the hallmark of Russian literature and literary criticism. This is especially true for the mid-nineteenth century, the period in which Baudelaire made his first appeareance in Russia. Influenced by such critics as Vissarion Belinsky, Nikolay Chernyshevsky, and Nikolay Dobrolyubov, the prevalent tendency in Russian criticism consisted of stressing political correctness (as it would nowadays be called) over aesthetic value.

There are concrete historical reasons accounting for this particular attitude. Because of censorship restrictions imposed by the autocratic government, fiction and poetry were left as the only outlets for discussing issues that in other nations would have been raised in the political press. The reading public was accustomed to looking for aesopian clues to contemporary problems in works of a seemingly purely aesthetic character. This encouraged the tendency for an instrumental reading even of such a poet as Baudelaire, who declared in his diary that he abhorred the idea of being considered a "useful man."[2] To be sure, a social approach to Baudelaire is not necessarily devoid of merit. Despite Baudelaire's declared contempt for utilitarian concerns, it would be mistaken to dismiss any such reading as incompatible with his intentions. Any isolated statement by Baudelaire is likely to be contradicted by other passages. It is worth noting that Baudelaire also condemned the idea of art for art's sake as a "puérile utopie" and praised the mediocre but "progressive" worker-poet Pierre Dupont.[3]

After an initial preoccupation with the decadent, Catholic, and modernist Baudelaire, Western criticism in recent years has begun to focus more on the social and political aspects of his work, thanks in part to the pioneering studies of Walter Benjamin. Neither Benjamin nor anyone else paid much attention to the fact that this approach was practiced in Russia long before it became fashionable in the West. Not only was Baudelaire translated earlier into Russian than into any other language, but it was in Russia that his oeuvre was for the first time subjected to a social reading. The earliest Russian readers and translators of Baudelaire may appear unsophisticated and naive in modern eyes. Yet, they still deserve credit as the forgotten pioneers of an approach to Baudelaire adopted in the West many years later.

FIRST ENCOUNTERS AND TRANSLATIONS

In March 1869, the venerable flagship journal of radical populism, Nekrasov and Saltykov-Shchedrin's *Otechestvennye zapiski* (Notes of the Fatherland), published the first Russian verse translation of a poem by Baudelaire. It was a rather free rendering of "Les Petites Vieilles" written by the populist poet and translator N. S. Kurochkin (1830–84). Incidentally, this first Russian verse translation of a poem by Baudelaire appeared in the same year as the first English translation. It was not, however, the first encounter of the Russian reading public with Baudelaire. Baudelaire's name had become known in Russia earlier than in any other nation outside France. The Russian press began to pay attention to Baudelaire some years before the *succès de scandale* of *Les Fleurs du Mal*, at a time when he was still relatively unknown even in his own country.

Baudelaire's presence in Russia began in September 1852, when the journal *Panteon* in St. Petersburg published his first essay on Edgar Allan Poe[4]—the first translation of a text by Baudelaire into any language. *Panteon*, incidentally, is also the journal in which Dostoyevsky had made his literary début eight years before with his translation of Balzac's *Eugénie Grandet*. Baudelaire's article was reviewed, not very favorably, in the conservative journal *Moskvitianin* by Apollon Grigoryev.[5] Baudelaire's second essay on Poe, the foreword to his 1856 edition of the *Histoires extraordinaires*, was also translated into Russian and appeared in the same year in *Syn otechestva* (Son of the Fatherland).[6] To be sure, these publications are more significant for the Russian reception of Poe than for that of Baudelaire. As W. T. Bandy has shown, Baudelaire largely plagiarized his first essay from two American sources.[7] Although the second essay is significantly more original than the first one, it did nothing to further Baudelaire's reputation in Russia, as his name was omitted and no reference was given to the edition of short stories he introduced. A rather remarkable alteration occurred with the account of Poe's alleged visit to St. Petersburg: obviously in order to blame Poe's problems on the strictness not of Russian but of Austrian laws, the Russian translator relegated the whole episode to Vienna.[8]

It was *Otechestvennye zapiski* that played the most significant role in introducing Baudelaire to the Russian reading public. This journal was not only responsible for bringing out the first Russian verse translations; it also published a critical essay about him as early as 1856. Karl Stachel, a Parisian correspondent, offered a survey of contemporary European poetry to the Russian reader in the form of a letter to the editor. Stachel seems to have been personally acquainted with Baudelaire, whom he introduced together with Philoxène Boyer, Théodore de Banville, and Pierre Dupont in an account seasoned with gossip and anecdotes. Baudelaire is presented as a rather young man not well known by the general public and neglected in the press but highly esteemed by the connoisseurs of the literary scene (Baudelaire's first major publications, his Poe edition of 1856 and *Les Fleurs du Mal* of 1857, had not yet appeared). Remarkably, Stachel's article also contains the first publication (in French) of the poem "Le Flacon," which appeared in France only a year later. Stachel seems to have received the manuscript from Baudelaire himself.[9]

Otechestvennye zapiski is hardly a journal that one would expect to promote French avant-garde poetry. In 1856, when Stachel's article appeared, the journal had reached a rather low point in its history. Once the leading organ of the Westernizers with Belinsky and Nekrasov as staff writers, it had lost them and much of its importance to its rival *Sovremennik* (The Contemporary) in 1847. After 1866, however, when *Sovremennik* was closed down by the authorities, *Otechestvennye zapiski* was to make a comeback as the leading populist journal of the 1870s under the editorship of Nekrasov and Saltykov-Shchedrin. *Otechestvennye zapiski*, even while playing second fiddle to *Sovremennik*, brought out some important works in the 1850s, among them Pisemsky's *One Thousand Souls* (1858) and Goncharov's *Oblomov* (1859).

The literary doctrine promulgated by such Russian radical journals of the period shaped to a large degree the reader's horizon of expectation for Baudelaire's poetry. The French poet appeared on the Russian stage in the unpoetic era of realist novelists, when utilitarian criticism preached social relevance over aesthetic quality. Poetry was considered a genre of minor importance—at best, it was useful as a weapon of agitation and social struggle. The civic poetry of the period is characterized by a formal eclecticism and frequent use of clichés. Little effort was wasted on questions of poetic technique or aesthetic innovation. The only new elements in poetry were the use of popular prosaisms and borrowings from vaudeville plays; satiric feuilletons, parodies, and epigrams became the preferred genres. The same criteria of social relevance applied to foreign poets as well: the more they could be connected with some revolutionary message, as in the case of Byron, Heine, or Béranger, the better they fared with the radical critics.

How could a Russian radical of the 1860s and 1870s be attracted to Baudelaire, a poet who seems to be an antipode of all these attitudes? It is true, of course, that Baudelaire had a brief "radical" phase in his life, although his revolutionary enthusiasm of 1848 proved to be short lived. His later contempt for the notion of democratic "progress" and any form of utilitarianism seems diametrically opposed to the views of his first Russian translators. But his hatred for the bourgeois society of France and Belgium, his focus on the downtrodden *Lumpenproletariat* of Paris, and the rebellious overtones in the cycle "Révolte" provided at least some common ground. It is safe to assume, also, that his first Russian translators did not know much about him. For a Russian reader of this time, Baudelaire was one of many contemporary minor French poets, less important, certainly, than a Béranger, who in Vasily Kurochkin's translation had become a popular Russian civic poet. Baudelaire was known mainly for the scandal that had been caused by the publication of *Les Fleurs du Mal* and his subsequent trial and conviction for "offense aux moeurs publics." The prosecution of the poet by the philistines of the Second Empire was bound to endear him to the Russian radicals, since it made him appear as a fellow victim of oppression by an autocratic government. Baudelaire's "immorality" could in this context be welcomed as a positive challenge to a reactionary system.

An early example of a Russian translation of Baudelaire that seems typical for the radical approach is D. D. Minayev's "Abel et Caïn," published in 1870 in the satirical journal *Iskra* (Spark).[10] Dmitry Dmitrievich Minayev (1835–89) had graduated from the St. Petersburg Military Academy and had worked after 1857 as a freelance writer for journals like *Sovremennik*, *Russkoe slovo*, and *Iskra*. Besides his own numerous poems, he published translations from Byron, Shelley, Heine, Molière, Hugo, Barbier, Vigny, Musset, and Dante's *Divina Com-*

media.[11] Minayev belonged to the category of political translators, who saw in a poem mainly a weapon and in the translated poet an ally in his social struggle. An exact rendering of the original syntax and form was his last concern, as he declared himself: "The translator is obliged to render only the idea, the impression, the bouquet of the original—otherwise he becomes a colorless toiler, a pedant of the letter. . . . The external similarity to the original makes a translation only impersonal."[12]

"Abel et Caïn," from the section "Révolte" of *Les Fleurs du Mal,* is one of Baudelaire's most revolutionary poems. The romantic cliché of Cain as a proud rebel, which can be traced back to Byron, acquires here a sociopolitical dimension as the fight between two hostile clans: the exploiting "race d'Abel" and the exploited "race de Caïn." However, Baudelaire's polemic rebellion seems as much metaphysical as political. God himself is condemned as the one who bears reponsibility for injustice on earth, and the poem ends with the defiant call to topple him: "Race de Caïn, au ciel monte, / Et sur la terre jette Dieu!" (Race of Cain, rise up to heaven, and throw God down to earth).

Of course, it was inconceivable that the censor would have passed the publication of such blasphemous words. It is interesting to observe how Minayev tried to make the poem more acceptable by eliminating its metaphysical dimension. Any mention of God is strictly avoided: "Dieu te sourit complaisamment" (God smiles at you complacently, line 2) becomes "Fei dobrye pokoi tvoi okhraniat" (Good fairies guard your rest), and the last two lines are rendered as

Племя Каина! Ты встанешь—и тогда-то
Под твоим напором дрогнет шар земной.

Tribe of Cain! You will rise—and one day
The Earth will shake from your onslaught.

The religious rebellion is, so to speak, secularized, and the revolutionary imperative is toned down to a less dangerous prophecy. Other images that might be too shocking in their realistic coarseness are replaced with nebulous romantic formulas. "Ah! race d'Abel, ta charogne / engraissera le sol fumant!" (Ah! race of Abel, your decaying carcass will fertilize the steaming soil) becomes "Plemia Avelia! Svetlo tvoe byloe, / No griadushchego zagadka nam temna" (Tribe of Abel! Your past is radiant, but your future is a dark riddle for us). At the same time, Minayev's translation is a typical sample of Russian civic poetry with all its stereotypes and clichés. Thus we can find "Vopl' detei svoikh i stony chakhlykh zhen" (Wailing of children and moaning of sickly women), which does not exist in Baudelaire's text, and Baudelaire's sober observation "Race de Caïn, ta besogne / N'est pas faite suffisament" (Race of Cain, your job is not done sufficiently) turns into another pathetic prophecy:

Племя Каина! Терпи, и иго злое
Грозно сбросишь ты в иные времена.

Tribe of Cain! Endure, and you will thunderously
Shake off the evil yoke at a future time.

Although Minayev tried to avoid trouble by eliminating all religious elements from the poem, the censor still reacted ungraciously. The editorial board of *Iskra* received a sharp warning against publishing once again such "socialist and tendentious" verses. Minayev managed to fool the authorities in one sense, however: Baudelaire's authorship went unnoticed. The poem was believed to be a creation by Minayev himself, disguised as a fictitious translation, as we can see from the censorship report: "It is said that this is a translation from French, but it is obvious that this poem is nothing else but a tendentious fabrication of the denunciatory poet Mr. Minayev."[13]

If Baudelaire appears in Minayev's rendition as a poet of social protest and revolutionary propaganda, we get a somewhat different picture in N. S. Kurochkin's seven translations, which were published between 1869 and 1872 in *Otechestvennye zapiski*.[14] Nikolay Stepanovich Kurochkin (1830–84) was the elder brother of Vasily Kurochkin, the well-known translator of Béranger and Shevchenko. He was a physician by training and served as an army doctor in the Crimean War before he became a member of the populist organization Zemlya i Volya (Land and Freedom). Together with his brother, he served as an editor of *Iskra* and later of *Otechestvennye zapiski,* where he published translations from Italian and French.[15]

Like Minayev, Kurochkin was not interested in a word-for-word rendering of the original. Some of his texts would have to be classified as poems based on Baudelairian motifs rather than as translations. The length of the Russian version always considerably exceeded that of the French text. For example, "Starushonki" ("Les Petites Vieilles")—the first verse rendition of a poem by Baudelaire ever to appear in Russia—more than doubles the number of lines of the original (176 instead of 84). The following excerpt from "Le Crépuscule du soir" (entitled "Nocturno" in the Russian translation) gives an impression of Kurochkin's approach:

Вот проституция—для беззаконной ловли,
Шлет тысячи своих погибших дочерей,
И расцветилися—с подвалом и до кровли
Дома терпимости сиянием огней.
Там оргия кипит ночная, там гулянка
Пойдет безумная до самого утра,
А тут безчестная неопытных приманка
Открыла свой притон азартная игра.
И тысячи людей спешат толпою праздной,
Не внемля голосу рассудка и стыда,
В притоны жалкие порока и соблазна,
Растрачивать и жизнь и силы—без следа.
(v. 21–32)[16]

Here comes prostitution—for her lawless hunting
She sends out thousands of her daughters who have perished,
And the public houses have come into bloom
From cellar to roof with the glow of fires.
A nightly orgy is seething there, a mad feast
Is going on 'til morning,
And there, the dishonest lure for the inexperienced,
Gambling, has opened its den.
And thousands of people hurry in an idle crowd,
Without heeding the voice of reason and shame,
To the pitiful dens of vice and seduction,
To squander their life and strength without a trace.

All this torrent of words is based more or less on the following lines in Baudelaire's poem:

La Prostitution s'allume dans les rues;
Comme une fourmilière elle ouvre ses issues;

Partout elle se fraye un occulte chemin,
Ainsi que l'ennemi qui tente un coup de main;
Elle remue au sein de la cité de fange
Comme un ver qui dérobe à l'Homme ce qu'il mange.

(v.15–20)

Les tables d'hôte, dont le jeu fait les délices,
S' emplissent de catins et d'escrocs, leurs complices

(v.23–24)

Prostitution is flaming up in the streets;
Like an anthill she is opening her outlets;
Everywhere she is clearing herself a secret path,
Like an enemy who is attempting an attack;
She is stirring in the bosom of the city of mud
Like a worm who steals from Man what he eats.
The tables d'hôte, the delight of which is gambling,
Are filling with whores and crooks, their accomplices.

As one can see, Kurochkin has a very free concept of translation indeed, to the point that Baudelaire becomes hardly recognizable. The translator both subtracts elements from the text and adds components of his own. One of the most striking features of Baudelaire's poetry, his use of allegory, is considerably tuned down in the Russian text. Neither "Prostitution" nor "Homme" is capitalized and no attention is paid to the elaborate images of prostitution as an anthill and a tapeworm. Whereas Baudelaire's text unfolds in an almost uninterrupted sequence of similes, comparisons, and metaphors (*comme* is the most frequently used word in *Les Fleurs du Mal*), Kurochkin has no use for figures of semantic indirection. He seems interested mainly in a straight portrait of urban vice, garnished with moralizing evaluations.

The rather unsavory details of Baudelaire's text, such as the image of prostitution as a worm stirring in a city of mud, are glossed over with a rhetoric of bombastic denunciation. Almost all of Kurochkin's additions, from adjectives to whole sentences, serve to express his indignation over the immoral spectacle he has to witness. Unlike some symbolists (Bryusov, for example, who also translated "Le Crépuscule du soir"), Kurochkin was hardly attracted by the glittering "beauty of evil." It is worth noting that the judgment of Baudelaire's first

Russian translator seems diametrically opposed to that of the tsarist censors and many of the future enemies of the French poet: Kurochkin read Baudelaire not as an immoral tempter but as a moralist and exposer of human depravity.

Besides the depiction of urban misery in poems like "Les Petites Vieilles" and "Le Crépuscule du soir,"[17] Kurochkin seems mostly drawn to Baudelaire's mood of hopeless pessimism, as his choice of translations indicates: haunted by ennui and taedium vitae ("Spleen"), and marked by the experience of transitoriness ("Le Portrait"), humanity can find relief only in the oblivion of death ("La Fin de la journée") or mental immobilism and stagnation ("Les Hiboux"). Kurochkin's own poetry seems itself to have been infected by Baudelaire's pessimism, as one can see from the poems that he published together with his translations:

А прежные мечты разбиты как химеры,
И сердцу все темно и мертвенно—без веры.[18]

And the former dreams are shattered like chimeras,
And all is dark and deathly for the heart with no faith.

Kurochkin's translations did not win the approval of the critic S. S. Okreits, who published a devastating review in the popular journal *Biblioteka*, pointing out that "the Russian public starts to think of Baudelaire as some sort of Fet (*nechto v rode Feta*), from whom the editorial staff of *Iskra* ordered some poems on various themes. . . . Besides the fact that the artistic imagery of Baudelaire's poems perished and dissolved in the crude chatter and moralizing of N. Kurochkin, it is vexing that the latter simply did not understand the most basic thoughts of the poet."[19] Some of Okreits' malevolence against Kurochkin might have been due to competition: the same issue of *Biblioteka* contained a sample of another early Russian translator of Baudelaire—Vladimir Sergeyevich Likhachev (1849–1910).[20] Likhachev, a prolific satiric poet and translator who became known mostly for his renderings of Molière, translated three of Baudelaire's poems into Russian.[21] Although he at least keeps the same number of lines as the original, his overall performance is hardly superior to that of Minayev or of Kurochkin. Baudelaire's famous last stanzas of "Le Voyage," the finale of *Les Fleurs du Mal* in the 1861 edition, take quite a different outlook in Likhachev's version:

О смерть! пора бы мне окончить этот путь!
Всего испробовал я в жизни понемногу—
И лямку скорбную наскучило тянуть:
Скорей в далекую, последнюю дорогу!

Я приготовился: пролей в меня свой яд—
И за тобою я пойду без сожалений,
Без слез, без ропота, пойду хоть в самый ад,
На муки страшные—для новых ощущений!

O death! it is time for me to finish this path!
I have tried everything in life a little—
I grew tired of toiling in mournful drudgery:
[Let's embark] sooner on the long, last journey!

I am prepared: pour your poison in me—
And I will follow you without regrets,
Without tears, without grumble, I will go even to hell,
To terrible torments—for new sensations!

In Baudelaire's original:

O Mort, vieux capitaine, il est temps! levons l'ancre!
Ce pays nous ennuie, ô Mort! Appareillons!
Si le ciel et la mer sont noirs comme de l'encre,
Nos coeurs que tu connais sont remplis de rayons!

Verse-nous ton poison pour qu'il nous réconforte!
Nous voulons, tant ce feu nous brûle le cerveau,
Plonger au fond du gouffre, Enfer ou Ciel, qu'importe?
Au fond de l'Inconnu pour trouver du *nouveau*!

O Death, old captain, it is time! let's lift the anchor!
This land bores us, o death! Let's get under way!
If the sky and the sea are black like ink,
Our hearts which you know are filled with rays!

Pour us your poison so that it comforts us!
We want, as long as this fire burns our brains,
To plunge to the bottom of the abyss, Hell or Heaven, what do we care?
To the bottom of the Unknown to find something *new*!

Likhachev's translation contains many features already observed in the work of Minayev and Kurochkin. As in Minayev, we find formulas that are more reminiscent of Russian civic poetry than of Baudelaire (*liamku skorbnuiu naskuchilo tianut'*—"I grew tired of toiling in mournful drudgery"), and we can feel the attempt to prevent confrontations with the censor by weeding out blasphemous passages. Likhachev avoids Baudelaire's dangerous equation of Heaven and Hell by leaving out any reference to Heaven. Like Kurochkin, he destroys the allegoric structure of the original: nothing is left of the sailing image or of Baudelaire's contrast of the black sky and sea with the light-filled hearts. Death seems more a fatalistically accepted ending for Likhachev than an impatiently desired departure to new shores. The shortcomings of this translation become cruelly evident if we confront it with Marina Tsvetayeva's rendering of the same passage:

Смерть! Старый капитан! В дорогу! Ставь вертило!
Нам скучен этот край! О Смерть, скорее в путь!
Пусть небо и вода—куда черней чернила,
Знай—тысячами солнц сияет наша грудь!

Обманутым пловцам раскрой свои глубины!
Мы жаждем, обозрев под солнцем все, что есть,
На дно твое нырнуть—Ад или Рай—едино!—
В неведомого глубь—чтоб *новое* обресть![22]

Death! Old captain! Let's set out! Set the sail!
We are bored by this land! Oh death, let's sooner depart!
May the sky and the water be much blacker ink,
Know, our breast radiates with thousands of suns!

Open your depths to the deceived sailors!
We crave, having surveyed all that exists under the sun,
To plunge down to your bottom—Hell or Paradise—the same!—
Into unknown depths, to find something *new*!

An English prose rendition only remotely approaches the splendor of Tsvetayeva's Russian, for example in the pun on *chernei* (blacker) and *chernila* (ink, derived from "black"). Tsvetayeva's, as it were, provides Baudelaire's image with a Russian etymological justification.

It becomes clear that Baudelaire's first Russian translators did not turn to his poetry *pour trouver du nouveau*. They seemed interested in him only inasmuch as he could be integrated in their own poetic world—be it as a revolutionary agitator or as a portraitist of the misery and hopelessness of modern urban life. In a general manner, the content of Baudelaire's poetry received more attention than its form. The impossibility of finding an adequate poetic expression in Russian for Baudelaire's innovative style reflects the general crisis of Russian poetry in the second half of the nineteenth century. Daring metaphors were not to the taste of this milieu. Even Baudelaire's dynamic evocation of modern urban life appears strangely muted and pale. Baudelaire's poetry seems entirely "domesticated" in its early Russian translations. Rather than being understood as a challenge and impulse to renovate an outdated poetic system, it was integrated into this system and thereby lost many features that we consider typically Baudelairean: emphasis on poetic craftmanship and form, and an elaborate rhetoric of unusual metaphors leading to a paradoxical new notion of the sublime that undercuts the traditional dichotomy of high and low style. Baudelaire's poetic revolution was largely ignored by his early Russian translators, who seemed mainly preoccupied with the alleged "message" of his poems and their relevance to the current situation—be it as revolutionary propaganda, as in the case of D. D. Minayev, or the pessimist doom and gloom of N. S. Kurochkin.

Despite a respectable number of translations published in various journals, Baudelaire was still at best a marginal figure in Russia. None of the translators discussed so far considered him of central importance. They saw him as one of many Western poets, and no one translated more than a few of his poems. This was to change, however, when the first Russian Baudelairean entered the literary scene—Petr Filipovich Yakubovich (1860–1911), to whom we now turn.

P. F. YAKUBOVICH: A POPULIST BAUDELAIREAN

Although honored in 1960 with a Soviet edition in the prestigious series Biblioteka Poeta,[23] Yakubovich hardly belongs to the pantheon of widely known Russian poets. He was more popular in his own lifetime, however, when his revolutionary romanticism struck a common chord with the Russian public and his heroic and tragic life endowed him in the eyes of his readers with the charisma of a martyr. By the turn of the century, Yakubovich had become a favorite poet of people with a rather middlebrow taste in poetry, such as Professor N. V. Bugayev, as we know from the memoirs of Andrey Bely, his son.[24]

Yakubovich's biography sounds like a textbook case of the exemplary, selfless revolutionary fighter. Born in 1860 in Novgorod province of impoverished gentry, Yakubovich attended St. Petersburg University, where he graduated in 1882 with a dissertation on Lermontov. His revolutionary poetry enjoyed great success among his fellow students, and he befriended, among others, the young and then still civic-minded N. M. Minsky and D. S. Merezhkovsky. In 1882, Yakubovich joined Narodnaya Volya, an organization that had gained notoriety the year before by murdering Tsar Alexander II. He tried to instill new life in the almost defunct movement by organizing a new party, the Young People's Will, which advocated and attempted a program of large-scale "economic" terror directed against leading capitalists. Some rather amateurish assassination attempts were thwarted by the numerous police informers who had penetrated the party.[25] Denounced by an informant, Yakubovich was arrested in November 1884. After three years of pretrial detention in the dungeons of the Peter and Paul Fortress, he was sentenced by the St. Petersburg military tribunal to be hanged but, in a Dostoyevskian turn of events, shortly before the scheduled execution, the sentence was commuted to eighteen years of forced labor. Yakubovich spent the following years in Siberia, first under hard conditions in Kara and the mines of Akatui and later as an exile in Kurgan. In 1900, he was allowed to return to St. Petersburg but remained under strict police surveillance until 1903. From 1904 on he worked with V. G. Korolenko as the literary editor of the populist journal *Russkoe bogatstvo* (Russian Wealth). During the 1905 revolution, he was again temporarily detained. Physically weakened and prematurely aged by his years of hardship, Yakubovich died in 1911.

Amazingly enough, Yakubovich managed not only to continue his literary activities throughout his detention, hard labor, and exile but also to publish his poems, stories, and articles. They were smuggled out of prison and appeared anonymously or under various pseudonyms (notably P. Ya. and Matvei Ramshev for poetry, L. Melshin for prose, and P. F. Grinevich for literary criticism); sometimes, his writings were disguised as fictitious translations from Italian or English. Most successful was his autobiographical novel, *V mire otverzhennykh* (In the World of Outcasts), which became a classic of nineteenth-century Russian "camp literature" and was translated into both German and French. Chekhov was so impressed with the book that he sent Yakubovich a copy of his *Sakhalin Island* with a personal dedication.

Inspired by Nekrasov with his rhetoric of anger and grief and thematic focus on the suffering masses, Yakubovich belongs to the civic school of nineteenth-century Russian poetry. Stylistically, his work is typical of the 1880s, a time dominated by the immensely popular Semyon Nadson, Yakubovich's colleague and friend at St. Peterburg University, who couched his civic ideals in a language of postromantic clichés. However, unlike Nadson's tired resignation which became the prevalent mood of the period, Yakubovich's poetry is distinguished by an impulsive idealism and revolutionary impetus. Struggle dominates Yakubovich's conventional imagery, where revolutionary agitation appears as tempestuous seas and ravaging thunderstorms, and a fearless and selfless fighter wrestles with the oppressive forces of darkness. There is, however, little optimism in Yakubovich's revolutionary vision. He entered the populist movement at a late stage, after both the devastating failure of the "going to the people" movement of the 1870s and the execution and arrest of many leading populists following the assassination of the tsar. If Yakubovich still advocated a struggle that seemed hopeless and pointless, it was because revolutionary heroism had become for him almost an aim in itself—the only way perhaps to avoid the pervading doom and gloom of the 1880s. As Richard Wortman put it in his study of the crisis of Russian populism: "[Yakubovich's] activism was one of despair, a last alternative to spiritual death. Struggle was the sole way of living meaningfully."[26]

Yakubovich's essentially conventional and conservative literary taste made him a bitter enemy of the symbolists, whose rise to prominence he witnessed with dismay. His view of poetry as "one of the weapons of social action, a service to the motherland and the ideal,"[27] caused him to reject anything that he perceived as "pure art." In numerous articles, he ridiculed the representatives of the new literary movement as "chirping literary sparrows."[28] The dislike was mutual: Yakubovich's poetry in its turn was referred to in the symbolist press as the "rhymed howlings of Mr. Yakubovich."[29] A quatrain written in 1900, dedicated to a "symbolist poet," illustrates Yakubovich's view of the new poetry as pointless intellectualism and an empty quest for technical virtuosity. At the same time, it reveals his own ideal of poetry, a sentimentalist vision of an overflow of feelings:

В искусстве рифм—уловок тьма,
Но тайна тайн, поверь, не в этом:

От сердца пой—не от ума,
Безумец будь, но будь поэтом![30]

In the art of rhyming there is a multitude of tricks,
But the mystery of mysteries, believe me, does not lie in this:
Sing from your heart, not from your intellect,
Be a madman, but be a poet!

However, Yakubovich exempted from his sweeping condemnation of modernism one poet who personified for many of his contemporaries everything that was loathsome or exciting (according to one's perspective) in the new poetry of the *fin de siècle*: Charles Baudelaire. Yakubovich discovered Baudelaire in 1879, when he was nineteen years old, through an article by Henry Céard in the radical journal *Slovo*.[31] It was from this article, one of the first extensive and benevolent discussions of Baudelaire published in the Russian press, that Yakubovich "personally learned about the existence of *Les Fleurs du Mal*."[32] Céard (1851–1924) was a naturalist writer and member of Zola's "groupe de Médan." Céard's view of Baudelaire as a realist rather than a decadent met with Yakubovich's approval, and he later used Céard's article as a foreword to the translations published in the 1887 edition of his poetry.

Almost immediately after his discovery of *Les Fleurs du Mal*, Yakubovich began to translate Baudelaire. Although his first attempts were published between 1879 and 1882 in the radical journals *Slovo* (Word) and *Delo* (Deed) and in the liberal *Vestnik Evropy* (Messenger of Europe), most of his translations were completed during his years of imprisonment in the Peter and Paul Fortress and the Siberian labor camps. As he later revealed in the foreword to his 1909 edition of *Les Fleurs du Mal*, "In these difficult years Baudelaire was for me a friend and consoler, and I, on my part, gave him much of the best of my heart's blood."[33]

Yakubovich's translations appeared in various journals and several book publications.[34] In total, he translated one hundred poems, roughly two-thirds of Baudelaire's lyrical oeuvre. Among the poems he did *not* translate are the six pieces condemned for obscenity by the French court in 1857 and the three poems constituting the section "Révolte" ("Le Reniement de Saint Pierre," "Abel et Caïn," and "Les Litanies de Satan"). This may seem surprising inasmuch as "Révolte" was later hailed as the most "revolutionary" section of *Les Fleurs du Mal*. The Soviet critic N. I. Balashov even called "Révolte" "the greatest masterpiece of French revolutionary poetry before the 'Internationale.'"[35] "Abel et Caïn," as we have seen, was used by the radical D. D. Minayev for purposes of political propaganda. In the foreword to his edition Yakubovich explained the absence of these poems by the "peculiar conditions of the Russian 'free word,'" which made such texts unfit for publication.[36] This excuse is not convincing, since by 1909 the poems in question had already appeared in various Russian translations. Another reason was perhaps more pertinent: Yakubovich also made clear that the poems of "Révolte" were not among his favorites. He called them "clamorous" (*kriklivye*) and claimed that their absence was not a loss for his translation. Since, paradoxically, it seems that the only professional revolutionary among Baudelaire's translators did not much care for Baudelaire's "revolutionary" poems, the reasons for his interest have to be found elsewhere.

In the foreword to his 1909 edition of *Les Fleurs du Mal,* Yakubovich described his adolescent discovery of Baudelaire thirty years earlier: "In 1879 *Les Fleurs du Mal* fell by chance into my hands and immediately captured me with its strange and powerful mood. A severe sadness wafted into my young soul from verses that had been condemned for immorality; a coarse, at times daringly open realism, by some artistic miracle, aroused [in me] only pure, noble feelings—pain, sorrow, horror, indignation—and lifted me high up from this 'tedious earth' to the eternally blue lands of the ideal."[37] Here Yakubovich seems to have followed two mutually conflicting strategies in his attempt to absolve Baudelaire from the charge of immorality. On the one hand, as one would expect from a disciple of Nekrasov, he stressed Baudelaire's "realism." The unadorned, "coarse" depiction of unpleasant reality must evoke in readers an emotional response and induce them to condemn that reality. But, on the other hand, moral indignation is not translated into a call to action: rather than a stimulus for revolutionary transformation, discontent with reality leads to escapist dreams. The romantic flight to the "eternally blue lands of the ideal" denotes a mere yearning for an unattainable utopia, an impulse toward what Hugo Friedrich has described as Baudelaire's "empty ideality."[38]

Escapist motifs are prevalent in many poems that Yakubovich selected for translation and publication. His first translation of three poems, published in September 1879 in *Slovo,* begins with "La Voix." This poem describes a choice made in early youth: to reject a voice that promised a hedonistic life filled with trite pleasures and to follow instead a voice advocating the life of a lonely outcast and dreamer, who dreamed of traveling "au-delà du possible, au-delà du connu." The following poem, "Le Portrait," laments the ravaging effect of time on female beauty, whereas "Le Vampire," the third poem, describes the persona's obsessive masochistic dependence on a vampire-like woman. Yakubovich seems to have liked this poem particularly, since he republished it three years later (March 1882) in *Vestnik Evropy*. "La Voix" could be connected at least marginally with the somewhat quixotic terrorist struggle of Narodnaya Volya. In the poem "V chas vesel'ia" ("In an hour of merriment," 1880), for example, Yakubovich proclaimed that "in the terrible, pitiless, fierce struggle one must curse the dream of happiness."[39] However, such a reading seems hardly possible for most other poems. Decadent motifs rather than social ones are prevalent in many of them.

A rather curious document of Yakubovich's idolatry of Baudelaire, which also sheds some light on his deeper motivation to undertake the translation, is the lengthy poem "Pamiati Sharlia Bodlera" (To the Memory of Charles Baudelaire), written in 1893.[40] It begins:

> В те дни, когда душа во тьме ночей бессонных
> Славолюбивых грез и дум была полна,—
> Из сонма чуждых муз, хвалой превознесенных,
> Одна явилась мне, прекрасна и бледна.

> In those days, when the soul in the darkness of sleepless nights
> Was filled with dreams and thoughts of glory,
> Out of a swarm of alien muses extolled by praise,
> She came to me, beautiful and pale.

The twelve stanzas that follow describe how the beautiful "winged friend" urges the poet to "unite [their] two names into one, and to pour her dreams, doubts, and torments submissively into the sounds of the north," how a cruel fate separates the two, before (almost like a second Anna Kern) the "pale Muse" appears again before the poet's eyes with enticing calls ("To me, o friend, o brother! To me!"), prompting him to follow her to the "land of sick visions, nightmares, horrors, and radiant dreams." Much of the imagery in the poem, the focus on "pale" faces, "grave vaults," "dark garrets," and "strange dreams," seems curiously reminiscent of the language of contemporary decadence. Unlike the decadents, however, who openly reveled in Baudelaire's morbid eroticism, Yakubovich took care to exonerate his idol from any suspicion of sexual depravity. The third stanza, with its attempt to present the French poet as a model of innocent chastity, stands paradigmatic for Yakubovich's bowdlerized vision of Baudelaire:

Лучистый, кроткий взгляд!.. Свободно обнажала
Она воздушный стан пред взором молодым,
Но не желаний рой, как грешница, рождала,
А мысли строгие, как чистый серафим.

A radiant, gentle look! . . . She uncovered freely
Her aerial figure before my young eyes,
Yet she did not, like a sinner, arouse a swarm of desires,
But only clear thoughts, like a pure Seraph.

Conspicuously absent from the poem is any indication of Baudelaire's critical realism, his bleak portrayal of the deprived underclass or his vitriolic scolding of the Parisian and Belgian bourgeoisie. Baudelaire's appeal for Yakubovich apparently did not lie exclusively, if at all, in any social or socialist "message" but rather in a self-identification, in the belief of having found, as the last line of the poem states, "a soul consonant with the anxiety of my feelings" (*trevoge chuvstv moikh sozvuchnaia dusha*).

Despite all his assertions to the contrary, one wonders whether it was not precisely Baudelaire's decadent features that most attracted the young Yakubovich. His insistent denial of any sexual allure in *Les Fleurs du Mal* is contradicted by his early interest in Baudelaire's sadomasochistic poems and by his portrayal of Baudelaire as a feminine object of (sublimated) desire. Albert Wehrle has even speculated whether a cynic of the time would not have found something "decadent" also in the imagery of Yakubovich's own rhetoric of social indignation, for example in his presentation in an 1897 book review of the populist "Muse of Revenge and Sorrow" as a "pale, bleeding woman lashed by the knout."[41]

Many decadent elements also are to be found in Yakubovich's first article about Baudelaire. The nine-page account of Baudelaire's life and work, published anonymously in December 1890 in *Severnyi vestnik* (Messenger of the North), was one of the first extensive critical assessments of Baudelaire to appear in a Russian journal. Its source, however, can easily be identified as Théophile Gautier's 1868 essay on Baudelaire, which served for half a century as the introduction to the standard French edition of Baudelaire's collected works.[42] Yakubovich copied verbatim whole passages from Gautier, frequently without proper acknowledgment (although Gautier's name is mentioned several times in the text). The article rather faithfully repeats many of Gautier's characterizations of Baudelaire and presents the poet as a dandy, renowned for his overly refined, bizarre taste, capricious behavior, and neurotic mind: "Nerves get irritated, the brain is burning, sensuality becomes strained—and the neurosis [misspelled in the Russian text as *nervoz*] comes with its strange unruliness and hallucinations of sleepless nights. Vague sufferings develop, unhealthy caprices, fantastic whims, loathing without reason, insane energy and an equally insane despair, finally, a craving for the stimulation of narcotics and a dislike for any sort of healthy nourishment."[43] Yakubovich translated this passage almost literally from Gautier.[44] A slight deviation from the French text occurs only with the expression "fantastic whims" (*fantasticheskie prichudy*) where Gautier has "dépravations fantasques." To accuse Baudelaire of depravity obviously went too far for Yakubovich.

Yakubovich's occasional mistranslations and deviations from Gautier's text indicate the difference between his thinking and the French parnassian's concept of "l'art pour l'art." Buried in the mass of Gautier quotations, we find ideas that are manifestly Yakubovich's own, such as the assessment of Baudelaire as a "deeply principled poet (*gluboko ideinyi poet*) in the noblest sense of this word."[45] Perhaps the most revealing passage is one that—falsely—asserts Baudelaire's alleged belief in the fundamental goodness of human nature. Yakubovich claimed that "in [Baudelaire's] opinion, man is essentially good (*po sushchestvu svoemu dobr*) and capable of moral rebirth, but at the bottom of even the purest souls a harmful element is hiding, inciting man to evil actions that are disastrous for himself."[46] Gautier had written, "Il ne pensait pas que l'homme fût né bon, et il admettait la perversité originelle comme un élément qu'on retrouve toujours au fond des âmes les plus pures, perversité, mauvaise conseillère qui pousse l'homme à faire ce qui lui est funeste."[47] By omitting the negation in Gautier's first sentence, Yakubovich inverted the meaning of the whole argument: Baudelaire's obsession with original sin obviously was alien to the Russian populist. However, despite Yakubovich's misreadings and "corrections" of Gautier, it seems evident that he quoted the French critic extensively because he agreed essentially with Gautier's general presentation of Baudelaire. Thus Yakubovich's position in 1890 seems hardly distinguishable from that of the soon-to-be-born symbolists, his future enemies. Ironically enough, the journal in which Yakubovich published his article, *Severnyi vestnik*, was to become a trailblazer of the New Spirit of the 1890s, something he could hardly have foreseen at that time.

The rise of modernism in the 1890s and Baudelaire's increasing notoriety in Russia as a quintessential decadent forced Yakubovich to reformulate his position. The fact that his favorite poet became the hero of his ideological and literary adversaries was irritating to him. For a while, he even hesitated to publish more translations because he was afraid of helping to promote a hateful cause. He overcame this fear only in 1901, when he declared in a note to the second volume of his poetry, "Not afraid anymore of playing into the hands of a disagreeable literary movement, I can present my work to the reader with a clear conscience—fully convinced that, with all its shortcomings, it can evoke only good and pure feelings."[48] A decisive moment had come in December 1894 when the Petrovskaia Biblioteka in Moscow published a volume with fifty-three poems by Baudelaire in Yakubovich's translation. This was the first volume consisting solely of Baudelaire's works ever to appear in Russia. Because the manuscript had been smuggled out of the Akatui prison, Yakubovich's authorship had to remain secret, and he was deprived of taking part in the preparation of the edition. The editorship was entrusted, without his knowledge, to the decadent poet Konstantin Balmont (later himself a translator of Baudelaire), who contributed a foreword to the book. Yakubovich later complained about the way Balmont handled his edition. He must have been particularly shocked when he read Balmont's introduction, a typical sample of decadent literary criticism in which Baudelaire's poetic world is seen as a hallucination of a "bewitched, dead kingdom" haunted by skeletons, gigantic coffins, and swarming poisonous plants.[49] When in 1896 Balmont suggested a second edition of the book, Yakubovich declined, irritated by the "decadent character" of his letter;[50] and he later expressed scorn and condescension for Balmont's poetic work: "Having very little talent, and feeling unconsciously (or perhaps even consciously) the whole naive primitivity (*dopotopnost'*) of his poetic taste, Mr. Balmont must have seized with a great joy the new 'symbolist' theories, giving him the right to write all sorts of nonsense under the tag of a profundity inaccessible to simple mortals, and we had one warped, affected, and insincere poet more."[51] The clash with Balmont was a harbinger of what was to become a major preoccupation for Yakubovich: the fight for the "correct" interpretation of Baudelaire.

Another source of irritation for Yakubovich was tsarist censorship. The censors mercilessly truncated many poems by cutting politically or religiously "harmful" expressions and passages and replacing them with dotted lines. The numerous omitted stanzas give the book almost an appearance reminiscent of Pushkin's *Eugene Onegin*. Any lines that even remotely could have evoked blasphemous associations were eradicated, among them such seemingly harmless expressions as "empty skies" (in "L'amour du mensonge"). Yakubovich later pointed out that a Russian reader unfamiliar with the original text must have been induced by such distortions to suspect the French poet of all sorts of indecencies, which could indeed only reinforce the common perception of Baudelaire as a decadent.[52]

In a letter to N. K. Mikhailovsky, the leading populist critic of the time, editor-in-chief of *Russkoe bogatstvo,* and himself an ardent anti-decadent, Yakubovich explained the necessity of defending Baudelaire from false accusations: "In recent years the best parts of our literature and society have adopted a most unfavorable opinion of Baudelaire, [seeing him] as the father and typical representative of contemporary decadence, symbolism, and other Russo-French absurdities. While I fully understand and welcome the hostility to these phenomena, I think, however, that Baudelaire is a slandered poet who was included in a company with which he does not rightfully belong."[53] Yakubovich's second article on Baudelaire, "Bodler, ego zhizn' i poeziia"(Baudelaire, His Life and Poetry), written at Mikhailovsky's request, was such a defense. It was published in April 1896 in *Russkoe bogatstvo* and later reprinted in the second volume of Yakubovich's collected poetry and in the 1909 edition of *Les Fleurs du Mal* (*Tsvety Zla*). Throughout, Yakubovich's attempts to clear the controversial French poet from the stain of decadence and to disassociate him from his symbolist followers are obvious. For tactical reasons, Yakubovich begins each of the four subchapters (about Baudelaire's life, poetry, his "soul," and his "idealism") by conceding some "unpleasant" sides but then proceeds to show that these "defects" were in reality quite harmless. For example, he mentions Baudelaire's drug abuse but insists at the same time that he was no de Quincey, who "would have laughed at his French imitator as at a small child."

In light of Yakubovich's own revolutionary engagement, his commentary on Baudelaire's political philosophy is interesting. He mentions Baudelaire's sympathy for the worker-poet Pierre Dupont and his revolutionary fervor of 1848, referring to Baudelaire's "general humanitarian principles and compassion for the working class." But he also stresses his later "reactionary" position, his "hostility to any kind of democratic utopias," and his propagation of "the Catholic religion and political absolutism." However, the reactionary views expressed in

Baudelaire's diaries should not be taken too seriously, according to Yakubovich, since they are irrelevant for our understanding of his "soul," the "key" to which is given only in the poetry of *Les Fleurs du Mal.*

Yakubovich concedes that there are indeed some "defects" (*iz"iany*) in Baudelaire's poetry, a certain "affectedness and strangeness" and a deplorable tendency sometimes to spoil the effect of a poem with an "unexpected or unpleasant image." Other "clearly decadent" features of Baudelaire are his preoccupation with the olfactory sense, love for cats, and preference for the artificial over the natural. Those secondary elements, according to Yakubovich, were isolated by his decadent imitators and blown out of proportion: "They artificially and intentionally expanded what was natural and sincere in Baudelaire, what was caused by the characteristics of his nature. As a result, over almost every line of their writings, a healthy reader must open his eyes wide, shrug his shoulders or even burst out laughing." But Yakubovich maintains that Baudelaire can in no way be confused with the contemporary symbolists: he is only "guilty" of symbolism insofar as he, like any poet, uses symbols in his poetry, and he is "decadent" only in the sense that he displays the heightened sensibility and refined style typical of periods of cultural "maturity" (another argument that Yakubovich appropriated from Gautier). As an example, Yakubovich quotes the tercets of the sonnet "Correspondances," which had become a favorite text of the symbolists, and adds: "Was it not from here that all these 'white peacocks' of ennui, the 'yellow dogs' of jealousy, and the other colorful absurdities of contemporary symbolism came forth? But what a huge difference even here between the imitators and their prototype!"[54]

It is useful to take a closer look at the evolution of Yakubovich's translation of "Correspondances," which he quotes as evidence for Baudelaire's proclaimed superiority over his decadent followers. The first version, published in *Severnyi vestnik* in 1891, when Yakubovich was still unconcerned with fighting the rising tide of modernism, seems itself strangely decadent. The last line of the poem ("Qui chantent les transports de l'esprit et des sens") is rendered as "They sing the feasts of love and the heat of voluptuousness" (*Poiut piry liubvi i sladostrast'ia znoi*).[55] Evidently disturbed by the *fin de siècle* eroticism of this imagery, Yakubovich later changed it to an optimistically energetic "They sing the ecstasies of feelings and the surf of good forces" (*Poiut ekstazy chuvstv i bodrykh sil priboi*). This was the version published in the 1895 edition and quoted in *Russkoe bogatstvo* as proof of Baudelaire's "nondecadence." A similar de-erotization happened to the "chairs d'enfant" in line 9, which changed from "a girl's cheeks" (*shcheki devushki*—*devushka* being a grown-up girl) in *Severnyi vestnik* to "a child's body" (*telo detskoe*). The second version is closer to Baudelaire's original but one wonders whether this change does not make the passage even more perverse. As one can see, Yakubovich's refutation of Baudelaire's decadence required for him a reinterpretation of the poetry itself.

The central focus of Yakubovich's critical attention was Baudelaire's "soul." In the same way as Byron was shaped by his revolutionary *Zeitgeist*, Baudelaire expressed, according to Yakubovich, the gloom and hopelessness typical of the reaction and depravity following the failed 1848 revolution. He thus became the "singer of the big cities," not as a cold observer but compassionately portraying the "unhappy, downtrodden, and deprived" with "love and tenderness." More generally, Baudelaire embodied the condition of modern man, the "sickly and at times downright psychopathological depths of his spirit," in which only a "poet or a doctor" could find his way. Yakubovich insists, however, that Baudelaire's focus on the dark sides of human nature was only a consequence of his deeper idealism. His description of Baudelaire's motivations seems rather a self-characterization:

> Although a deep sceptic and misanthrope, Baudelaire is not a singer of unconditional despair. At the bottom of his soul, he always carries a saving fire, which illuminates his path and prevents him from being submerged in the unclean mud of life. One could not say that it is a particular religious feeling, a belief in the immortality of the soul, in a recompense beyond the grave; even less is it some social ideal. But we do not know, however, another poet (perhaps with the exception of Shelley), in whom there lived such a passionate impulse toward an ideal, admittedly a vague, unclear ideal, not expressed in any real formulas, but nevertheless bright, radiant, and undying.[56]

If Yakubovich hoped with such formulations to convert the "best parts of our literature and society" to a more positive view of Baudelaire, his attempt was not entirely successful. Many of his colleagues remained unconvinced or even were hostile. A typical example is the Marxist critic Andreyevich (i. e., Evgeny Andreyevich Solovyov, 1867–1905), who dismissed Yakubovich's characterization of Baudelaire's "idealism" as sheer nonsense: "There was no ideal whatsoever in Baudelaire, neither vague nor unvague, neither clear nor unclear, neither 'expressed' nor unexpressed." Andreyevich called Baudelaire "the most decadent of all decadents," and even his alleged compassion for the poor seemed suspect: "There is less love and tenderness here than excitement over the smell of decay."[57] Yakubovich thus found himself in the uncomfortable situation of waging war on two fronts. The symbolists criticized his lack of aesthetic understanding of Baudelaire—Ellis, the chief Baudelairean among the Russian symbolists, called his translations "far-fetched, arbitrary, clumsy, and coarse"[58] —and, doubtless more painful for him, his own peers on the political left accused him of naively idealizing a decadent poet.

An interesting example of this battle over Baudelaire is provided by Yakubovich's polemic controversy with F. D. Batyushkov (1857–1920), an editor of the "legal Marxist" journal, *Mir Bozhii* (God's World). Yakubovich initiated the argument himself by accusing *Mir Bozhii* of being soft on decadence, since it committed the indecencies of serializing Merezhkovsky's novel *Resurrection of the Gods, Leonardo da Vinci* and showing symbolism in a favorable light in an article by A. Bogdanovich.[59] *Mir Bozhii* retaliated with a review by F. D. Batyushkov of Yakubovich's 1901 poetry edition, drawing attention to the fact that Yakubovich himself was guilty of promoting a decadent poet. Batyushkov accused Yakubovich of "systematically distorting" Baudelaire in his translations by glossing over his decadent features in a mistaken attempt to make him look more idealistic. In Batyushkov's opinion, Baudelaire did not need Yakubovich's false idealization to be appreciated by the Russian public; although undoubtedly a "poet of decadence" and a writer of "pure art," he was a great artist in his own right, and Yakubovich would have done better to pay more attention to the elaborate intricacies of his form.[60] Yakubovich was deeply offended by these attacks, less by the critique of his translation as technically inadequate—a point that he was ready to concede—than by the portrait of his favorite poet as a decadent. In an angry reply published in *Russkoe bogatstvo*, he defended his view of Baudelaire and accused Batyushkov of a "hostile" and "tendentious" attitude.[61] A second article by Batyushkov, written in a more conciliatory tone,[62] was not able to soothe Yakubovich, who continued the controversy with him in private correspondence.[63] Yakubovich's letters show that he saw himself as the victim of unfair attacks and of a campaign orchestrated against him by the editorial board of *Mir Bozhii*.

The argument between Yakubovich and Batyushkov over Baudelaire's decadence makes for rather amusing reading. The *pièce de résistance* and yardstick for judging Baudelaire's decency was his treatment of sexuality. A lot of ink was spilled, for example, on the exact meaning of *sage* in the opening line of the poem "Madrigal triste" ("Que m'importe que tu sois sage?"), translated by

Yakubovich as "May your mind not shine with sharpness" (*Pust' tvoi um ostro-toi ne blistaet*). Batyushkov claimed that *sage* refers not to mental capacities but to the virtuous behavior (or lack thereof) of the woman addressed in the poem, and he quoted Yakubovich's translation as an example of the latter's sentimental "softening" of Baudelaire. Yakubovich maintained in his counterarticle that the primary meaning of *sage* is "wise" rather than "well-behaved," which led the two critics to an extensive argument over the use of *sage* in French literature back to Montaigne, including digressions about such expressions as *sage-femme* (midwife). Yakubovich finally conceded that Batyushkov might be correct in his interpretation of the passage,[64] although he added that this still did not make of Baudelaire an apostle of immorality. Arguments on a similar scale were fought over whether the poem "Une nuit que j'étais près d'une affreuse Juive" is about two women (Batyushkov) or just one (Yakubovich); here it was Batyushkov who finally conceded defeat.[65] The third hotly debated poem was "La servante au grand coeur dont vous étiez jalouse." Batyushkov accused Yakubovich of trying to conceal a possible lewd meaning by omitting "dont vous étiez jalouse" in his translation, while Yakubovich maintained that this expression was really of no importance and only added by Baudelaire because he needed a rhyme with *pelouse*.

Although this quibbling over Baudelaire's "decadence" seems rather an exercise in futility, Batyushkov certainly was not wrong when he called Yakubovich's translations "subjective." Yakubovich, curiously enough, tried to justify his deviations from the originals with purely aesthetic arguments. In the foreword to the 1909 edition of *Tsvety Zla*, he named "beauty" and "poeticity," along with the "ideological content" (*ideinoe soderzhanie*), as his main guiding principles.[66] Characteristically, he refrained from any discussion of what such notions as beauty or poeticity meant to him since he regarded them as self-evident, atemporal constants. Unlike Baudelaire, he did not waste thought on the historical relativity and shifting character of such concepts.

Not surprisingly, Yakubovich's translations are most successful when there is some common ground between Baudelaire's poetry and his own. Although one might think that there is little to unite the two poets who, in many respects, seem more like antipodes, both Yakubovich and Baudelaire have roots in European romanticism. Both of them admired Byron and Lermontov. To be sure, for Baudelaire, romanticism was only a starting point that he soon and radically transcended, whereas Yakubovich used it as a reservoir of ready-made imagery for his epigonous poetic style.[67] It is not by chance that Yakubovich found the more conventionally romantic poems by Baudelaire, such as "L'Homme et la mer" or the famous "Albatros," compatible with his own sensibility. The stock romantic image of the lonely rebel in confrontation with the raging sea and the allegorical representation of the poet as a lofty bird floating high above the hostile world can be found also in Yakubovich's own poetry, although with more overtly political overtones.[68] Yakubovich's romantic understanding of Baudelaire is noticeable also in the 1896 essay, where he asserted that "Baudelaire's lofty view of the poet as a priest (*zhrets*) and prophet is one of the most attractive themes of his poetry."[69] The symbolists would not have disagreed with that.

Yakubovich was more ambivalent toward the morbid and decadent side of Baudelaire's "romantic agony." While perhaps subconsciously attracted by these features, he tried to mitigate the shock of Baudelaire's sadistic eroticism and necrophilia. A good example is the poem "Une nuit que j'étais près d'une affreuse Juive / Comme au long d'un cadavre un cadavre étendu" (A night when I was with a hideous Jewess like a corpse stretched out along a corpse), which Yakubovich rendered as

> С ужасной еврейкой, прекрасной, как мертвый
> Изваянный мрамор, провел я всю ночь,
> Как труп, возле трупа простертый . . .[70]

> With a hideous Jewess, beautiful, like dead
> Chiseled marble, I spent the entire night,
> Like a corpse stretched out along a corpse . . .

The obvious function of the "parnassian" insertion *prekrasnoi, kak mertvyi izvaiannyi mramor* ("beautiful, like dead chiseled marble") is to neutralize Baudelaire's provocative and shocking imagery. *Prekrasnoi* (beautiful) serves to counterbalance *uzhasnoi* (hideous) in the first line, even as it rhymes with it, and *mertvyi* (dead) prepares and motivates the following picture of the two corpses.

The poem provides also a good example of Yakubovich's neglect of form. In order to accommodate his various additions, he has to extend considerably the number of verses. As a result, Baudelaire's sonnet extends to twenty-one lines in his translation. While Yakubovich found it unnecessary to pay attention to the intricacies of the sonnet structure, his idiosyncratic attitude toward Baudelaire's form took a peculiar and rather unexpected turn in his treatment of the *Petits poèmes en prose*. The "revolutionary" significance of this new genre, highlighted by modern critics as Baudelaire's breakthrough to modernist anti-poetry,[71] was obviously lost on Yakubovich, who put the only two prose poems he ever translated ("L'Etranger" and "Les bienfaits de la Lune") into rhymed dactylic and iambic verse. He justified his choice with the argument that "Baudelaire was such a master of prose that under his hand it sounds often better than verse, and if the translator has any hope of conveying in the Russian language this intoxicating and at the same time frightful music, it can be only in verse."[72]

Familiarization is a characteristic feature of Yakubovich's approach to translation. Rather than understanding Baudelaire's poetry as a challenge to an outdated poetic system, he integrated it into his own aesthetic convention, essentially defined by Pushkin and Lermontov, Nekrasov and Nadson. Not all of Baudelaire's poetry easily lends itself to an adaptation to Yakubovich's own style. His approach becomes especially problematic with Baudelaire's "symbolist" poems, such as the above-mentioned "Correspondances," the second stanza of which he translated as follows:

Как людных городов стозвучные раскаты
Сливаются вдали в один неясный гром,—
Так в единении находятся живом
Все тоны на земле, цвета и ароматы.[73]

As the resounding peals of human cities
Blend in the distance in one obscure thunder—
So are in a living unity
All tones on earth, colors and scents.

In the original:

Comme de longs échos qui de loin se confondent
Dans une ténébreuse et profonde unité,
Vaste comme la nuit et comme la clarté,
Les parfums, les couleurs et les sons se répondent.

Like long echoes blending in the distance
In a dark and deep unity,
Vast like the night and like clarity,
The perfumes, colors and sounds respond to each other.

Baudelaire's urbanism seems to have made such a lasting impression on
Yakubovich that he evokes it even when there is no base for it in the original.
The distant roar of the city provides a convenient "realistic" setting for the phenomenon of correspondences, while the mysterious and paradoxical third line
is omitted completely from the translation. Obviously unsatisfied himself with
this solution, Yakubovich later changed the stanza to

Как эхо дальнего стозвучные раскаты
Волною смешанной в ущельях гор плывут,
Так голоса друг другу подают
Все тоны на земле, цвета и ароматы.[74]

As the resounding peals of a distant echo
Float as a combined wave in mountain gorges,
So voices pass on to each other
All tones on earth, colors and scents.

The transfer of the scenery from the city to the mountains, which looks like a return to the stock imagery of romantic landscape painting, does not do much to
enhance the quality of the translation.

Besides this affinity to the romantic heritage, Yakubovich also was sympathetic to Baudelaire's depiction of the Parisian underclass. A translation that he
himself considered among his most successful ones is "Pirushka triapichnikov"
("Le Vin des chiffonniers").[75] Stanzas 4–6 of the poem read as follows in Yakubovich's version:

Старик, до времени согнутый и седой,
Измолотый трудом, заботой и нуждой,
Уставший подбирать вонючие тряпицы,
Отрыжку грязную прожорливой столицы,
Так он идет домой, в свой угол бедняка,
Пропитан запахом приятным погребка,

С толпой товарищей, и их усы седые
Висят, как пред полком знамена боевые!
Пред ними солнца блеск, и флаги, и цветы . . .
И в шумной оргии—о, светлые мечты!—
Победных кликов, труб несут они свободу
И воскресенья весть усталому народу![76]

An old man, prematurely hunched and grey,
Ground down by work, worry and want,
Tired of picking up stinking rags,
The dirty belch of the gluttonous capital,
So he walks home, to his poor man's hut,
Steeped in the pleasant smell of the wine-cellar,
With a crowd of companions, and their grey moustaches
Hang like war banners in front of a regiment!
Before them the brightness of the sun, flags, and flowers . . .
And in the noisy orgy—o radiant dreams!—
Of victory calls and trumpets, they bring freedom
And the message of resurrection to the tired people!

In Baudelaire's original:

Oui, ces gens harcelés de chagrins et de ménage,
Moulus par le travail et tourmentés par l'âge,
Ereintés et pliants sous un tas de débris,
Vomissement confus de l'énorme Paris,
Reviennent, parfumés d'une odeur de futailles,
Suivis de compagnons, blanchis dans les batailles,
Dont la moustache pend comme les vieux drapeaux.
Les bannières, les fleurs et les arcs triomphaux
Se dressent devant eux, solennelle magie!
Et dans l'étourdissante et lumineuse orgie
Des clairons, du soleil, des cris et du tambour,
Ils apportent la gloire au peuple ivre d'amour!

Yes, these people harried by sorrow and labor,
Ground down by work and tormented by age,

Broken and hunched under a heap of debris,
Jumbled vomit of the enormous Paris,
Come back, perfumed with a smell of casks,
Followed by companions, whitened in battles,
Whose moustache hangs like old flags.
The banners, flowers, and triumphal arches
Rise before them, solemn magic!
And in the dizzying and luminous orgy
Of the bugles, the sun, the shouts and the drum,
They bring glory to the people drunk with love!

The subjective character of Yakubovich's approach is easily recognizable: his main emphasis lies on the revolutionary message of the poem, which is taken at its face value rather than as the nebulous fantasies of an intoxicated Parisian *clochard*. The depiction of social misery is more concrete and adorned with additional details: Yakubovich's ragpicker, for example, is *prematurely* aged, and Baudelaire's rather abstract "vomissement confus" becomes an unsavory "dirty belch" (*otryshka griaznaia*). On the other hand, the ragpicker's grandiose alcoholic hallucinations—"solennelle magie!"—turn into "radiant dreams" of "freedom" and "resurrection." The gray moustaches of his comrades are no longer slackly hanging simple "old flags," but become "war banners" carried in front of a "regiment." As Efim Etkind has pointed out, the rhyme *svobodu-narodu* (people-freedom) in the last two lines is an almost "phraseological sign" of Russian nineteenth-century civic poetry.[77] However, such militant and revolutionary notes are the exception rather than the rule in Yakubovich's translations.

It is curious to note that, despite Yakubovich's idolatry, Baudelaire's oeuvre exerted little influence on his own poetry. Clearly Baudelairean, however, is the occasional use of the decidedly un-Russian word *splin* (spleen).[78] The feeling of tedious doom that the expression conveyed, the anxiety of being "submerged in the filthy mud of life," are as much a product of the historical and biographical circumstances of Yakubovich's own situation as they are Baudelaire's doing. Baudelaire may have provided the image of the lyric persona in the double role of executioner and victim that opens and closes one of the most popular of Yakubovich's early poems, "Bitva zhizni" (The Battle of Life, 1880):

Ах, без жизни проносится жизнь вся моя! . . .
  Увлекаемый мутною тиною,
Я борюсь день и ночь, сам себе—и судья,
  И тюрьма, и палач с гильотиною.[79]

Alas, my whole life drags on lifelessly! . . .
  Carried along in a turbid slime,
I am fighting day and night, and I am my own judge,
  And prison, and executioner with a guillotine.

This image of self-destruction seems inspired by Baudelaire's "Héautontimorouménos" ("Je suis la plaie et le couteau! / Je suis le soufflet et la joue! / Je suis les membres et la roue, / Et la victime et le bourreau!"—"I am the wound and the knife! I am the slap and the cheek! I am the limbs and the wheel, and the victim and the executioner!"). However, if Baudelaire's text is addressed to a female figure, Yakubovich's image is placed in the revolutionary context of his time. His self-loathing is caused by his inability to live up to the great revolutionary heritage of the past (the poem was written before he joined Narodnaya Volya). Yakubovich's persona suffers from the repudiation of the ghastly specters of his fallen "brothers and friends," who reproach him for "singing sorrowful songs" instead of seeking a heroic death in battle. Thus, although grisly and cruel images occur in both Baudelaire's and Yakubovich's poetry, they serve different purposes. Yakubovich operated within the boundaries of a conventional poetic discourse in order to convey a specific message. He chose to agitate readers but not to shock them. Because he felt that bizarre images could only spoil the effect of a poem, he domesticated Baudelaire, the revolutionary champion of modernity, and rendered him an epigonous descendant of Byron or Shelley. Yakubovich thus became the victim of his own anti-modernism: his ideological blinders and hatred for anything that smacked of symbolism prevented him from fully understanding the phenomenon of Baudelaire.

In spite of all the negative criticism that he received from various sides and although he himself acknowledged certain shortcomings in his translations, Yakubovich was convinced until the end of the correctness of his approach. In the foreword to his 1909 edition of *Les Fleurs du Mal*, he declared that "among the hundreds of poems of such intricate content and original style as Baudelaire's, I know that in my translation there will be found not a few unsuccessfully rendered lines, stanzas, and perhaps even entire pieces. . . . But the general poetic physiognomy of my favorite poet, the spirit of his poetry (and in this lies my ambition as a translator) are rendered, I hope, truthfully."[80] Not all critics disagreed with Yakubovich on this account. Amidst all the negative voices, we can also find some encouraging ones. Perhaps most surprising and noteworthy is the fact that Valery Bryusov, chef d'école of the symbolists and certainly one of Yakubovich's ideological adversaries, had a few words of praise for him. In his review of Ellis' 1904 translation of *Les Fleurs du Mal*, Bryusov made an honorable mention of Yakubovich, whose version he found superior to that of his symbolist colleague: "In Russian literature we have the conscientious and in many respects valuable work of Mr. P. Ya[kubovich], who has translated more than 200 poems by Baudelaire. Mr. P. Ya[kubovich]'s translations give the Russian reader, if not a complete, then at least a sufficiently clear and faithful idea of Baudelaire's poetic work."[81] To be sure, Bryusov's praise of Yakubovich was probably motivated in part by his own agenda, namely his intention of dealing a blow to Ellis. Nevertheless, there seem to have been some mutual positive feelings between Bryusov and Yakubovich. Bryusov became aware of Yakubovich's Baudelaire translations as early as 1895, when he commented on them in a letter to V. K. Stanyukovich.[82] Yakubovich's opinion of Bryusov was slightly more benevolent than the one he held of the other decadents, since he acknowledged in Bryusov a certain idealism: "By the way, we have to point out that even in the realm of decadent fantasies, Mr. Bryusov, in our view, favorably distinguishes himself from his colleagues: although he sometimes develops ugliness and vulgarity to monstrous dimensions, one can see that he is sincerely imbued with an idealistic mood, the naive dream of some great task in store for him and the other 'symbolists.'"[83] One wonders whether Yakubovich would have been heartened to learn that Bryusov became a communist after 1917.

Yakubovich was successful in converting some of his political peers on the left to his view of Baudelaire. Maxim Gorky's positive opinion of the French poet was certainly shaped by Yakubovich, whom he held in high esteem as a selfless revolutionary fighter. In his 1896 article "Pol' Verlen i dekadenty" (Paul Verlaine and the Decadents), an obituary of Verlaine and a scathing attack on the French decadents, Gorky quoted a few lines by Baudelaire in Yakubovich's translation and spoke approvingly of Baudelaire high morality and critique of the French bourgeoisie. In *The Life of Klim Samgin*, the hero rebuts as a "narrow view" the opinion that "the revolutionary and ex-convict Yakubovich-

Melshin should not have translated Baudelaire."[84] Another Baudelairean among the Russian Marxists was Anatoly Lunacharsky, later the Communist commissar of culture and education, who praised Yakubovich's translations in dithyrambic terms, claiming that "with his almost impeccable and at times downright astonishing translation of these poems, ravishing with a depth of color, sharpness of image, and intensity of feeling, Mr. P. Ya[kubovich] has rendered an enormous service to Russian literature."[85]

Yakubovich's Baudelairism deserves attention as an interesting phenomenon in the history, or prehistory, of Russian modernism. The fact that a poet who is commonly considered the father of modern poetry and a patriarch of symbolism was discovered and appreciated by a populist revolutionary prompts a new look at the relationship between modernism and radicalism. In spite of the anti-positivist orientation of the decadents and symbolists, some links unite them to nineteenth-century radicals. An iconoclastic attitude toward conventional values was certainly shared by the radical nihilists of the 1860s as well as the decadents of the 1890s and the modernist avant-garde of the twentieth century. Like Nietzsche, Baudelaire appealed to members of both the progressive and the decadent camps (characteristically, the two major Russian Marxist Baudelaireans, Gorky and Lunacharsky, were also admirers of Nietzsche).[86] Yakubovich himself was no Nietzschean. In his polemic article against *Mir Bozhii*, he criticized the Russian Marxists for their flirtation with Nietzschean and symbolist ideas, accusing them of treating the people (*narod*) with contempt.[87] But he was nevertheless shaped by the same spiritual climate as were Nietzscheanism and decadence. His early reception of Baudelaire's poetry in the 1880s, with his interest in its escapist, morbid, and perverse features, reveals a decadent *in statu nascendi*. In this sense, the young Yakubovich was hardly distinguishable from his colleagues and friends, D. S. Merezhkovsky and N. M. Minsky, who subsequently became his enemies. Only later, when decadence had become notorious as a literary doctrine, did Yakubovich revert to a more populist concept of Baudelaire; and could then salvage the purified ideal of his favorite poet only by willfully ignoring the decadent features that perhaps had originally attracted him.

In the context of Baudelaire's international reception, Yakubovich emerges as a unique figure. At a time when, both in France and in Russia, the prevalent view of Baudelaire was that of a cold aestheticist and dandy interested mainly in new, bizarre forms of beauty, refined sensual pleasures, and narcotic "paradis artificiels," the Russian populist's focus on Baudelaire's suffering "soul" and "heart," on his "tenderness" and "compassion" seems at odds with critical opinion. Yakubovich's view of Baudelaire may appear one-sided and naive in many respects. One could argue, however, that he was ahead of his time: he anticipated what was later said by a critic whom certainly nobody would suspect of naïveté or a lack of aesthetic refinement—Marcel Proust: "En réalité le poète que l'on prétend inhumain, d'un aristocratisme un peu niais, a été le plus tendre, le plus cordial, le plus humain, le plus 'peuple' des poètes" ("In reality, this poet considered inhuman, of a somewhat silly aristocratism, was the most tender, most cordial, most human, most 'popular' of poets").[88] It is a credit to the Russian populist Yakubovich that he recognized and defended this "human" side of Baudelaire at an early stage of his reception, even if he failed to understand or rejected the implications of Baudelaire's aesthetic modernity.

THE MARXIST VIEW

Since Marx and Engels never developed a coherent theory of literature (and also, incidentally, never mentioned Baudelaire in their writings), it is not surprising that no unified Marxist view of the literary process in general, or of Baudelaire in particular, surfaced in Russia before the 1930s. An artificial unity was reached only after party authorities imposed Socialist Realism as the sole correct Marxist-Leninist approach to art. In comparison with the denunciatory rhetoric of later Stalinist hacks, the Russian Marxist critics of the prerevolutionary era appear relatively sophisticated and tolerant in their approach to contemporary avant-garde literature.

Not all Russian Marxists shared Lunacharsky's and Gorky's positive view of Baudelaire. G. V. Plekhanov (1856–1918), the "father" of Russian Marxism, even categorically condemned Baudelaire in his article "Evangelie ot dekadansa" (The Gospel of Decadence), published in 1909 in *Sovremennyi mir (Modern World)*. Plekhanov tried to refute the assertion made by the decadent poet and critic N. M. Minsky that social critics and modernists could be allies in the struggle for freedom and justice. Plekhanov for his part did not want such allies and he pointed to Baudelaire as a chief example to explain his reluctance. He conceded that Baudelaire did take a revolutionary position in 1848 but the reason for doing so, according to Plekhanov, was simply the fact that he was unable to "swim against the tide." The waves of the popular uprising washed him "totally unexpectedly" into the revolutionary camp before he reverted to the reactionary he was before. Baudelaire only turned into a revolutionary because of his spinelessness.

Plekhanov's approach of linking artistic value with "progressive" ideological content, in a cruder form, was later to become the hallmark of official Soviet criticism.

Plekhanov's rejection and Lunacharsky's enthusiasm mark the opposite ends of a rather wide spectrum of Marxist opinions on Baudelaire. Many critics took an intermediate position: they did not share Plekhanov's harsh judgment, but neither did they try to make of Baudelaire a genuine revolutionary. In a survey of modern French poetry published in 1896 in the legal Marxist journal *Novoe slovo* (New Word), Evgeny Degen characterized Baudelaire as a disillusioned anti-romantic still clinging to some tenets of romanticism. He explained his decadent features as a reaction to the historical circumstances and type of society he lived in, pointing out that Baudelaire "had even properly developed moral notions, but no stimulus for a honest activity. The difficult life conditions of French society in the 1840s and 50s explain the moral isolation, the social pessimism and indifferentism of the small group of 'lone' *intelligenty* to which Baudelaire belonged."[89] In his book *Kriticheskie nabroski* (Critical Sketches), M. Mogilyansky found a few words of praise for Baudelaire's "humane and progressive (*svobodoliubivye*) thoughts," which had to be distinguished from the later "monstrous forms" that his poetry took under the influence of his "shattered nerves." By calling Baudelaire the "voice of the insulted and injured," Mogilyansky drew an implicit connection between Baudelaire and Dostoyevsky. His cult of suffering, while seen as a positive feature, nevertheless also aroused the suspicion of the Russian critic: "Baudelaire had the bad luck to be the voice of human conscience for all unhappy, suffering, and fallen people, for all insulted and injured. If, in focusing on compassion with everything suffering, fallen, criminal, and depraved, he at times went as far as if he loved it, let us not forget that he also loved and poeticized his own sufferings. . . . Here we will stop, for we have reached again the realm of pathology."[90]

Two leading representatives of what was later to become the "vulgar sociological" school of the 1920s, P. S. Kogan (1872–1932) and V. F. Friche (1870–1929), tried to approach the phenomenon of Baudelaire from a Marxist point of view. In his 1904 article "Sharl' Bodler," Kogan described Baudelaire as an idealistic character who was too weak to resist the fascination of evil, but who was able to recognize his own depravity in tormenting moments of self-knowledge. In his bright moments, Baudelaire turned from a singer of evil into a "truthful realist, a preacher of humanity and exposer of vice." He showed compassion for the predicament of the downtrodden masses in the capitalist metropolis but lacked understanding for the "great historical events that took place under his eyes: the struggle between the exploiters and the exploited."[91] V. F. Friche interpreted Baudelaire as a frustrated intellectual and typical product of the new capitalist society, where the triumphant bourgeois class reduced the intelligentsia to a servant role and subjected everything, including art and literature, to the law of supply and demand. Baudelaire, according to Friche, was an adversary of this new order. Friche's sociological approach to Baudelaire's modernity seemed almost to anticipate Walter Benjamin: "The oppressing power of the moneyed bourgeoisie, the pitiful situation of the intelligentsia, doomed to a bohemian existence, the overpowering structure of the big city, the extreme irritability caused by the whole modern way of life—all this disposed the poet to look at life as an evil nightmare, an assemblage of horrors. And the future—a freer, brighter and more radiant future—was not something Baudelaire believed in."[92]

A tendency that becomes more and more noticeable in the populist and Marxist criticism after the turn of the century was to separate Baudelaire from his decadent followers. Perhaps influenced by P. F. Yakubovich, the new critics drew a distinction between Baudelaire, of whom they partially approved, and the literature of the fin de siècle, which they considered detestable. Kogan's position seems fairly representative:

> In recent times, as we know, Baudelaire, who was proclaimed a poet of vice and depravity in his own time, has begun to be "rehabilitated." But few of these belated worshippers of the poet had the correct attitude to their task. Instead of restoring the better and nobler elements breathing in his poetry, the so-called decadent school declared him to be its forefather; it accepted only the perverse and sickly; devoid of the Baudelairean idealism and the deep grief of the poet over the injustice of the world and suffering humanity, Baudelaire's epigonous followers feasted their eyes upon the images of vice themselves and began to draw these pictures for their own sake.[93]

The best informed and most sophisticated article on Baudelaire to be published in a Russian Marxist journal was written by the St. Petersburg University professor Evgeny Anichkov (1866–1937). His study "Bodler i Edgar Po" came out in 1909 in *Sovremennyi mir*.[94] Unlike the verbal excesses of the various self-proclaimed Baudelaireans, Anichkov's style was soberly professorial and detached, but nevertheless sympathetic to Baudelaire. He proved to be well acquainted with Baudelaire's biography and complete work, including his diaries, literary and art criticism, and the short novella "La Fanfarlo" (Anichkov was the only Russian critic ever to comment on this text). In an overview, Anichkov outlined Baudelaire's and Poe's position in European literary history between romanticism and symbolism and dwelled on the differences between Baudelaire and Baudelairism. Unlike Théophile Gautier and the critics of the fin de siècle, Anichkov defined the essence of Baudelaire's poetry not as decadence, but as "modernity" (*sovremennost'*). He pointed out that in his aesthetics of modernity, Baudelaire is diametrically opposed both to the romantics and to Gautier's parnassian aestheticism. Anichkov explored the implications of modernity in Baudelaire's representation of the urban landscape, of women and human suffering. He asserted that Baudelaire has nothing in common with "so-called realism." His art is not representational but, like that of the symbolists, requires active reader participation: "A poet who creates symbolist images necessarily assumes that his reader is himself able to create mentally, to find associations and similarities; in this lies the mission of symbolism."[95] Sixty years before Jean Starobinski, Anichkov paid attention to Baudelaire's allegorical self-portrait of the artist as a comedian.[96] In discussing the prose poems "Le Vieux Saltimbanque" and "Une mort héroïque," Anichkov pointed to the fact that, unlike Poe, Baudelaire was tormented by self-doubt with regard to the question "Why poetry?" (which explains, according to Anichkov, why the self-assured Poe and his notion of beauty were so important to Baudelaire). The figure of the comedian, "not only a caricature of the poet, but his own brother," becomes an image of the alienated and paradoxical status of the writer in capitalist society. In his final paragraph, Anichkov tried to distinguish Poe's and Baudelaire's symbolism from that of their "conscious and unconscious imitators," who care "only for the external, as children and savages grab for fake glitter." For them, according to Anichkov, symbolism is nothing but a technique, an allegorical way of representation. For Poe and Baudelaire, however, symbolism meant more than that: not only was it "a means to penetrate into the abyss of human emotions and potentialities of the soul," it was also "a means of thinking according to the laws of world creation. To create symbolistically meant for them to create anew."[97]

In the Soviet period, such a sophisticated approach to Marxist literary criticism was no longer possible. Some Marxist critics revised their earlier, favorable opinion of Baudelaire for the worse, as if to repent for their prerevolutionary sins. In the first edition of the *Great Soviet Encyclopedia* (1927), P. S. Kogan presented Baudelaire as the offspring of a family of "mentally ill" people. We learn that because of his wrong class origin Baudelaire was unable to understand, let alone join, the workers' movement and instead escaped into an artificial world of aesthetism and narcomania. Baudelaire's seeming revolutionary fervor of 1848, Kogan explained, was only triggered by his interest in the aesthetic effects of death and destruction. Kogan's revised position reflected the new "party line" on Baudelaire. Like everything else in the now defunct Soviet system, the reception of Baudelaire in the Soviet Union was dominated by party interference. The fortune of the poet depended on the fluctuations of the official policy on literature and culture. In the comparatively liberal climate of the 1920s, there still existed a plurality of opinions and Baudelaire could even be praised in print. As Stalinism set in, he vanished from the Soviet literary scene for half a century. No book by Baudelaire appeared in Russia throughout the ascendancy of Lenin, Stalin, and Khrushchev.

To be sure, Baudelaire was not without friends even among the Soviet establishment. Lunacharsky, who in the 1920s became the commissar of education and culture in the Bolshevik government, attempted to "rehabilitate" Baudelaire as a social critic. He wrote the entry on Baudelaire in the first Soviet Literary Encyclopedia, where he spent a lot of time explaining Baudelaire as a product of his period, characterized by the decline of bourgeois culture and by social hopelessness. These historical factors are responsible, according to Lunacharsky, for Baudelaire's "moral and aesthetic dandyism." He mentions that in the year 1848, "democratic and almost revolutionary notes began to appear in Baudelaire's poetry," which Lunacharsky detected in such poems as "Le Crépuscule du soir," "Le Crépuscule du matin," and "Le Vin des Chiffonniers," but that these notes "soon expired in an even more sinister despair." Nevertheless, Lunacharsky thought that it would be misguided to identify Baudelaire as a decadent, as had been frequently done. He underlined Baudelaire's mastery of the poetic form, with which he overcame his despair, transforming it into a work of art:

> Before us, there is a poet who knows that life presents darkness and pain, that it is complicated, full of abysses. He does not see a ray of light before him, he knows no way out. But he did not despair, did not fall into depression. On the contrary, it is as if he took his heart firmly in his hands. He tries

to maintain a certain high calm in everything, tries, as an artist, to prevail over his milieu. He does not cry. He sings a manly and bitter song precisely because he does not want to cry. Later poets of this decadent type completely lost such a balance and such a stern cut-glass quality of form.[98]

The manly wish "not to cry" might have been conveyed to Lunacharsky less by Baudelaire than by P. F. Yakubovich: "I am not crying" or "we won't cry" are formulas that occur in the poetry of the populist revolutionary.[99] Although Lunacharsky's approach to Baudelaire may seem somewhat old-fashioned and sentimental (poetic modernity was not his concern), his attitude differed positively from the new voices of Soviet criticism. Despite his official position, Lunacharsky did not express the views of the communist literary bureaucracy. Evidently, his tolerant liberalism had become outdated by the late 1920s. In the same year the article on Baudelaire appeared in print, Stalin removed Lunacharsky from his post. The encyclopedia containing his article was later stigmatized as "formalistic," its publication halted, and the existing volumes withdrawn from circulation. Rather than Lunacharsky's, it was Kogan's presentation of Baudelaire in the *Great Soviet Encyclopedia* that was to set the tone for thirty years to come.

Still, although a sort of persona non grata, Baudelaire never fell totally out of favor even in Stalin's time. A small selection of his poetry, notably from the cycle "Révolte," continued to appear in various anthologies of Western "revolutionary" and "atheist" poetry. The Soviet ritual "jubilee approach to literature" was applied also to him. Two brief articles appeared in the Soviet press on the occasion of his 115th(!) and 120th birthdays. L. Rapoport, in *Knizhnye novosti* (Book News), dwelled proudly on the long tradition of Russian translations of Baudelaire, starting with Kurochkin and the political prisoner Yakubovich, and also quoted from Lunacharsky's "splendid article" (although he did not indicate where this article had been published). Aside from Lunacharsky, he also recommended Kogan's contribution in the Soviet encyclopedia. More interesting is V. Aleksandrov's 1941 jubilee article in *Literaturnoe obozrenie* (Literary Review). "V. Aleksandrov" was the pseudonym of the literary critic Vladimir Borisovich Keller (1898–1954). The author turned out to be well acquainted not only with Baudelaire's poetry but also with his critical writings and correspondence. He makes an attempt to rehabilitate Baudelaire from his decadent reputation by collecting quotations that show the French poet as a social critic of the bourgeois society. He dwelled notably on Baudelaire's article on the worker-poet

Pierre Dupont and pointed out that Karl Marx himself had quoted Dupont in *Das Kapital*. Aleksandrov gave a rather detailed account of Baudelaire's involvement in the revolution of 1848 and asserted that, contrary to current opinion, Baudelaire did not lose all his revolutionary spirit in his later life. As evidence for that, he mentioned the sympathetic portrayal of poor people in Baudelaire's prose poems.

Even after the coming of Khrushchev's "thaw," Baudelaire's status in the Soviet Union changed only gradually. The publication of his works remained as restricted under Khrushchev as it was under Stalin. Ironically, it was only in the late 1960s, when the thaw had already fizzled and the Brezhnevite stagnation had set in, that his poems finally reappeared in Russia after a hiatus of fifty years. Baudelaire was one of several Western modernists rehabilitated and cleared for publication in the 1960s, along with Kafka, Rilke, Camus, and T. S. Eliot. In order to justify Baudelaire's publication, the Soviet literary authorities had to present him as a politically correct author. The resulting campaign for Baudelaire's rehabilitation looks like a late vindication of Yakubovich's and Lunacharsky's views. From a depraved bourgeois decadent, the French poet metamorphosed into a progressive humanist and an honorary member of the Soviet pantheon of critical realists. The new positive attitude certainly was an improvement compared to the former rejection of Baudelaire and had the beneficial effect of making the poet once more accessible to Russian readers. On the whole, however, it amounted to hardly more than another application of the old nineteenth-century radical notions of social relevance, resulting in a literary criticism bristling with stereotypes and clichés. More sophisticated attempts to read Baudelaire as a social critic, such as those of Walter Benjamin, were ignored.

In 1966, the first Soviet edition of Baudelaire's poetry came out, edited by Efim Etkind. It was a small volume containing one hundred poems translated by Vilgelm Levik, Pavel Antokolsky, Ariadna Yefron (Marina Tsvetayeva's daughter), and others. In his foreword, Antokolsky mentioned that Baudelaire had been first discovered in Russia by the populists who allegedly called him a "French Nekrasov,"[100] and he also quoted a poem by the Communist Louis Aragon in praise of Baudelaire—all this in an effort to make the publication politically acceptable. The view of Baudelaire as a "French Nekrasov" seems to be an idea not of nineteenth-century populists but of post-Stalinist Soviet literary critics. No evidence has been found that Yakubovich, or any other Russian populist for that matter, ever called Baudelaire a "French Nekrasov" (although it is true that Valery Bryusov described Nekrasov as a Russian Baudelaire).[101] In any event, it is safe to assume that the Soviet reading public did not flock to Baudelaire because of his populist credentials. The first Soviet edition of Baudelaire was an instant success. As we know from Valentin Katayev, the 50,000 copies were sold out within hours.[102] In 1970, a Russian edition of *Les Fleurs du Mal* appeared in the prestigious series Literaturnye Pamiatniki (Monuments of Literature) of the Soviet Academy of Sciences. Baudelaire at last had become academically respectable. The edition, also published in 50,000 copies, contains almost all of Baudelaire's poetic oeuvre in verse, with the notable exception of four of the poems that had been banned by the French court in 1857 because of alleged obscenity ("Lesbos," "Femmes damnées [Delphine et Hyppolyte]," "A celle qui est trop gaie," and "Les Métamorphoses du vampire"). It seems that the theme of lesbian love was still considered too risqué for the Soviet readers of the 1970s. In a brief foreword to the volume, the chairman of the editorial board of the series Literaturnye Pamiatniki, N. I. Konrad, announced that it was time to take a new approach to many things that had been looked at differently "not long ago." Baudelaire, he revealed, had now been reappraised also in France by "the most progressive circles of French society; and among them in the forefront—the Communists." It was time to free Baudelaire from his modernist image and establish him as a "classic."

As if the first entire publication of *Les Fleurs du Mal* in the Soviet Union were not sensational enough, the editors offered an additional publicity stunt by proclaiming that their arrangement of the text realized for the first time in history Baudelaire's own wishes for the definitive, third edition of his book. A closer look reveals that this grandiose claim is based solely on the omission of one single poem ("La Lune offensée") from the arrangement of Jacques Crépet's 1922 edition of *Les Fleurs du Mal* (Crépet had already questioned the inclusion of this poem). The Soviet scholars did not deem it necessary to mention that Crépet himself later repudiated the principles of this edition and in 1942 brought out a new critical edition which was based on Baudelaire's 1861 version, the last one to appear in the poet's lifetime. The reconstruction of the "definitive" posthumous edition of *Les Fleurs du Mal* according to Baudelaire's intentions has long been abandoned by Western Baudelaire scholars as an impossible chimera. The Soviet resurrection of Crépet's fifty-year-old project shows evidence of a rather naive provincialism. The edition contains a programmatic afterword by N. I. Balashov, entitled "Legenda i pravda o Bodlere" (Legend and Truth about Baudelaire), which was intended to put the French poet into the correct ideological perspective. The author attacked Baudelaire's "wrong friends" for describing him as a modernist or decadent (without mentioning that his Stalinist detractors made the same claim). The "truth" (*pravda*) about Baudelaire, according to Balashov, was that he was an unrelenting adversary of bourgeois society, who created with his cycle "Révolte" the "greatest masterpiece of French revolutionary poetry before the 'International.'" The Soviet critic showed that Baudelaire's anti-liberalism was shared by Marx and Engels and had therefore a progressive rather than a reactionary significance.[103] He singled out Baudelaire's anti-American remarks and his raging hatred of Belgium for special praise. Balashov's article, as the authoritative expression of the new party line on Baudelaire, was later spread to other satellite nations of the Soviet Union. In 1976, it was republished in East Germany.

In spite of all its shortcomings and heavy-handed political slanting, the Soviet publication of *Les Fleurs du Mal* remains an important event. It marked the definitive rehabilitation of Baudelaire in Russia. Starting in the 1960s, the French poet once again became a legitimate subject of academic inquiry in literature departments all over the Soviet Union. Before that time, he had been practically ignored in the Soviet academic world, with the exception of a bizarre 1946 article by N. G. Protsenko, who, faithful to the "anti-cosmopolitan" spirit of that period, claimed that Baudelaire was indebted to Russian literature as the first French translator of Pushkin. Now, scholars and graduate students from the Ukraine to Siberia and from Leningrad to Georgia and Kazakhstan started to investigate various aspects of Baudelaire's oeuvre. Many of these studies were not overly concerned with Baudelaire's political correctness. Instead of extolling the poet as an anti-capitalist hero, most researchers prefered to focus their attention on more technical questions. Dissertations were written, for example, on Baudelaire's art criticism (O. Timasheva, Moscow State University, 1973) and on the linguistic and stylistic expression of the category of time in Baudelaire's work (V. Sychkov, Leningrad State University, 1977).

A new, benevolent approach also became evident by the fact that the Soviet Union participated in the colloquium held on the one-hundredth anniversary of Baudelaire's death. The well-known writer Valentin Katayev (1897–1986) was sent to Brussels as the Soviet delegate. He gave a sentimental speech about Baudelaire's significance for Russian literature and his ongoing "third birth" in the Soviet Union (the first and second births having been his discovery by the populists and the symbolists). Perhaps the most direct expression of the changing party line on Baudelaire can be observed by comparing the different editions of the *Great Soviet Encyclopedia*. While in the first edition, Baudelaire had been introduced as the offspring of a mentally deranged family, the presentation of Baudelaire in the latest, third edition of 1970 began with the information that the poet "was born into the family of a participant in the Great French Revolution." The article, written by O. I. Ilinskaya, ends with a critique of the "bourgeois historians of literature," who "cultivate mainly the aesthetic sides of Baudelaire's work." At the same time, Ilinskaya praises the Marxist approach of Lunacharsky and Gorky, who is quoted as having said of Baudelaire that "he lived in evil, loving the good" (*on zhil vo zle, dobro liubia*). This pronouncement by Gorky, a figure of high authority in the world of Soviet literature, obviously was calculated to convey legitimacy to Baudelaire. Ilinskaya did not seem to be aware of the rather piquant fact that in reality she was citing not Gorky, but—*horribile dictu!*—the decadent poet Konstantin Balmont. Gorky had plagiarized this line from a poem that Balmont included in his introduction to Yakubovich's 1895 edition of Baudelaire.[104]

The new party line on Baudelaire was followed closely by D. D. Oblomievsky, whose book on French symbolism, published in 1973, contains a chapter on Baudelaire. The author drew a neat distinction between Baudelaire's "progressive" and "reactionary" features. For example, he commended the poet for the "militant atheism" of the cycle "Révolte" but criticized his later "religious rebirth" as a defection from the cause of human progress into the camp of decadence.[105] The most extensive Soviet study of Baudelaire (more than 300 pages) was M. L. Nolman's book *Sharl' Bodler. Sud'ba, estetika, stil'* (Charles Baudelaire. Fate, Aesthetics, Style), published in 1979; the book was hailed as a "turning point" by the Soviet press.[106] In his introduction, the author promises an "objective" investigation of Baudelaire, based on a Marxist position (the terms *objective* and *Marxist* are treated as synonyms). Nolman presents this approach as all the more necessary and urgent in that the bourgeois scholars of Baudelaire, according to Nolman, have the deplorable habit of ignoring or distorting the historical facts. Instead they interpret Baudelaire "in the spirit of religious-mystical metaphysics and morals, traditional biographism and Freudian psychoanalysis, updated with existentialist philosophy. Very fashionable are also formalist-structuralist analyses, which drive from the Baudelairean poetry its living soul."[107] Titles like Georges Blin's *Le sadisme de Baudelaire*, according to Nolman, "speak for themselves."

Nolman's thesis of Baudelaire as an adversary of capitalist society corresponds to N. I. Balashov's *mot d'ordre* but he avoided the pitfalls of Balashov's apodictic oversimplifications. He too refered with patriotic pride to the Russian populists who discovered Baudelaire, and he named Gorky and Lunacharsky as the paragons of a Marxist approach to Baudelaire (predictably, he cited once more Gorky's plagiarized Balmont quotation). At the same time, he ventured some cautious critique of the Stalinist attitude toward Baudelaire, deploring Soviet criticism that "until the mid-fifties" did not judge the French poet as "objectively" as Gorky and Lunacharsky did. In his attempt to rehabilitate Baudelaire, Nolman tried to show that some of the seemingly decadent or symbolist features of the poet are grounded in a progressive worldview. The sonnet "Correspondances," for example, is not a manifesto of symbolism but "a polemic against vulgar materialism in philosophy," and Baudelaire's predilection for the artificial over the natural has nothing to do with decadence but should be understood as a protest against something specifically bourgeois: contrived "naturalness."[108] But even Nolman could not avoid following Oblomievsky's example. He too was forced to distinguish between the "positive" and "negative" Baudelaire: "The strong and the weak sides of Baudelaire's aesthetics, coming from the same source—the fight with the decline of bourgeois culture that had set in—and unseparable at the time of their appearance, can now be critically taken apart, and everything healthy, really valuable can be separated from delusions, from the sick and decadent."[109] As is frequently the case with Soviet literary critics, one wonders whether Nolman really believed what he said or whether he was just trying to score political points. In any event, he could hardly have published his study without engaging in this sort of rhetoric. The real purpose of the book was perhaps a different one: the patient reader is rewarded with numerous excerpts from an unpublished translation of *Les Fleurs du Mal* by the former futurist and imagist poet Vadim Shershenevich (1893–1942), quoted from a manuscript given to Nolman shortly before the poet's death.[110]

There is evidence that the officially prescribed Soviet attitude toward Baudelaire was not shared by everyone. The poet seemed to enjoy a continued popularity in underground literary circles, where poetry was evaluated and practiced without regard to the orthodox Socialist Realist dogma. Gennadii Aigi (born 1934), the Chuvashian who has emerged in recent times as a leading Russian avant-garde poet, opened his poem "Bodler" (1956) with the words

Не вы убивали не вы побеждали
не вашего поля

Недаром вы слушать его не умели
диктовало откуда-то что-то
места своего не имея[111]

Not you were killing not you were winning
a field not yours

Not by chance could you not listen to him
something was dictating from somewhere
not having its place

Vy (you), presumably referring to the philistines of the Second Empire who were unable to "listen" to Baudelaire, might as well be an apostrophe to the philistines of the Soviet literary establishment, where there was "no place" for Baudelaire either (as there was no place for Aigi himself). In the 1970s and 1980s, Baudelaire the societal outcast and *poète maudit* became the topic of several Soviet poems.[112] His critique of societal norms was hardly understood as anti-capitalist propaganda, as the Soviet literary functionaries would have liked to have it. Baudelaire's predicament seemed in many ways emblematic of the fate of the poet in Soviet society, and writing about Baudelaire became an aesopian way of addressing contemporary literary issues. Baudelaire the social critic turned into a figure that could be used for criticizing the realities of Soviet life. The ending of Igor Zhdanov's poem "Bodler" (1978) tells in a veiled fashion how the Soviet literary bureaucrats turned the French poet postmortem into a monument of political orthodoxy:

Его при жизни
                    крупным матом крыли.
Когда он умер—
                    вскрыли и зарыли
Поглубже,
                    чтоб никто не раскопал.
Пятьсот статей разумных написали,

Убогий холм цветами забросали,
Железными,
Чтоб дождь не растрепал.

While he was alive they abused him with foul language.
When he died, they dissected and buried him,
Deeper, so that nobody could dig him out.
They wrote five hundred learned articles,
They showered his squalid grave with flowers,
Made of iron, so that rain could not scatter them.

In a play of multiple ironies, the social approach to Baudelaire, initiated by the nineteenth-century radical populists, was still operative in Russia. The emphasis shifted, however, from the content or form of his poetry to his persona. The mythical presence of the *poète maudit* served as a weapon in the struggle with a system that had fetishized social relevance and thereby turned it into an empty shell. Paradoxically, the social relevance of Baudelaire turned out to be his resistance to any form of officially prescribed social relevance.

With the collapse of communism, the orthodox Soviet approach to literary criticism has become discredited. It seems unlikely that a Marxist view of Baudelaire will be making much headway in Russia anytime soon. Whether any other approach to Baudelaire's oeuvre—decadent, modernist, postmodernist—will have an appeal in post-totalitarian Russian society remains to be seen. One wonders whether the introduction of a market economy with its spread of a Western-style pop culture will not ultimately be detrimental to serious poetry. The abolition of censorship in Gorbachev's glasnost, contrary to what one might have expected, produced no outpouring of new Baudelaire editions. A first Ukrainian translation of *Les Fleurs du Mal* came out in 1989 in Kiev. In Russian, only a small provincial volume appeared in 1991 in Rostov-na-Donu, featuring a still "politically correct" foreword by N. I. Balashov. Somewhat incongruous with this message, the book is illustrated by Yu. E. Belov with surrealistic and rather decadent looking photo montages. Moscow street hucksters in 1993 were peddling a probably pirated reprint of *Tsvety Zla* (text of the 1970 edition) made in Estonia, together with pornographic literature and Western detective stories. They were hoping, so it seems, to cash in on Baudelaire's still "scandalous" market appeal. However, the prose poems and Baudelaire's diaries have not been republished in Russian since 1910. Baudelaire's critical writings fared somewhat better: in 1986, an illustrated volume with Baudelaire's collected art criticism appeared in 30,000 copies. This was the first time these texts were translated into Russian.

Disillusionment with social relevance is a phenomenon that is not occurring for the first time in Russian intellectual history. In this respect, our own fin de siècle bears some striking resemblance to the spiritual climate that reigned in Russia a hundred years ago. It is to this decadent reception of Baudelaire that we now turn.

The Decadent Response

The term *decadence* has become known as both the pejorative tag and the proudly accepted distinction and battle cry of a current that originated in the 1880s in France and later spread to many European literatures of the fin de siècle. No universally accepted definition of decadence and its exact temporal boundaries exists.[1] In Russia, the situation is further complicated by the fact that its first proponents used the term more or less interchangeably with symbolism. The Russian decadent movement of the 1890s was not an exact copy of the earlier French *décadence*. Like the following mystic generation of Russian symbolism, it has been characterized as a "relatively more solemn and metaphysical" phenomenon than its Western counterpart.[2] If decadence in Western Europe can be understood as a reaction against the materialism, positivism, and utilitarianism of the predominant nineteenth-century bourgeois culture, Russian decadence was also directed against the sterile dogmatism of the radical intelligentsia, which was increasingly perceived as inadequate to deal with any of Russia's problems. Both French and Russian decadence are characterized by a cluster of negative attitudes, notably the rejection of democratic "progress" and the escape from reality into an artificial world of aesthetic gratification; the propagation of an aristocratic, elitist individualism and contempt for the *profanum vulgus*; and a value system that replaces nature by artificiality, health by morbidity, normality by perversity, optimism by pessimism, religion by blasphemy, morality by the "beauty of evil," and vitality by the glorification of death. By the same token, language turns from a rational tool of communication into an allusive "music" and object of beauty.

Baudelaire is usually credited with an important role in this development, although he had no unified theory on the subject of *décadence*. With character-istically Baudelairean inconsistency, the term seemed for him sometimes to have a negative and sometimes a positive connotation.[3] However, many readers understood titles like *Les Fleurs du Mal* or *Les Paradis artificiels* as paradigmatic for central tenets of decadence, and Baudelaire the extravagant Parisian dandy and consumer of narcotics provided an easy role model for the decadent lifestyle. At the same time, the French poet became a favorite target for indignant anti-decadent attacks, which often made the mistake of confusing literary legend with reality and taking the decadent Baudelairism for the real Baudelaire. It was this decadent legacy that prompted Henry James to observe, "Les Fleurs du *Mal*? Non, vous vous faites trop d'honneur. What you call *evil* is nothing more than a bit of rotting cabbage lying on a satin sofa."[4]

It is important to stress that this Baudelairism owes as much to Baudelaire's followers in France and elsewhere as to the poet himself, if not more. The essay by Théophile Gautier that introduced the standard edition of Baudelaire's works and from which P. F. Yakubovich had so freely borrowed played an important role in establishing a decadent reading of Baudelaire. Equally important were Paul Bourget's influential *Essais de psychologie contemporaine* (1883), which appeared in 1888 in a Russian translation. The chapter devoted to Baudelaire is titled "Théorie de la Décadence" and discusses Baudelaire's "nihilism" in connection with the general symptom of "nausée universelle" and sinister prophecies about the coming spiritual bankruptcy of mankind. In 1884, Joris-Karl Huysmans published his famous novel *A rebours*, which was destined to become the bible of European decadence. In this book, Huysmans lavished praise on the author of *Les Fleurs du Mal* in expressions that were in themselves an interesting demonstration of decadent style. He claimed that Baudelaire had "reached the realms of the soul where the monstrous vegetations of thinking multiply . . . where aberrations and sickness, the mystic Tetanus, the hot fever of lewdness, the typhoids and vomits of crime reside. . . . He has revealed the morbid psychology of the spirit in the October of sensations."[5]

The impact of this sort of language in Russia was enormous. It mobilized a violent reaction from the side of both reactionary and progressive forces, which felt threatened in their essence by what they perceived as a message of cynicism and disillusionment. At the same time, it touched a chord with the increasing number of people who felt similarly ill at ease with tsarist conservativism and the ideology of the left opposition. Alongside with Nietzsche, Baudelaire emerged as a major figure in this development. He was seen, depending on one's perspective, as a main culprit or a main hero in the new culture of the fin de siècle.

BAUDELAIRE AND THE GENESIS
OF RUSSIAN DECADENCE

In a certain sense, Russian decadence started long before the term was officially acknowledged as such in the literary manifestoes of the 1890s. A homegrown tradition of decadence is visible already in the pessimistic atmosphere of the 1880s. It is not by chance that such later champions of decadence as N. M. Minsky (1855–1937), D. S. Merezhkovsky (1865–1941), and K. D. Balmont (1867–1942) all started their literary careers in this period. Even the work of such a stout anti-decadent as P. F. Yakubovich, as we have seen, contains elements that could be described as decadent. This is hardly surprising if we keep in mind the character of this decade and the type of literature it produced. The period was characterized by a general sense of crisis, malaise, and *bezvremen'e* (stagnation, literally "timelessness"), exacerbated by the fierce political reaction to the killing of Tsar Alexander II in 1881 and by the death or silence of virtually all the great Russian novelists around 1880. Tired resignation, a melancholy feeling of personal impotence, and a sense of "no way out" became the dominant feature of both the civic and the "pure art" poetry of these years. The immensely popular poet Semyon Nadson, who died of consumption in 1887 at the age of twenty-four, perhaps exemplifies these tendencies most typically. D. S. Mirsky has described Nadson's idealistic but bloodless rhetoric as "the low-water mark of Russian poetical technique" and his great popularity as "the low-water mark of Russian poetical taste."[6]

Baudelaire's pessimism and "Spleen" seemed in this context to correspond to a widespread mood among the Russian intelligentsia and became the central point of identification for his Russian readers in the 1880s. This point dominates the translations of lawyer, author, and literary critic Sergey Arkadyevich Andreyevsky (1847–1919),[7] who published his rendition of five Baudelairean poems in the liberal *Vestnik Evropy* (Messenger of Europe).[8] Andreyevsky is known most of all for his posthumously published *Book of Death*, which Mirsky has characterized as "one of the finest achievements of Russian prose."[9] It is interesting to compare Andreyevsky's approach to translating

Baudelaire with that of the populist N. S. Kurochkin, Baudelaire's first Russian translator. A comparison of their versions of "Spleen [IV]" shows that Andreyevsky followed the original more closely and refrained from moralizing insertions. The juxtaposition of the last stanza in Kurochkin's and Andreyevsky's translation's shows the superiority of the latter's approach.

Kurochkin:

> Тогда в душе моей—процессий погребальных
> Ряд мрачный тянется. И немощен и наг
> Мой ум—пред ужасом проклятых и печальных
> Вопросов, траурный свой выкинувших флаг . . .

> At this moment in my soul funeral processions
> In a gloomy file drag on. And powerless and naked
> Is my mind—before the horror of accursed and sad
> Questions, which have hoisted their mourning flag . . .

Andreyevsky:

> Тогда немых гробов я вижу вереницы
> И плачу над своей растерзанной Мечтой,
> А Скорбь меня сосет со злобою тигрицы
> И знамя черное вонзает в череп мой!

> At this moment I see rows of mute coffins
> And I weep over my lacerated Dream,
> And Sorrow sucks me with the spite of a tigress
> And thrusts a black banner into my skull!

In the original:

> —Et de longs corbillards, sans tambours ni musique,
> Défilent lentement dans mon âme: l'Espoir,
> Vaincu, pleure, et l'Angoisse atroce, despotique,
> Sur mon crâne incliné plante son drapeau noir.

And long hearses, without drums and music,
March past slowly in my soul: Hope,
Defeated, weeps, and atrocious, despotic Anguish
On my bent skull plants its black flag.

Whereas in Kurochkin's version, the poet is haunted by "accursed questions"—
a dear cliché of nineteenth-century Russian radical literature—Andreyevsky
renders the allegoric structure of the original more successfully. He is the first
Russian translator who paid attention to Baudelaire's technique of capitalizing
nouns. "Espoir" and "Angoisse" are correctly understood as personifications,
although *Mechta* (dream) and *Skorb'* (sorrow) are not semantically exact translations. Andreyevsky also neglects the fact that they are the *only* agents in the
poem (*Hope* is crying, not the persona, who seems an entirely depersonalized,
empty stage for a fighting match between hostile powers). Andreyevsky's
vaguely exotic image of a tigress is hardly appropriate[10] (one wonders, too, why
a tigress would "suck" somebody), but at least the last line is rendered felici-
tously. Baudelaire's final tableau becomes even more painful in Andreyevsky's
version, where the flag of "Spleen" literally seems to penetrate the poet's brain.

Melancholy, tiredness, and pessimism are the predominant features of
many Russian Baudelaire translations of the 1880s. Even Baudelaire's dynamic
evocation of modern urban life seems strangely muted and pale. The "fleuves
de charbon" streaming out of the chimneys in the poem "Paysage" are reduced
to a simple *chernyi dym* (black smoke) in Semyon Nadson's translation, and
Baudelaire's explosive imagery turns into worn-out, post-romantic clichés:

И на призыв певца весна меня обвеет,
Весна волшебных грез и солнце чистых дум . . . [11]

And invoked by the singer, spring is wafting around me,
The spring of magic dreams and the sun of pure thoughts . . .

One would hardly guess that this is Nadson's reading of the following lines
from Baudelaire's "Paysage":

Car je serai plongé dans cette volupté
D'évoquer le Printemps avec ma volonté,

De tirer un soleil de mon coeur, et de faire
De mes pensers brûlants une tiède atmosphère.

For I will be plunged in the [sensual] pleasure
Of evoking Spring with my will,
Of pulling a sun out of my heart, and of making
Of my burning thoughts a mild atmosphere.

Interestingly enough, it was less Baudelaire's *Les Fleurs du Mal* than his *Petits poèmes en prose* that seemed to have had the greatest impact on the Russian "predecadence" of the 1880s. The genre of the prose poem with its fragmentation and oxymoronic subversion of the traditional prose-verse dichotomy proved to have a special appeal in this period of crisis. It seemed to offer a way out of the stagnation that had affected traditional verse poetry. Furthermore, miniatures had become a prevalent trend in prose writing after the breakdown of the great novelistic form. This can be observed in the works of such various writers of the 1880s as Garshin, Chekhov, Saltykov-Shchedrin, and even Lev Tolstoy.

An important event of December 1882 was the publication of Turgenev's last work in *Vestnik Evropy,* a collection of fifty *Stikhotvoreniia v proze* (Poems in Prose), which Merezhkovsky later hailed as a crucial stage on the road to symbolism. With their use of "musical" prose and their predominant mood of Schopenhauerian pessimism and *memento mori,* Turgenev's prose poems indeed share many common elements with the decadent spirit of the time. Although Turgenev never mentions Baudelaire in his literary criticism or in any of his letters, there can be no doubt that he was at least partially inspired by him, as can be seen already from the generic title *Stikhotvoreniia v proze,* which introduced the Baudelairean notion of the *poème en prose* into Russian literature.[12] Besides some rather vague common motifs, striking parallels exist in the mode of reading that Baudelaire and Turgenev recommend for their prose poems. Both of them suggest in their forewords a random, nonsequential approach. Echoing Baudelaire's advice to cut one's reading wherever one wants without paying attention to a "superfluous plot,"[13] Turgenev also recommends an aleatory approach: "My dear reader, do not run through these poems one after the other (*spodriad*): you will probably get bored—and the book will fall from your hands. Read them separately: today one, tomorrow another—and one of them, perhaps, will arouse something in your soul."[14] The predominance of the fragment over the whole has been described by Paul Bourget and later by Nietzsche as a central aspect of the decadent worldview.[15]

Turgenev's *Stikhotvoreniia v proze* were not the first prose poems to appear in Russia. The first Russian translation of Baudelaire's prose poems had come out a few years earlier. In 1878, the journal *Zhivopisnoe obozrenie* (Art Review) published five of them—"Le Don des fées," "Les Yeux des pauvres," "Le Joujou du pauvre," "Le Vieux Saltimbanque," and "La Corde"—under the title "*poemy v proze.*"[16] The editors attached a brief introductory statement, in which the new genre, perhaps in accordance with the journal's primary function, was characterized as "poems in prose, providing ready-made subjects for paintings, and serving with their style as a link between prose and poetry." The selection of the texts with its focus on poverty seems to indicate a "populist" rather than a "decadent" view of Baudelaire. The excerpts quoted from Baudelaire's foreword are curiously distorted in the Russian translation, highlighting the author's "idealism" in a manner worthy of a P. F. Yakubovich.

Six years after this initial publication, D. S. Merezhkovsky, who was at the time nineteen years old, published his translation of twelve prose poems by Baudelaire in the journal *Iziashchnaia literatura* (Belles-Lettres).[17] In an introductory note, the young translator claims that, besides their "elegance of form and novelty of content," these texts are of special interest to Russian readers because of Turgenev's recently published *Stikhotvoreniia v proze.* He points out that it was not Turgenev but Baudelaire who "invented" the new genre. The fact that two such different writers both made use of the same literary device indicates, according to Merezhkovsky, that the genre of the prose poem has a great future. Although Merezhkovsky did not neglect the poverty-theme (after all, he still belonged to the camp of civic poets at that time), his selection also contains many pieces of a more decadent character. His commentaries indicate a heightened interest in the purely aesthetic qualities of Baudelaire's language. In comparison with the earlier publication in *Zhivopisnoe obozrenie,* the focus of attention seems to shift from content to form. Merezhkovsky ends his introduction with the remark: "I have to add that Baudelaire's language, because of its conciseness, force and audacity, does not yield easily to translation, and I would therefore consider my task fulfilled even if it turned out that I succeeded in rendering only an insignificant part of the original's beauty."

Another early proponent of Baudelaire's prose poems in Russia was Viktor Ivanovich Bibikov (1863–92), a prose writer whose "coarse self-castigation and eccentric moods," according to the *Russian Biographical Dictionary,* are imitative of the French *décadence.*[18] In 1890, Bibikov published a book entitled *Tri portreta. Stendal'-Flober-Bodler* (Three Portraits. Stendhal-Flaubert-Baudelaire), which contains, after a brief biographic note, excerpts from Baudelaire's diaries and letters as well as twenty prose poems. Bibikov claims that the *Petits poèmes en prose* are Baudelaire's best work. It is interesting to note that in the whole book not even one verse poem is quoted. It seems that in Bibikov's opinion, the days of verse poetry were numbered.[19]

Merezhkovsky was less extreme than Bibikov in his predilection for the prose poem. He continued to write verse poetry and also translated four poems by Baudelaire into Russian verse: "L'Invitation au voyage," "Chant d'automne," "L'Albatros," and "Spleen [III]."[20] His adaptation of "L'Invitation au voyage," under the title "Golubka moia" (My Little Dove), became popular in the 1880s as a gypsy romance.[21] The novelty of Merezhkovsky's approach can best be highlighted if we confront his translation of "L'Albatros" with Yakubovich's rendering of the same poem. Incidentally, Merezhkovsky and Yakubovich were friends in their youth. (One wonders whether it was Yakubovich who initially drew Merezhkovsky's attention to Baudelaire!) As late as 1888, Merezhkovsky sent Yakubovich, then in a labor camp in Siberia, a copy of his first volume of poetry, *Stikhotvoreniia*, which contained his translations of "L'Invitation au voyage," "Chant d'automne," and "L'Albatros," with the dedication "to my dear colleague Yakubovich as a sign of deep respect."[22]

Baudelaire's allegoric "Albatros" is an anthology piece par excellence and one of the most famous poems in the French language (although not everybody would agree that it is Baudelaire's best):

L'Albatros

Souvent, pour s'amuser, les hommes d'équipage
Prennent des albatros, vastes oiseaux des mers,
Qui suivent, indolents compagnons de voyage,
Le navire glissant sur les gouffres amers.

A peine les ont-ils déposés sur les planches,
Que ces rois de l'azur, maladroits et honteux,
Laissent piteusement leurs grandes ailes blanches
Comme des avirons traîner à côté d'eux.

Ce voyageur ailé, comme il est gauche et veule!
Lui, naguère si beau, qu'il est comique et laid!

L'un agace son bec avec un brûle-gueule,
L'autre mime, en boitant, l'infirme qui volait!

Le Poète est semblable au prince des nuées
Qui hante la tempête et se rit de l'archer;
Exilé sur le sol au milieu des huées,
Ses ailes de géant l'empêchent de marcher.

The Albatross

Frequently, to amuse themselves, the men of the crew
Catch albatrosses, vast birds of the sea,
Which follow, indolent travel companions,
The ship gliding over the bitter abysses.

As soon as they deposit them on the planks,
These kings of the azure, awkward and ashamed,
Let their big white wings pitifully
Like oars trail alongside them.

This winged voyager, how clumsy and weak he is!
He, once so beautiful, how comical and ugly!
One is irritating his beak with a cutty,
Another is aping, limping, the cripple who used to fly!

The Poet resembles the prince of clouds
Who haunts the storm and laughs at the archer;
Exiled on the ground amidst jeers,
His giant wings hinder him from walking.

In Yakubovich's translation:

Альбатос

Когда в морском пути тоска грызет матросов,
Они, досужий час желая скоротать,

Беспечных ловят птиц, огромных альбатросов,
Которые суда так любят провожать.

И вот, когда царя любимого лазури
На палубе кладут, он снежных два крыла,
Умевших так легко парить навстречу бури,
Застенчиво влачит, как два больших весла.

Быстрейший из гонцов, как грузно он ступает!
Краса воздушных стран, как стал он вдруг смешон!
Дразня, тот в клюв ему табачный дым пускает,
Тот веселит толпу, хромая, как и он.

Поэт, вот образ твой! Ты также без усилья
Летаешь в облаках, средь молний и громов,
Но исполинские тебе мешают крылья
Внизу ходить, в толпе, средь шиканья глупцов.[23]

The Albatross

When on the sea journey boredom nags at the sailors,
Wishing to while away the time of leisure,
They catch careless birds, the huge albatrosses,
Which so love to accompany the ships.

And see, when the beloved tsar of the azure
Is put on the deck, his two snowy wings,
Which were able to soar so lightly against the storm,
Trail shyly like two big oars.

The swiftest of hunters, how heavily he treads!
The ornament of aerial lands, how ridiculous he has suddenly become!
Mocking him, one is blowing in his beak tobacco smoke,
Another amuses the crowd by limping like he does.

Poet, here is your image! You too without effort
Fly in the clouds, amidst lightning and thunder,

But gigantic wings hinder you
From walking below, in the crowd, amidst the hissing of fools.

In Merezhkovsky's translation:

Альбатос

Во время плаванья, когда толпе матросов
Случается поймать над бездною морей
Огромных, белых птиц, могучих альбатросов,
Беспечных спутников отважных кораблей,—

На доски их кладут: и вот, изнемогая,
Труслив и неуклюж, как два больших весла,
Влачит недавний царь заоблачного края
По грязной палубе два трепетных крыла.

Лазури гордый сын, что бури обгоняет,
Он стал уродливым, и жалким, и смешным,
Зажженной трубкою матрос его пугает
И дразнит с хохотом, прикинувшись хромым.

Поэт, как альбатрос, отважно, без усилья
Пока он—в небесах, витает в бурной мгле,
Но исполинские, невидимые крылья
В толпе ему ходить мешают по земле.[24]

The Albatross

During the sailing, when a crowd of sailors
Happen to catch over the abyss of the seas
Huge, white birds, the mighty albatrosses,
The carefree companions of brave ships,

They put them on the deck: and see, growing faint,
Timorous and awkward, like two big oars,

The recent tsar of a land beyond the clouds drags
Over the dirty deck two trembling wings.

The proud son of the azure, who outstrips the storms,
He has become ugly, pathetic and ridiculous,
A sailor scares him with a lit pipe
And mocks him with guffaws, pretending to be limping.

The Poet, like the albatross, bravely, without effort
Hovers in the stormy haze, as long as he is in the skies,
But gigantic, invisible wings
Hinder him from walking in the crowd on earth.

While the two translations share some common features (the rhyme *matrosov - al'batrosov*, for example, which does not exist in the original, but seems to be dictated by the Russian language),[25] the two translators offer different interpretations of the poet's lonely estrangement from the human world. Yakubovich tries to provide rational explanations for the fate of the pitiable albatross. Unlike Merezhkovsky, he provides a motivation for the action of the sailors (they suffer from *toska* [melancholy, boredom]). The immorality of their behavior is emphasized by the fact that they are torturing a bird that is their voluntary companion. Yakubovich asserts that albatrosses love to accompany ships (*kotorye suda tak liubiat provozhat'*), a far cry from Baudelaire's "indolents compagnons de voyages" and Merezhkovsky's "careless companions" (*bespechnye sputniki*). The poet suffers from the same problem, being hissed at by a stupid mob of "fools." The situation is different in Merezhkovsky's version. Here, the albatross is not simply a victim of insensitive tormentors. Its fate seems the logical consequence of its fundamental alienation from the human race. This is true also for the poet, who is less disturbed by hissing blockheads than by the crowd of people in general. As the ruler of a transcendental kingdom "beyond the clouds" (*tsar' zaoblachnogo kraia*), he can have nothing in common with this world of common mortals.[26]

While both translations seem relatively successful, there is a noticeable difference in tone. Merezhkovsky is much more detached and cool: Baudelaire's and Yakubovich's exclamations in stanza three become a sober statement of fact, as does Yakubovich's apostrophe to the poet at the beginning of stanza four (here, Merezhkovsky is closer to the original). An important stylistic feature of Baudelaire escaped the attention of both translators: the integration of prosaisms into the poetic diction. Neither Yakubovich nor Merezhkovsky found an adequate solution for the vulgar expression *brûle-gueule* (a short clay pipe, or cutty), probably because they were both guided by a "high" ideal of poetry. Merezhkovsky's version of the poem seems more aesthetically appealing, however. A dominant formal feature of his translation is the numerous enjambements and the peculiar use of syntax, with which he achieves an iconic representation of the albatross's indolent flight over the sea. Note that the first two stanzas consist of a single, uninterrupted sentence.

French symbolism played a major role, along with Nietzsche's influence, in Merezhkovsky's conversion from his populist "love of the people" to a detached aestheticist individualism. Baudelaire certainly was an important figure for him at that period, and motifs from *Les Fleurs du Mal*, like the symbol of the "cold sun" (from "De profundis clamavi"), occur in his own poetry of the time.[27] However, Baudelaire did not prove to be an "eternal companion" in later years. Unlike some later Russian symbolists, Merezhkovsky was mostly concerned with Baudelaire's ennui and aesthetic escapism and paid no attention to him as a religious thinker. In the metaphysical search and apocalyptic mysticism that became predominant in Merezhkovsky's thought after the turn of the century, Baudelaire plays no visible role. This is perhaps not surprising: Baudelaire's radical notion of the fall and original sin could hardly be perceived as helpful in an attempt to rehabilitate the flesh.

Baudelaire comes up only indirectly in Merezhkovsky's influential lecture "On the Causes of the Decline and on the New Trends of Contemporary Russian Literature" (1892, published 1893). The French poet is named twice, in connection first with Poe and later with Dostoyevsky: "Already Baudelaire and Edgar Poe said that the beautiful has to *astonish* somewhat, that it has to seem unexpected and rare. . . . You will agree that Dostoyevsky had this criminal curiosity for rebellious thought, this audacity to encroach on the most sacred objects of duty and faith, this demonic element, which Baudelaire, with regard to Byron, calls 'le satanique.'"[28] Merezhkovsky's references to Baudelaire's aesthetic of the bizarre and to his blasphemous satanism are characteristic of the pattern of decadent reception. A similar view of Baudelaire emerges also from the poem "Novoe iskusstvo" (New Art) from the cycle "Konets veka" (End of the Century), which Merezhkovsky published in 1892 in the collection *Simvoly*.

Baudelaire is presented there as a successor of Edgar Allan Poe and embodiment of the fin de siècle spirit:

И сумрачный Бодлэр, тебе по музе брат,
На горестный напев откликнуться был рад;
Зловешей прелестью, как древняя Медуза,
Веселых парижан пугала эта муза.
Зато ее речей неотразимый яд,
Зато ее цветов смертельный аромат
Надолго отравил больное поколенье.
Толпа мечтателей признала в опьяненьи
Тебя вождем, Бодлэр . . . Романтиков былых
Отвага буйная напоминала в них . . .[29]

And the gloomy Baudelaire, your brother in poetry,
Was pleased to respond to the sorrowful tune;
With an ominous beauty, like an ancient Medusa,
Did this Muse frighten the gay Parisians.
But then, the irresistible poison of her speeches,
The deathly aroma of her flowers
Poisoned for a long time to come the sick generation.
The crowd of dreamers, in an intoxicated state,
Recognized you as their leader, Baudelaire . . . Their stormy
Bravery evoked memories of the romantics of former times . . .

In the same year that Merezhkovsky's *Simvoly* came out, *Vestnik Evropy* published an important milestone in the reception of French symbolism in Russia: Zinaida Vengerova's article "Poety simvolisty vo Frantsii" (Symbolist Poets in France). Vengerova (1867–1941), sister of the well-known literary scholar S. A. Vengerov, tried to present the French symbolists less from a partisan than from an objective approach. Her article, mainly devoted to Verlaine, Mallarmé, Rimbaud, Laforgue, and Moréas, also contained a paragraph on Baudelaire, who is presented as their forerunner and as the "first real decadent." Vengerova's emphasis on Baudelaire's neurotic sensitivity is, once again, reminiscent of Théophile Gautier. Vengerova also wrote the entry on Baudelaire in the *Brokgauz-Efron Encyclopedia*, which had appeared a year before the *Vestnik Evropy* essay. Besides the discussion of Baudelaire's decadent features, his dandyism and focus on the "decay of the human soul," which are reported rather sympathetically, Vengerova also underlined his "idealism": "They accused the poet himself of the depravity that he described, not understanding that behind the passionate contempt, with which Baudelaire depicts the fall of man, there is hidden a deep love for the ideal of good and truth."[30] Among the "best pieces" of *Les Fleurs du Mal,* Vengerova named "L'Albatros," "L'Homme et la mer," and "Les Petites Vieilles," and she points to "P. F. Ramshev's" (i.e., P. F. Yakubovich's) translations in *Severnyi vestnik.* Attention is also paid to *Petits poèmes en prose,* with an excerpt from "Enivrez-vous" quoted in French, and to *Les Paradis artificiels.* Baudelaire's diaries are referred to only indirectly, with a quotation documenting his contempt for nature and for women.

It is noteworthy that a Russian reader of 1891 had access to this relatively well documented and benevolent source, at a time when few of Baudelaire's works had been translated. In later years, Vengerova wrote two more articles on Baudelaire—a twenty-page survey of his life published in *Literaturnye kharakteristiki* and the entry on Baudelaire in *Novyi entsiklopedicheskii slovar',* which is more extensive than the first version and contains a bibliography of Russian translations. Her judgment of Baudelaire seems not significantly altered, but we can detect a heightened consciousness of Baudelaire's importance for contemporary modernism. If in 1891 Baudelaire had been simply a "renowned French poet," he was now a "renowned French poet, the patriarch (*rodonachal'nik*) of contemporary aesthetism and decadence."[31]

The characterization of Baudelaire as a decadent became the predominant feature of Russian Baudelaire criticism of the 1890s. Friends and foes alike insisted on his decadence (with the notable exception, of course, of P. F. Yakubovich—but even he was influenced by Gautier). Baudelaire's name frequently comes up together with that of another writer whom the Russian decadents and symbolists discovered as one of their predecessors: F. M. Dostoyevsky. A good example is A. N. Engelgardt's 1892 article on Baudelaire in *Vestnik inostrannoi literatury* (The Messenger of Foreign Literature). In his "Society and Literature Chronicle of the West," Engelgardt gave an account of the polemic dispute that arose in France over a planned monument for Baudelaire. In 1892, the revue *La Plume* started a fund to erect a statue of Baudelaire in Paris. Many leading writers of the day endorsed the project but it was attacked by the influential critic Ferdinand Brunetière, according to whom a Baudelaire in bronze would be a "scandal, or rather a sort of obscenity."[32] Since the poet is "not well known in Russia," Engelgardt presented his readers with an extensive characterization of Baudelaire, called a "decadent amidst the parnassians." The enumeration of his decadent features—his neuroses, predilection for the literature of the late Latin Empire, contempt for all "philanthropists, progressists, utilitarianists, and utopists," his aestheticism and love for the artificial, perfumes, and cats—sounds once more like a paraphrase of Gautier. More interesting is the comparison with Dostoyevsky. Engelgardt's approach to decadence contained idealistic and moralizing overtones: "If we define decadence as the poetry of dirt, as the 'flowers of evil,' as the striving, in the representation of evil and the perversion of nature, to arouse through opposition the bright picture of the good, as the striving to illuminate the 'two abysses' of the human soul, according to Dostoyevsky's expression, its 'satanic depths' and the boundless distances (*dali*) of the ideal, then Baudelaire has to be called the father of decadence in France."[33] Similar ideas were expressed also in the more lowbrow press. In 1894, the popular and rather pedestrian journal *Knizhki "Nedeli"* devoted an article to the "first decadents," focusing on Baudelaire and Verlaine. The author sees "discord" (*razlad*) as the main feature of modernist poetry. Baudelaire's work is characterized by sharp, unresolved "dissonances" and "contradictions." The critic explained: "Baudelaire's poetry is a poetry of discord, both internal—that is, the discord of the poet with himself, and external—the discord of the poet with the surrounding world. The disintegration of elements, characteristic for the literature of decadence, is clearly visible in his poetry."[34] The reviewer asserted that, unlike the poetry of Verlaine, Baudelaire's poetry does contain philosophical thoughts, and he recommended it for readers interested in the condition of modern humanity and its "dual, disarranged nature." Verlaine, in comparison, was treated as a poet of pure art.

An emphasis on Baudelaire's insight into the dark abysses of the human soul rather than on formal criteria seems characteristic for many decadent Russian followers of Baudelaire. A notable exception to this rule was Prince A. I. Urusov (1843–1900), a wealthy Moscow lawyer and connoisseur of French literature with a special predilection for Flaubert and Baudelaire. In his reminiscences, Konstantin Balmont calls Urusov "one of the main popularizers (*rasprostraniteli*) of Baudelaire's poetry in Russia, and one of the first who provided moral support for the representatives of the movement in poetry which received from the crowd the condemning name of decadence."[35] Urusov's approach to Baudelaire was that of a parnassian aestheticist. His commentaries show him as perhaps the first explicitly "nonreferential" reader of Baudelaire's poetry in Russia: "Baudelaire is interesting as the creative composer of images and sounds, as an artist who contains in himself an architect—in the well-proportioned construction of poems, a musician—in the melody and harmony of the verse, a painter—in the splendor of colors, a sculptor—in the relief of details and roundedness of the whole, and an actor—in the creation of moods."[36] According to Urusov, it is impossible to translate Baudelaire's poems, because of their "full harmony of form and content."[37] He made only a few prose translations: some pages from "Notes nouvelles sur Edgar Poe," four prose poems ("L'Etranger," "Chacun sa chimère," "Les Yeux des pauvres," "Les Bienfaits de la lune"), and two prose versions of poems from Les Fleurs du Mal ("L'Ennemi," "Le Balcon").[38]

Urusov played an important role not only in the Russian reception of Baudelaire but also in the French. He edited, together with Mallarmé, the volume Le Tombeau de Charles Baudelaire, published by the revue La Plume in 1896. Urusov included in this book his French essays on "L'architecture secrète des Fleurs du mal" and "Les trois textes des Fleurs du mal," written in his "neigeuses et paisibles retraites villageoises, si éloignées de Paris!" They are the first serious study of the composition of Les Fleurs du Mal and remain a pioneering and seminal work of Baudelaire criticism. Urusov's interest in the "architecture" of Les Fleurs du Mal, that is, the sequential arrangement of the poems independently of the chronology of their composition, had a lasting impact on Russian symbolist poetry. The cyclization of poems in larger frames became a hallmark of this movement, starting with Balmont's and Bryusov's poetry collections of the 1890s. Since both Balmont and Bryusov were acquainted with Urusov, the idea seems not too far-fetched that it was he and thus ultimately the example of Baudelaire's Fleurs du Mal that started the Russian symbolist tradition of carefully composed "books of poetry."[39]

Although the decadent discovery of Baudelaire may appear one-sided in some respects, it still left an important legacy. By the mid-1890s the stage was set for a new era in Russian poetry, characterized by the predominance of aesthetics over political concerns. For the first time, Baudelaire was appreciated as a groundbreaking figure in the history of modern poetry. Rather than with Béranger, Barbier, or Dupont, his name was now associated with Verlaine, Rimbaud, and Mallarmé. The sharpened awareness of the aesthetic qualities of his work evolved along with the understanding of poetry as creation rather than simple entertainment or propaganda. The dawning Silver Age, as it later became known, was to produce some of the greatest Russian poetry since the age of Pushkin. After a hiatus of half a century, characterized by sterile didacticism and neglect of form, poetry was again at the forefront of the Russian literary scene.

BALMONT: THE MUSIC OF DECADENCE

Perhaps the most important legacy of Urusov in Russian literature is his effect on someone who was to become a major poet of the Silver Age: Konstantin Dmitrievich Balmont (1867–1942). It was Urusov, according to Balmont's own testimony, who cured him of his distaste for French literature by introducing him to Flaubert and Baudelaire and who made him attentive to the "musicality of sounds," the most celebrated feature of Balmont's poetry. The encounter with Urusov was a turning point in Balmont's life: "Urusov helped my soul become free, helped me to find myself."[40] A polyglot, tireless globe-trotter, and extremely prolific writer, Balmont achieved tremendous popularity in turn-of-the-century Russia with both his formal virtuosity and his predilection for daring erotic themes.

Baudelaire is the only French poet who was of any importance to Balmont. In his opinion, symbolism owed everything to the Germanic world—England, America, Scandinavia, and Germany—and not to France. Balmont dismissed Verlaine (whose languorous musicality seems so similar to his own) and Mallarmé as "highly overrated" poets. Baudelaire, however, was an exception, although Balmont saw him mainly as a successor of Edgar Allan Poe. He stated that "Baudelaire developed some thoughts which Poe was unable to express, or did not have time to finish saying, he gave to symbolism a particular color, which received in the history of literature the designation 'decadent,' and he wrote a whole array of original poems which widened the field of symbolist poetry."[41]

The sense of decadent pessimism that invaded Balmont's poetry in the early 1890s was certainly in part influenced by Baudelaire. A good example is the sonnet "Koshmar" (Nightmare) in the collection *Pod severnym nebom* (Under Northern Skies, 1894), where, in a "luxuriant alcove full of fragrance," the persona is confronted with a woman who turns out to be a "soulless wild animal" gazing at him with the "half-closed eyes of a snake."[42] A similarly spooky atmosphere permeates Balmont's foreword to Yakubovich's 1895 edition of Baudelaire, which provides a good example of Balmont's peculiar approach to literary criticism. The text reads like an extended hallucination that seems only vaguely connected with certain motifs from *Les Fleurs du Mal*. The main emphasis lies on death and decay. The reader is carried off to a "bewitched land" full of "poisonous evaporations," with towering "gigantic coffins" in a ghastly landscape gloomily illuminated by a "dead, cold moon."[43] Poor Yakubovich must have been bewildered when he read in the foreword to his volume that "no roses bloom here, no nightingales fly to this place. The air is poisoned, only ill-omened owls can breathe it; the soil is defiled, and there are only poisonous plants growing on it, with gloomy and fantastic outlines. Even the refined fragrances which fill this dead, enchanted kingdom are so strange, so enigmatic, that, providing a moment of enjoyment, they instantly demand a bitter retribution, they trouble the soul, quench the will, and inspire thoughts and actions that are followed by repentance." [44]

The last word indicates that, despite all his "poisonous flowers" and bizarre morbidity, Balmont did not (yet) advocate a decadent immoralism. Like so many other Russian commentators, he found it necessary to stress Baudelaire's "idealism." His foreword culminates in a poem, which, after running through the gamut of decadent aestheticism and "beauty of evil," repudiates its own initial position and ends on a morally edifying note:

Его манило зло, он рвал его цветы,
Болотные в себя вдыхал он испаренья,
    Он в грязной тине преступленья
    Искал сиянья красоты.
Исполнен странного немого упоенья,
В вертепах низости, среди толпы чужой,
Скорбел он чуткою тревожною душой.
И там, где пьяное бесстыдство хохотало,
Циничной шуткою приветствуя порок,
    Он был от пошлости далек,
В его уме живом мечта мечту рождала.
Незримые цветы он собрал,—и венок,
    Венок печальный и позорный,
Он возложил на нас, украсив им себя.
    Он свет зажег в пучине черной,
    Он жил во зле, добро любя.[45]

He was lured by evil, he plucked its flowers,
He inhaled its swampy exhalations,
    In the filthy slime of crime
    He searched for the shining of beauty.
Filled with a strange, mute intoxication,

In the dens of baseness, amidst an alien crowd,
He grieved with a sensitive, anxious soul.
And there, in the laughter of drunken shamelessness,
Which greeted vice with a cynical joke,
　　He was far from vulgarity,
In his living mind one dream gave birth to another.
He collected invisible flowers—and he laid on us a wreath
　　A sad and shameful wreath,
Adorning himself with it.
　　He lit a light in a black abyss,
　　He lived in evil, loving the good.

Balmont omitted this poem from the revised version of the foreword, which he published in 1904 under the title "O 'Tsvetakh zla'" (On the "Fleurs du Mal") in his essay collection *Gornye vershiny* (Mountain Peaks). The most striking difference from the text of 1894 is the absence of any moralizing elements, and even a certain pose of provocative amoralism. This is hardly surprising if we remember Balmont's evolution from musically languorous doom and gloom in the 1890s to his partly Nietzschean decadent emotionalism in the early years of the twentieth century. If in 1894 Balmont had some words of praise for Baudelaire's "prayerlike attitude to the Good" (*molitvennoe otnoshenie k Dobru*), ten years later this quotation emerges in a rather different context: "If the highest final goal of this man, who is walking on the paths of Evil, coincides with the goal of reaching an ultimate all-encompassing harmony, I love him for the fact that in the smoke and laughter of contradictions he conserves in himself a *prayerlike attitude to the Good.* However, if he lives in the world of Evil simply because he wants to live in the world of Evil, I love him for his integrity (*tsel'nost'*)."[46] The "immoral" second sentence was added in 1904.

In 1899, Balmont devoted a second hymn to Baudelaire, which has some striking similarities with Yakubovich's poem "Pamiati Sharlia Bodlera." Both texts are written in iambic hexameters (perhaps imitating the structure of Baudelaire's alexandrines), and both celebrate the French poet as a personal idol revealing himself to his worshiper in a supernatural apparition:

Как страшно-радостный и близкий мне пример,
Ты все мне чудишься, о царственный Бодлер,
Любовник ужасов, обрывов и химер![47]

Like a frightful-joyful and close example
You keep appearing to me, oh kingly Baudelaire,
Lover of horrors, precipices and chimeras!

The five stanzas that follow deal with Baudelaire's "heavy yellow spleen"; his knowledge of Woman as a demon and of the Demon as the "spirit of beauty"; his familiarity with the "secrets of mystical poisons," "gigantic cities," and the "kingdom of ice";[48] his "symphony of perfumes, sounds and colors"; and his wanderings through "destroyed worlds" as a "black, ghostly, outcast monk." At the end, like Yakubovich, Balmont expresses the wish to fuse his soul with Baudelaire's:

Пребудь же призраком навек в душе моей,
С тобой дай слиться мне, о маг и чародей,
Чтоб я без ужаса мог быть среди людей!

As a ghost remain eternally in my soul,
Allow me to merge with you, oh magician and sorcerer,
So that I can be without horror among people!

Several of Balmont's poems of this period are clearly inspired by Baudelaire. In the same volume that contains his hymn to the French poet, *Goriashchie zdaniia* (Burning Buildings, 1900), we find a poem with the title "Al'batros." Unlike Baudelaire's allegoric bird of the same name, Balmont's albatross is not caught and humiliated but keeps floating proudly above the "nightly desert of the seas." The poem "Akkordy" (Chords) in *Tishina* (Silence, 1898) is an attempt to emulate Baudelaire's "Les Phares," a line from which is quoted as the epigraph to the text ("C'est un phare allumé sur mille citadelles"). Like Baudelaire, Balmont enumerates a series of great painters, but only two of them, Goya and Leonardo da Vinci, coincide with those in Baudelaire's poem. Balmont's view of the artist is rather different from Baudelaire's, as comparison of the endings reveals: whereas Baudelaire sees art as an expression of human dignity in the face of God's eternity ("Car c'est vraiment, Seigneur, le meilleur témoignage / Que nous puissions donner de notre dignité / Que cet ardent sanglot qui roule d'âge en âge / Et vient mourir au bord de votre éternité!" — "For this is really, o Lord, the best testimony that we can give of our dignity, this ardent sob which rolls from age to age and comes to die at the verge of your eternity"), Balmont revels in aggressive forebodings of a coming Nietzschean *Übermensch*:

Мне снились волхвы откровений, любимцы грядущих времен,
Воззванья влекущих на битву, властительно–ярких знамен.
Намеки на сверхчеловека, обломки нездешних миров,
Аккорды бездонных значеньем, еше не разгаданных снов.[49]

I dreamt of soothsayers of discoveries, the favorites of coming times,
Appeals of imperiously bright banners summing to battle,
Allusions to the superman, fragments of supernatural worlds,
Chords of still uninterpreted dreams, bottomless with meaning.

Like Baudelaire, Balmont also devoted a poem to cats: "Moi zveri" (My Animals) in *Tol'ko liubov* (Only Love, 1903). In the first half of the poem, he tries to outdo Baudelaire once more by focusing on tigers, leopards, and panthers rather than just plain house cats. The second half is vaguely reminiscent of Baudelaire's "Les chats" with its hints of magic power sparkling in the cats' eyes. Balmont points out that not only he but also the "terrible Edgar" (Poe) and the "tragic Baudelaire," his "two brothers," were lovers of cats. The casual manner in which Balmont puts himself in the same company with these geniuses shows that, unlike Baudelaire, he was not suffering from pangs of self-doubt:

Два гения, влюбленные в мечтанья,
Мои два брата в бездне мировой,
Где нам даны безмерные страданья
И беспредельность музыки живой.[50]

Two geniuses in love with dreams,
My two brothers in the world abyss,
Where immense sufferings are given to us
And the boundlessness of living music.

A persistent element in all of Balmont's commentary on Baudelaire is the semantic field of magic. Baudelaire is called a "magician" and "sorcerer," a "powerful demon" and "ghost," the ruler of a "bewitched kingdom." The poem devoted to Baudelaire is preceded by a hymn to Hermes Trismegistos,[51] master of occult sciences, which echoes Baudelaire's "Satan Trismégiste" in his opening poem to *Les Fleurs du Mal*. This emphasis on the irrational, suggestive elements in Baudelaire's poetry is characteristic of Balmont's attitude: unwilling or unable to engage in a distanced, logical, and analytical discourse, he lets himself be enthralled by Baudelaire's "music," and by "fusing" his soul with Baudelaire's he sets the strings of his own lyre in motion.

This approach is also characteristic of Balmont's translations. In total, he translated six poems by Baudelaire into Russian—"La Beauté," "La Géante," "Le Balcon," "Les Litanies de Satan" (in a condensed version), "La Mort des amants," and "Le Gouffre"[52]—a rather small amount compared with his huge output of translations (including the complete poetry of Shelley and Poe). Balmont's selection of texts provides a cross section of decadent themes, highlighting the terrible charm of beauty ("La Beauté"), provocative eroticism and bizarre monstrosity ("La Géante"), allusive musicality ("Le Balcon"), blasphemous satanism ("Les Litanies de Satan"), the praise of death ("La Mort des amants"), and an oppressive feeling of *angst* ("Le Gouffre").

Perhaps the most famous of these six poems is "La Mort des amants." With its morbid beauty and delicate musicality the sonnet was of a special appeal to the fin de siècle. Huysmans made it one of the favorite poems of his decadent hero des Esseintes in *A rebours*, and Villiers de L'Isle-Adam and Debussy both put it to music.[53] Balmont offers an extensive paraphrase of what he perceives as the "hidden story" (*skrytaia poema*) behind the text in his essay "Elementarnye slova o simvolicheskoi poezii" (Elementary Words on Symbolist Poetry). "La Mort des amants" is presented there as a perfect example of a symbolist poem. Every line, according to Balmont, is a "whole image, a complete chapter of a story, and another poet, Musset, for example, would have made from such a subject a long declamatory narrative." But not Baudelaire: "The symbolist poet shuns such commonly accessible devices; he takes the same subject, but forges it into shining chains, gives it such a force of compression, such a laconism of a stern and at the same time tender dramatism, that the ambition of the artistic idea cannot go further."[54]

Balmont's translation of "La Mort des amants" tries to do justice to the musical qualities of the original:

Смерть любовников

Постели, нежные от ласки аромата,
Как жадные гроба, раскроются для нас,
И странные цветы, дышавшие когда-то
Под блеском лучших дней, вздохнут в последний раз.

Остаток жизни их, почуяв смертный час,
Два факела зажжет, огромные светила,
Сердца созвучные, заплакав, сблизят нас,
Два братских зеркала, где прошлое почило.

В вечернем таинстве, воздушно-голубом,
Мы обменяемся единственным лучом,
Прощально-пристальным и долгим, как рыданье.

И Ангел, дверь поздней полуоткрыв, придет,
И, верный, оживит, и, радостный, зажжет
Два тусклых зеркала, два мертвые сиянья.[55]

The Death of the Lovers

Beds, tender from the caresses of fragrances,
Like greedy coffins, are opening for us,
And strange flowers, which once breathed
Under the splendor of better days, will sigh for a last time.

The remainder of their life, sensing the hour of death,
Will light two torches, huge luminaries,
The consonant hearts, having begun to weep, will unite us,
Two brotherly mirrors, where the past was resting.

In the evening mystery, aerily-blue,
We exchange a unique ray,
An intense farewell, long like a sob.

And an Angel will later come, half opening the door,
And, faithful, he will revive, and, joyful, he will light
The two tarnished mirrors, the two dead radiances.

In the original:

La Mort des amants

Nous aurons des lits pleins d'odeurs légères,
Des divans profonds comme des tombeaux,
Et d'étranges fleurs sur des étagères,
Ecloses pour nous sous des cieux plus beaux.

Usant à l'envi leurs chaleurs dernières,
Nos deux coeurs seront deux vastes flambeaux,
Qui réfléchiront leurs doubles lumières
Dans nos deux esprits, ces miroirs jumeaux.

Un soir fait de rose et de bleu mystique,
Nous échangerons un éclair unique,
Comme un long sanglot, tout chargé d'adieux;

Et plus tard un Ange, entrouvrant les portes,
Viendra ranimer, fidèle et joyeux,
Les miroirs ternis et les flammes mortes.

The Death of the Lovers

We will have beds full of light fragrances,
Divans, deep like tombs,
And strange flowers on shelves,
Which blossomed for us under more beautiful skies.

Vying with each other to use their last warmth,
Our two hearts will be two vast torches,
Which will reflect their double light
In our two spirits, these twin mirrors.

An evening made of pink and mystical blue,
We will exchange a unique flash of lightening,
Like a long sob, all fraught with farewell;

And later an Angel, half opening the doors,
Will come to revive, faithful and joyful,
The tarnished mirrors and the dead flames.

Balmont's translation, like most of his poetry, is aesthetically attractive, although it becomes clear that he does not pay attention to an exact rendering of the formal and semantic features of the original (Baudelaire's irregular scheme of rhymes in the tercets, for example, becomes regular in the Russian version). As a general tendency, Balmont seems to sentimentalize Baudelaire's rather abstract sonnet: *nezhnye* (tender) and *laski* (caresses) are nowhere to be found in the original. (Are they inspired by Balmont's oxymoronic "tender dramatism?") In the second line, he tries to outdo Baudelaire once more with graves that are "greedy" instead of being simply "deep." Baudelaire's second stanza, which seems like a celebration of duality with its succession of paired objects (deux coeurs, deux flambeaux, doubles lumières, deux esprits, miroirs jumeaux) is rendered only approximately. The sentimental line seven is entirely Balmont's invention. It is perhaps typical for his preoccupation with sound that he deems it necessary to introduce an acoustic element even in Baudelaire's completely "silent" text. The tercets display especially well Balmont's virtuoso mellifluousness with their smoothly running succession of composite adjectives.

A rather interesting text in its own genre is Balmont's revelation of the alleged "hidden story" behind "La mort des amants." It reads like a prose variation of his verse translation with many added details stemming from Balmont's own fantasy. Unrestrained by any formal scheme, Balmont can give free flow to his evocation of a beautifully decadent *Liebestod*. Since the text is too long to be quoted in full, the following excerpt may suffice as an illustration: "The death of lovers is always wrapped in mystery. But one has to think that, if they decided to part with such a *unique* thing as their life, they had deep reasons for it, making their death doubly tragic and beautiful. They grew tired of life, or they cannot live any longer. Having withdrawn from all people, in this room, where they had loved so much, in the semitransparent haze of the evening, mystically mysterious and aerially blue, they bent down on the bed, which will be their tender grave, in order to unite in one embrace love and death."[56]

In a provocative reading of "La Mort des amants," Fredric Jameson observed that the euphoria of ressurrection seemingly suggested in the conclusion of the poem is undermined by the dissolution and assimilation of the subjects to the tawdry kitsch objects of a Victorian boudoir. He compared Baudelaire's technique to that of our contemporary photorealism, featuring the shiny, mirroring surfaces of the alluring dream-objects of consumerism, where the postmodernist sublime has become entirely absorbed in the "production and reproduction of the image and of the simulacrum."[57] In a similar fashion, Balmont uses Baudelaire's poems for the production of decadent "dream-texts." In endless permutations, he combines and recombines the clichés of the decadent universe, similar to the rampant growth of the "poisonous plants" which he evokes in his hallucinatory paraphrase of *Les Fleurs du Mal*, adding yet another variation to the never-ending, ongoing "supertext" of his own poetic oeuvre.

BRYUSOV: A "COLD WITNESS"

Balmont was not the only Russian decadent to be interested in "La Mort des amants." Valery Yakovlevich Bryusov (1873–1924), the self-proclaimed leader of Russian decadence in the 1890s, wrote no fewer than four translations of this text between 1894 and 1900. Unlike Balmont, Bryusov always had a keen interest in French literature. He has been called "le plus français des écrivains russes" by a French critic,[58] and it comes as no surprise that Baudelaire played an important role in his life and work. Zinaida Vengerova's article in *Vestnik Evropy* proved to be a catalyst for his creative development. In an autobiographical note of 1909, Bryusov underlined the importance of the French symbolists for his writing: "I began to write verses very early, but only at age thirteen did I definitely recognize myself as a poet. The acquaintance, at the beginning of the 1890s, with the poetry of Verlaine and Mallarmé, and soon also Baudelaire, opened a new world to me. Under the impression of their work, I created those verses which first appeared in print (1894–95)."[59] In 1895, Baudelaire was the most prominent member in Bryusov's poetical pantheon, together with Verlaine and Tyutchev (whom he "discovered" *after* the French symbolists):

О милый мой мир: вот Бодлер, вот Верлен,
вот Тютчев—любимые, верные книги.[60]

Oh my dear world: here is Baudelaire, here Verlaine,
Here Tyutchev—beloved, true books.

The young Bryusov was particularly impressed with the decadent, "scandalous" features of *Les Fleurs du Mal,* and an aesthetic of cynical immoralism, contempt for nature and healthiness, the cult of death, and a morbid eroticism climaxing at times in perverse necrophilia became the hallmark of his own poetry. Certain motifs like Baudelaire's comparison of a pair of lovers to two corpses in "Une nuit que j'étais près d'une affreuse Juive" can be found in numerous variations in Bryusov's poetry of the 1890s. The rhyme *gub-trup* (lips-corpse), for example, occurs no fewer than four times.[61] Baudelaire's influence can be felt also in Bryusov's view of woman as a demonic temptress as well as in his representation of lovemaking as a form of sadomasochist torture.[62]

Explicit references to Baudelaire are rather rare in Bryusov's oeuvre of the 1890s. His name comes up once in the three miscellanies *Russkie simvolisty,* which catapulted Bryusov to scandalous fame in 1894–95. Volume three contains Bryusov's translation of a poem by Prisca de Landelle, entitled "Nadpis' na ekzempliar Bodlera" (Inscription on a Copy of Baudelaire), which stresses Baudelaire's amoralist aestheticism.[63] Three years later, we find an original poem by Bryusov with the title "A la Charles Baudelaire,"[64] featuring a "dirty cavern" with "purulent beer-puddles" and a situation that seems vaguely reminiscent of Baudelaire's "Une nuit que j'étais près d'unc affrcusc Juive." The persona lying in the "dark darkness of the night" with his "drunk woman friend" has visions of a "pale ghost" of a woman hovering about as a "crying, crying spirit." In Bryusov's defense it has to be mentioned that he was self-critical enough not to publish the poem.

Like Balmont, Bryusov was also intrigued by Baudelaire's blasphemous "Litanies de Satan." In 1900, he both translated the poem and wrote an imitation of it in his own style. Unlike Baudelaire's submissive attitude to Satan, Bryusov displays in it the proud self-glorification that became a typical feature of both his and Balmont's poetry. In the last stanza he even depicts himself as Satan's equal:

Я равен тебе, обреченной судьбой,
Лик с ликом могу упиваться тобой,
    О дьявол, владыка, покорствуй![65]

I am your equal, doomed by fate,
Face to face I can revel in you,
    Oh devil, master, be submissive!

Bryusov's unpublished notebooks contain a total of eleven translations of poems by Baudelaire[66] written between 1894 and 1900: "La Mort des amants" (four versions), "A une passante," "Le Revenant," "Parfum exotique," "Sed non satiata," "Le Mort joyeux," "Les Yeux de Berthe," and "Les Litanies de Satan." Of special interest are his four different versions of "La Mort des amants." They demonstrate Bryusov's obvious fascination with this text. Repeatedly he came back to it and wrestled with its form without ever being satisfied (the second version is even qualified as *plokho* [bad] in the notebook). A comparison of the four texts shows interesting parallels to Bryusov's own creative development during the 1890s. The first version, far from Baudelaire's original, is dominated by a somewhat naive exoticism and eroticism. The text features an array of plants that are nowhere to be found in Baudelaire. The two quatrains read as follows:

Ласкающих кроватей аромат
Глубокие, как тайный склеп, диваны
Магнолии, акации, тюльпаны
Огни цветов и сладострастный яд.

Последний жар желаний и услад,—
Как факелы, проникшие в туманы,
Зажжет сердца—и этот свет багряный
Два зеркала—две мысли отразят.

The fragrance of caressing beds
Deep divans like a secret crypt
Magnolias, acacias, tulips
Fires of flowers and voluptuous poison.

The last glow of desires and delights,
Like torches penetrating the fog,
Will light the hearts—and this crimson light
Will reflect two mirrors—two thoughts.

In February and March 1896, we find two new attempts. While the first stanza still features a nebulous exoticism, although without the "voluptuous poison" of 1894, the second stanza introduces an attempt at symbolist allegorization, couched in the typically Bryusovian mood of defiant pride:

И мы, вдвоем с тобой, в смертельном аромате:
Я—светоч истины, ты—факел красоты—
Два ярких зеркала,—две дерзкие мечты . . .
И этот гордый сон восторгов и объятий!

And we, the two of us together, in the fragrance of death:
I—the torch of truth, you— the flare of beauty—
Two bright mirrors,—two daring [day]dreams . . .
And this proud dream of delights and embraces!

A month later the allegory has disappeared, and we find ourselves in the "ante-room of Nirvana":

Зажгутся в нас сердца при странном аромате
Последней вспышкою в предверии нирваны
Две мысли отразят их свет полубагряный,
Живые зеркала восторгов и объятий!

Our hearts will flare up in a strange fragrance
As a last flash in the anteroom of Nirvana
Two thoughts will reflect their half-crimson light,
Living mirrors of delights and embraces!

Finally in 1900 the translation begins definitely to resemble Bryusov's "parnass-ian" style of his later period. The tone is rather detached and lofty, as is empha-sized by the longer meter (ponderous iambic hexameters instead of the pen-tameter used in the 1894 version, which was closer to Baudelaire's *décasyllabes*). A striking feature of the vocabulary is the use of Church Slavonic archaisms (*nevedomyi, lozhe, zlato*), which serve to underline the rhetorically high style of the translation:

Кровати опьянят нас теплым ароматом,
Нас примут, как гроба, глубокие диваны,
И странные цветы задышат пред закатом . . .
(Растили их для нас неведомые страны).

И будем мы вдвоем на ложе сладко смятом,

Предчувствием конца невыразимо пьяны . . .
И взоры отразят сердец огонь багряны,
Как факел зеркало—каким-то резким златом.

Beds will intoxicate us with a warm fragrance,
Deep divans, like tombs, will receive us,
And strange flowers will begin to breathe before sunset . . .
(Unknown countries grew them for us).
And we will be together on the sweetly rumpled couch,
Drunk beyond expression with the foreboding of the end . . .
And our glances will reflect the crimson fire of the hearts,
Like a torch a mirror—with some sharp gold.

The "sharp gold" of the last line (not existent in Baudelaire's text) forms a telling contrast to the watercolor-like fluidity of Balmont's impressionist imagery. Baudelaire's mirror-lined funeral parlor comes with Bryusov's translation in a gilded deluxe version. Did he later find this text too tawdry? In any event, Bryusov never published any of his translations of "La Mort des amants." The poem is not included in his anthology of French lyric poets of the nineteenth century (*Frantsuzskie liriki XIX veka*, 1909), which contains six poems by Baudelaire in his translation. It seems that he lost interest in "La Mort des amants" after 1900, when other aspects of Baudelaire became more important to him.

After the turn of the century, Bryusov established himself as the main spokesman for a strictly literary, nonreligious understanding of symbolism. He challenged the assumption that symbolist art necessarily had to express a connection with a metaphysical beyond. Himself the offspring of an agnostic merchant family, Bryusov harbored little sympathy for transcendentalist mysticism. He publicly attacked the notion of theurgic poetry, propagated by the mystic symbolists, as a violation of the freedom of art.[67]

With his cult of form and insistence on dispassionate craftmanship, Bryusov shows a certain affinity to the French parnassian movement. He has indeed sometimes been characterized as a parnassian rather than a genuine symbolist. It is worth pointing out, however, that it is not how Bryusov saw himself. He claimed to be a symbolist, and he even explicitly criticized the parnassian notion of "l'art pour l'art" (like Baudelaire, incidentally, who had condemned it as a "puérile utopie").[68] In his programmatic speech "Kliuchi tain" (Keys to the Mysteries), which was published in the opening number of the symbolist journal *Vesy* (Libra) in 1904, Bryusov asserted that true art could not exist for itself but had to be grounded in life. A beautifully crafted marble statue or sonnet is "dead," according to Bryusov, if it does not express a deeper human urge. The positive meaning of art, Bryusov explains in this article, is not the pursuit of a sterile beauty but of a specific form of cognition. Art allows us to break out of the "blue prison" of existence in special moments of "clearing" (*prosvety*), "moments of ecstasy, of supernatural intuition, which give us another understanding of the world phenomena, penetrating deeper behind their outer crust into their very heart (*serdtsevina*)."[69]

Bryusov's concept of penetrating beyond the surface should not be confused with the platonism of the mystic symbolists. Bryusov was less concerned with metaphysical essence than with the specific perception of the world made possible through poetic "intoxication." With its aesthetic rather than religious spiritualism, Bryusov's theory of art seems close to Baudelaire's. Bryusov must have been familiar with the passage in *Les Paradis artificiels* where Baudelaire discusses "this mysterious and temporary state of the spirit, where the depth of life, bristling with its multiple problems, reveals itself entirely in the spectacle, however natural and trivial, before our eyes,—where the first random object becomes a speaking symbol."[70]

Baudelaire was to remain an important figure for Bryusov throughout his career. If in his early years Bryusov had been attracted by the scandalous features of *Les Fleurs du Mal*, he later identified mostly with the anti-romantic side of Baudelaire, his rejection of sentimental effusions, and his conscious laboring with the poetic form—all tenets embodied in Bryusov's work during those years. In his well-known programmatic poem "Poetu" (To the Poet) of 1907, Bryusov expressed his wish to be a "cold witness," for whom everything in life, including his own suffering, is only a "means for clear-singing verse."[71] In the foreword to his 1909 anthology of French poetry, Bryusov emphasized Baudelaire's protest against romanticism: "To romantic sentimentality, Baudelaire opposed the cold analysis of feelings; to the rhetoric of the romantics—the sobriety of language; to their conventional morality—a paradoxical, but well thought-out worldview; to their attraction to the past—his love for modernity."[72] Bryusov himself proved to be a "cold witness" in his literary criticism, where he cultivated a soberly detached, professorial tone. His approach to Baudelaire was that of a literary scholar. The most extensive discussion can be found in his notes to the *Frantsuzskie liriki* edition, where Bryusov places Baudelaire in context and stresses at the same time his originality and modernity:

> Baudelaire occupies an isolated place in French poetry. A romantic by up-bringing, a parnassian by style, a realist by method, he did not belong to any school, he created his own. He is not a poet who relates personal grief and joy in his verses; but neither is he a calm reconstructor of historic and exotic pictures: he is the first poet of modernity. Baudelaire had the courage to embody in poetry, in verse, the whole complexity, the whole contradictoriness of the soul of modern man. He looked at the dark side of the soul and found beauty and poetry, where before him they saw only repulsiveness: in evil, vice, and crime. At the same time, Baudelaire was one of the first to create the poetry of the modern city, the poetry of modern life, its trivialities, its horror, its mystery. Baudelaire perceived the truth that the realist writers brought with them, but his sharp eyes were always fastened beyond reality, in the hope of seeing something greater. For this reason, Baudelaire's images frequently turn into symbols.[73]

The Baudelairean themes highlighted by Bryusov—life in the urban metropolis with its anonymous crowds and paradoxical "beauty of evil"—also figure prominently in his own work. Several of his poems are directly inspired by Baudelaire. Baudelaire's sonnet "A une passante" (which figures among Bryusov's unpublished translations of the 1890s), featuring a fleeting and abortive potential erotic encounter with an anonymous passerby, spawned two different poems: "Prokhozhei" (To a passerby [1900]) and "Vstrecha" (Encounter [1904]). The first is written in a more decadently sensual and the second in a more melancholically detached mood, carrying Baudelaire's last line as an epigraph ("O toi que j'eusse aimée, ô toi qui le savais").[74] "Le Paradis artificiel" appears as the title of a poem in the collection Zerkalo tenei (Mirror of Shadows [1909]), describing Baudelaire's drug-generated mood of "béatitude calme et immobile" evoked in the epigraph.[75] The poem "Sed non satiatus" (after Baudelaire's "Sed non satiata," which Bryusov translated in 1896) originally provided the title of the entire collection Sem' tsvetov radugi (Seven Colors of the Rainbow, 1912).[76] The more narrowly sexual content of Baudelaire's "Sed non satiata" is extended in Bryusov's "Sed non satiatus" to a sort of Faustian quest for total experience.

The only text that seems somewhat incongruous with Bryusov's focus on modernity and his nonmystic conception of Baudelaire is his foreword to Ellis's translation of *Les Fleurs du Mal* (1908). Probably as a concession to Ellis and in an attempt to find some common ground with the mystic translator, Bryusov does not make any reference here to Baudelaire's modernist urbanism. Instead of placing Baudelaire in the context of the French poetry of his time, as he did in the introduction to his own translations, he discusses Baudelaire, using Ellis's millennarian rhetoric, in the context of the entire spiritual history of humanity. Bryusov's text sounds almost like a parody of Ellis's high-pitched style. Two poems, "La Beauté" and "Correspondances," according to Bryusov, express the "limits of Baudelaire's poetry, and perhaps of all poetry." They represent not only the fundamental ideals of Baudelaire but those of all humanity: "Beauty" and "Mystery." While the classical world venerated the first and Christianity the second principle, Baudelaire, according to Bryusov, was one of the few who sought to reconcile these "eternal contradictions" by "embodying the mystery in clear beauty." Baudelaire's poems are perfect in form and at the same time a "forest of symbols, a temple with living pillars." Bryusov assures us that Baudelaire was not interested in Evil for its own sake but for its "Beauty and Infinity." In his poems, Bryusov proclaims, Baudelaire gives us access to the "bottomless depths of the human soul."[77] Later, Bryusov did not seem to feel comfortable with this kind of language. In any event, he did not include this text in the edition of his complete works, where his other commentaries on Baudelaire were republished. Of the two poems named as central for Baudelaire, "Correspondances" and "La Beauté," only the latter proved to be important for Bryusov. He never attempted to translate the former, and, aside from his foreword to Ellis's edition of Baudelaire, he never made any reference to the theory of correspondences so dear to the mystic symbolists.

The selection of Baudelaire's poems that Bryusov translated for his book *Frantsuzskie liriki*—"La Beauté," "Parfum exotique," "Le Rebelle," "Le Revenant," "Le Crépuscule du soir," "Abel et Caïn,"[78] —shows a continuous interest in Baudelaire's blasphemous and rebellious features, aside from the Bryusovian preoccupation with urban life and the "beauty of evil" and a continued proclivity toward exoticism and ghastly morbidity. With a total number of six published translations (aside from the eleven unpublished ones in the 1890s notebooks), Baudelaire occupies a comparatively modest position in Bryusov's total output of translations, which includes separate editions of Verlaine and Verhaeren. The only other Baudelairean text translated by Bryusov is the cynical "Choix de maximes consolantes sur l'amour."[79]

Bryusov's approach to translation is the opposite of Balmont's impressionism. He believed in the necessity of a "scientific" method. The outer appearance of his books of translation betrays the conscientious scholar, who equips his texts with ample introductions, commentaries, notes, and bibliographies. Bryusov explained his method of translation in various theoretical writings.[80] Every poem, Bryusov showed, is composed of a series of basic elements such as style, syntax, imagery, meter, rhyme, rhythm, puns, and sound structure. Since it is impossible to render all these features, the translator has to select the element(s) considered the most important as the focus of translation. Usually these are the meter and the imagery, but in certain poems, sound patterns or rhymes can be more important. The problem with this formalist theory lies in the fact that a good poem constitutes an organic whole and not simply a sum of individual elements, which makes it often difficult to isolate specific elements at the expense of others. Bryusov's "scientific" practice of translation sometimes results in a certain dryness and pedantry. Nevertheless, Bryusov's translations, with their conscientious attempt to preserve as faithfully as possible the dominant semantic and formal features of the original, certainly rank among the more successful Russian renderings of Baudelaire. A good example is an excerpt from "Le Crépuscule du soir" (part of which has already been discussed in N. S. Kurochkin's 1869 translation):[81]

> Cependant des démons malsains dans l'atmosphère
> S'éveillent lourdement, comme des gens d'affaire,
> Et cognent en volant les volets et l'auvent.
> A travers les lueurs que tourmente le vent
> La Prostitution s'allume dans les rues;
> Comme une fourmilière elle ouvre ses issues;
> Partout elle se fraye un occulte chemin,
> Ainsi que l'ennemi qui tente un coup de main;
> Elle remue au sein de la cité de fange
> Comme un ver qui dérobe à l'Homme ce qu'il mange.
> On entend çà et là les cuisines siffler,
> Les théâtres glapir, les orchestres ronfler;
> Les tables d'hôte, dont le jeu fait les délices,
> S'emplissent de catins et d'escrocs, leurs complices,
> Et les voleurs, qui n'ont ni trêve ni merci,
> Vont bientôt commencer leur travail, eux aussi,

Et forcer doucement les portes et les caisses
Pour vivre quelques jours et vêtir leurs maîtresses.

But pernicious demons in the atmosphere
Wake up heavily, like businessmen,
And bump in their flight against the shutters and roofs.
Through the lights tormented by the wind
Prostitution is flaming up in the streets;
Like an anthill she is opening her outlets;
Everywhere she is clearing herself a secret path,
Like an enemy who is attempting an attack;
She is stirring in the bosom of the city of mud
Like a worm who steals from Man what he eats.
Here and there one hears the kitchens whistle,
The theatres yelp, the orchestras snore;
The tables d'hôte, the delight of which is gambling,
Are filling with whores and crooks, their accomplices,
And the thieves, which have no truce or mercy,
Will soon begin their work also,
And gently force open doors and coffers,
To live for a few days and to dress their mistresses.

Но злые демоны, раскрыв слепые очи,
Проснувшись, как дельцы,—летают в сфере ночи,
Толкаясь крыльями у ставен и дверей.
И проституция взымает меж огней,
Дрожащих на ветру, свой светоч ядовитый . . .
Как в муравейнике, все выходы открыты;
И, как коварный враг, который мраку рад,
Повсюду тайный путь творит себе Разврат.

Он, к груди города припав, неутомимо
Ее сосет.—Меж тем восходят клубы дыма
Из труб над кухнями; доносится порой
Театра тявканье, оркестра рев глухой.
В притонах для игры уже давно засели

Во фраках шулера, среди ночных камелий . . .
И скоро в темноте обыкновенный вор
Пойдет на промысл свой,—чтоб можно было снова
Своей любовнице дать щегольнуть обновой.[82]

But evil demons, opening their blind eyes,
Having woken up like dealers, fly in the sphere of the night,
Bumping with their wings against shutters and doors.
And prostitution raises amidst the fires,
Trembling in the wind, her poisonous torch . . .
Like in an anthill, all outlets are open;
And, like a perfidious enemy, who is glad about darkness,
Everywhere Vice clears himself a secret path.

Pressing himself to the bosom of the city, he tirelessly
Sucks it.—Meanwhile puffs of smoke rise
From the chimneys over the kitchens; at times one hears
The yelping of a theatre, the deaf roar of an orchestra.
In the gambling dens already a while ago took their seats
Cardsharpers in tailcoats, amidst nightly camellias . . .
And soon in the darkness the ordinary thief
Will go about his business—so that again
His mistress can flaunt a new dress.

Bryusov's translation certainly renders the original much better than does Kurochkin's moralizing transposition. However, in certain details we can observe a curious similarity between Bryusov and Kurochkin. Bryusov also hesitates to translate literally the image of prostitution as a tapeworm, probably because he finds this connotation too unaesthetic and vulgar. Instead, he resorts to a much less original poetic cliché, evoking a snake that the city nourishes with its bosom. A similar fate is reserved for Baudelaire's "catins" (whores), who are upgraded to "nightly camellias" in Bryusov's translation.[83] The vulgar "catins" proved to be a cause of uneasiness for various Russian translators of this text. Ellis rendered them as "cocottes," which, although semantically accurate, belongs to an overly elevated stylistical register, whereas Yakubovich, similar to Kurochkin, resorted to a pathetically moralizing "fallen women."

Bryusov is visibly fascinated with the aesthetics of evil. He seems particularly enthralled by the fantastic imagery of the poem. Baudelaire's "démons malsains" acquire additional attributes in his translation, such as "blind eyes" and "wings," and Bryusov's prostitution is brandishing a "poisonous torch." With the personified "Vice" (*Razvrat*), Bryusov adds another allegoric creature to the text. Baudelaire's uncanny "soundtrack" with its representation of urban culture (restaurant, theatre, concert hall) as a bestial whistling, yelping, and grunting is adequately rendered in Bryusov's translation. On the other hand, Bryusov does not seem to care much about Baudelaire's explanations of the criminal activity of his thieves. "Pour vivre quelques jours" does not count for him. As his only motivation he names the procurement of luxurious clothing to satisfy the vanity of a mistress. The elements of social criticism present in Baudelaire's text are passed over in favor of the aesthetic thrill afforded by the spectacle of vice.

A text that deserves special attention is Bryusov's translation of the sonnet "La Beauté." The selection of Baudelairean poems in *Frantsuzskie lirikie* begins with this text. Bryusov's interest in "La Beauté" had been longstanding: as early as the notebooks of 1894, we find fragments of an attempted translation.[84] In his critical writings, Bryusov repeatedly referred to this poem. In the foreword to Ellis's edition of *Les Fleurs du Mal,* he named "La Beauté" together with "Correspondances" as the most central expression of Baudelaire's worldview and of the concerns of humanity in general. A rather ambiguous view of "La Beauté" emerges from the article "Kliuchi tain," where Bryusov quotes parts of the poem in French. The text does double duty in his argument against the philosophy of "l'art pour l'art" by providing both a negative and positive example. Bryusov criticizes the message of "immobility" uttered by the sphinx-like persona of the poem and claims that this message is contradicted by Baudelaire's own poetic practice: "The human spirit cannot reconcile itself with rest. 'Je hais le mouvement qui déplace les lignes'—says Baudelaire's Beauty. But art is always a quest, always an upsurge, and Baudelaire himself poured in his refined sonnets not deathly immobility but whirlpools of anguish, despair, and damnation."[85]

The ambiguity between a parnassian and an anti-parnassian reading reflects a common pattern in the reception of "La Beauté." Like "Correspondances," "La Beauté" has been subjected over the years to various and conflicting interpretations. Traditionally, the poem has been regarded as a document of Baudelaire's allegiance to the parnassian movement with its celebration of detached, "cold" beauty. Critics such as P.-G. Castex and Antoine Fongaro challenged this assumption and suggested that Baudelaire, rather than celebrating impassionate beauty in this poem, exposes it as a dangerous temptation which is hostile to life, an enticing and at the same time pernicious "flower of evil."[86] The poem's persona itself raises difficulties of interpretation: Is it a woman? A statue? Or, as has been recently suggested, a woman model *posing* as a statue in the studio of a sculptor?[87] On the textual level, "La Beauté" not only evokes but exemplifies beauty with a rich pattern of phonic intrumentation and internal rhymes:

La Beauté

Je suis belle, ô mortels! comme un rêve de pierre,
Et mon sein, où chacun s'est meurtri tour à tour,
Est fait pour inspirer au poète un amour
Eternel et muet ainsi que la matière.

Je trône dans l'azur comme un sphinx incompris;
J'unis un coeur de neige à la blancheur des cygnes;
Je hais le mouvement qui déplace les lignes,
Et jamais je ne pleure et jamais je ne ris.

Les poètes, devant mes grandes attitudes,
Que j'ai l'air d'emprunter aux plus fiers monuments,
Consumeront leurs jours en d'austères études;

Car j'ai, pour fasciner ces dociles amants,
De purs miroirs qui font toutes choses plus belles:
Mes yeux, mes larges yeux aux clartés éternelles!

Beauty

I am beautiful, o mortals! like a dream of stone,
And my breast, where everybody bruised himself in turn,

Is made to inspire to the poet a love
Eternal and mute like matter.

I sit enthroned in the azure like an incomprehensible sphinx,
I join a heart of snow to the whiteness of swans;
I hate the movement which displaces the lines,
And never I cry, and never I laugh.

The poets, before my grand attitudes,
Which I seem to borrow from the proudest monuments,
Will pine away their days in austere studies;

For I have, to fascinate these docile lovers,
Pure mirrors which make all things more beautiful:
My eyes, my big eyes of eternal clarity!

In Bryusov's translation:

Красота

О смертный! как мечта из камня, я прекрасна!
И грудь моя, что всех погубит чередой,
Сердца художников томит любовью властно,
Подобной веществу, предвечной и немой.

В лазури царствую я сфинксом непостижным;
Как лебедь, я бела, и холодна, как снег;
Презрев движение, любуюсь неподвижным
Вовек я не смеюсь, не плачу я вовек.

Я—строгий образец для гордых изваяний,
И, с тщетной жаждою насытить глад мечтаний,
Поэты предо мной склоняются во прах.ю

Но их ко мне влечет, покорных и влюбленных,
Сиянье вечности в моих глазах бессонных,
Где все прекраснее, как в чистых зеркалах.[88]

Beauty

O mortal! like a dream of stone, I am beautiful!
And my breast, which will ruin all in turn,
Torments the hearts of the artists imperiously with a love
Similar to matter, eternal and mute.

In the azure I rule as an inscrutable sphinx;
Like a swan, I am white, and cold, like snow;
Despising movement, I admire the immobile;
Eternally I do not laugh, I do not cry eternally.

I am the stern model of proud sculptures,
And, with a vain craving to satiate the hunger of dreams,
The poets bow before me in the dust.

But they are attracted to me, submissive and in love,
By the radiance of eternity in my sleepless eyes,
Where everything is more beautiful, as in pure mirrors.

The parnassian style of Baudelaire's poem was likely to strike a sympathetic chord in Bryusov, who applied to his translation the same insistence on formal craftmanship. Baudelaire's laconic parallelisms in the second stanza become in Bryusov's version an artful chiasmatic construction (*Kak lebed'–kak sneg, Vovek–vovek*). The symmetrical structure "freezes" the flow of the line and achieves thereby an iconic representation of the idea of immobility on the syntactic level. Bryusov's verses seem to congeal to ice. The stony goddess Beauty appears even more aloof, monumental, and destructive than in Baudelaire's original. She "destroys" (*pogubit*) rather than simply "hurts," and she is presented as the "stern model" for "proud sculptures" (whereas in Baudelaire's text, she seems to *imitate* them). The poets, rather than "studying" her, prostrate themselves in the dust as if in front of an Asian potentate. The lofty tone of Bryusov's translation is reinforced by slavonicisms like *glad* instead of the common *golod* (hunger). In the fourth line, Bryusov skillfully exploits the possibilities for sound play offered by the homophony of *veshchestvo* (matter) and *vechnyi* (eternal). This is an adequate rendering of a text rich in phonic instrumentation and internal rhymes. Although Bryusov had voiced certain reservations as to the "content" of "La Beauté" in his article "Kliuchi tain," insisting that the function of art could not be reduced to the expression of an immobile beauty, he found the poem clearly appealing. The sonnet became an apt expression of his own poetic style, which had evolved from youthful provocative decadence to a sort of marmorean neoclassicism. With its dehumanizing features, Bryusov's translation seems to celebrate rather than to denounce a superhuman and inhuman beauty.[89]

The sonnet "La Beauté" has a special significance for Russian symbolism, since it was translated not only by Bryusov but also by three other symbolist poets—Balmont, Ellis, and Vyacheslav Ivanov. Balmont's version, published in the collection *Iz chuzhezemnykh poetov* (From Foreign Poets), came out in the same year as Bryusov's (1909). It looks almost like a reply to Bryusov's text:

Красота

Стройна я, смертные, как греза изваянья,
И грудь, что каждого убила в час его,
Поэту знать дает любовь и с ней терзанье,
Безгласно-вечное, как вечно вещество.

В лазури я царю как сфинкс непостижимый;
Как лебедь бледная, как снег я холодна;
Недвижна Красота, черты здесь нерушимы;
Не плачу, не смеюсь, мне смена не нужна.

Поэты пред моим победно-гордым ликом
Все дни свои сожгут в алкании великом,
Дух изучающий пребудет век смущен

Есть у меня для них, послушных, обаянье,
Два чистых зеркала, где мир преображен:
Глаза, мои глаза, бездонное сиянье.[90]

Beauty

I am well-proportioned, o mortals, like the dream of a statue,
And my breast, which killed everybody in his hour,

Gives the poet knowledge of love and, with it, torment,
Voicelessly eternal, eternal like matter.

In the azure I rule like an inscrutable sphinx;
Pale like a swan, I am cold like snow;
Beauty is immobile, the features inviolable here;
I do not cry, not laugh, I do not need change.

The poets before my victoriously proud face
Will burn all their days in great craving,
The studying spirit will be forever confused;

I have for them, the obedient ones, a charm,
Two pure mirrors, where the world is transfigured:
Eyes, my eyes, bottomless radiance.

Balmont's aesthetics are diametrically opposed to Bryusov's parnassian ideal of polished monumentality: he loves everything fluid, soft, and vague. He believed in "inspiration" more than in poetic craftmanship and never revised a line in his poems. Bryusov's ethos of conscientious formal labor was as alien to him as the notion of a poetry cast in marble or bronze. It is interesting to note that the image of the sphinx appears in Balmont's own poetry not as a symbol of impassionate beauty but as a frightening "nightmare made of granite," a monstrous blind head looming in the desert, representing in its eternal immobile monotony the "enemy of beauty."[91] Under these circumstances, it seems almost surprising that Balmont would translate such a poem as "La Beauté." Did he see in it, like some modern critics, an image worthy of horror rather than admiration? Even a furtive glance at Balmont's translation reveals that this is hardly the case. Balmont's attitude toward Baudelaire's sphinx is a positive one. However, he could reach this positive judgment only by profoundly transforming Baudelaire's poem and making it palatable to his own poetic taste.

The word *stone* is conspicuously absent from Balmont's translation. His vision of beauty is not a "dream made of stone" (*un rêve de pierre*), but the "daydream (*greza*) of a statue." The heavy "stoniness" of the original gives way to the immaterial fluidity of mere imagination. Faithful to his musical ideal of poetry, Balmont pulls out all the stops of phonetic instrumentation. The play with *veshchestvo* and *vechnyi* noted in Bryusov's translation is expanded by Balmont to a sort of magic incantation based on sound repetition (*Bezglasno-vechnoe*, *kak vechno veshchestvo*), featuring Balmont's trademark, composite adjectives. It becomes clear that Balmont is not overly concerned with a faithful rendering of Baudelaire's syntax. The monumental parallelisms of the second stanza dissolve in the pleasant flow of his lines. Their tone seems more reminiscent of a folksong (*Kak lebed' blednaia, kak sneg ia kholodna*—"like a swan pale, like snow I am cold"). The choice of *blednaia* (pale) instead of the metrically possible and more exact *belaia* (white) seems entirely conditioned by Balmont's concern for sound effects—*blednaia* harmonizes better with the preceding *lebed'* (swan). Balmont's "sorcellerie évocatoire" culminates in the last stanza, devoted to the seductive charm of Beauty. Here Balmont is visibly in his element. Rather surprisingly, in light of his neglect for formal exactitude, he even manages to maintain the syntactic movement of the tercet, climaxing in the last line of the poem with the double evocation of the hypnotizing, "bottomless" eyes of Beauty.

Unlike Balmont, whose love for Baudelaire seems to have been more of a transitory infatuation, Bryusov remained faithful to his French idol for his entire life. In his later years, he seemed to gravitate back to a more decadent view of Baudelaire. The poem "Bodler" (Baudelaire, 1923), consisting of seven quatrains and written a year before his death, provides a sort of *summa* of his lifelong fascination with the French poet. With its combination of homeric and biblical myth, nineteenth-century history, exotic geography, social satire, decadent stock imagery, and science fiction, "Bodler" provides a good example of Bryusov's eclectic approach to poetry. Any theme was good enough for him as long as it could be turned into "clear-singing verse." In a sort of intertextual montage, Bryusov integrates quotes and reminiscences from various Baudelairean poems in his text. His choice of examples ("Moesta et errabunda," "Les Litanies de Satan," "Abel et Caïn," "Une Charogne," "Lesbos") shows Bryusov's continuing fascination with the dark and rebellious side of Baudelaire's poetry. His portrayal of Baudelaire as a societal outcast, who prophesies the coming doom of a corrupt empire, acquires additional political overtones if we remember that in the meantime Bryusov had become a member of the Communist Party of the Soviet Union. The poem begins:

Давно, когда модно дышали пачули,
И лица солидно склонялись в лансье,
Ты ветер широт небывалых почуял,
Сквозь шелест шелков и из волн валансьен.[92]

A long time ago, when the smells of patchouli were fashionably breathing,
And faces were solidly bowing to the lancier,
You sensed the wind of fantastic latitudes,
Through the rustling of silks and from waves of Valenciennes lace.

The text is replete with all sorts of exotic sounding words (*pachuli, lans'e, valans'en,* etc.) as well as elaborate sound effects such as *skvoz' shelest shelkov* (through the rustling of silks). In the six stanzas that follow, Baudelaire is presented as an unacknowledged prophet in the corrupt society of the Second Empire, whose blood he sucks in as a "vampire" (rhyming with "Empire"). After he has hardened it in the "crucible of thought," it appears in his poems as "steel of verse." Like a black lightening, Baudelaire flashes through the sky with his hymns to Satan and to the tribe of Cain. "Grieving like Ulysses," he is an "exile from a coming planet." Finally he dies on Mount Nebo, seeing the promised land that was not given to him. The poem ends with the slightly resigned note: *Maiak mezh tvoikh 'maiakov',—no komu*? ("A beacon among your 'beacons'—but to whom?"). One wonders whether this element of wistfulness was not partially prompted by Bryusov's musings about his own career path from decadent *enfant terrible* and aloof leader of Russian symbolism to the job of a literary bureaucrat in the Soviet Union's People's Commissariat of Enlightenment. Remarkably, Baudelaire stayed a faithful companion to Bryusov throughout these various metamorphoses of his literary existence.

ANNENSKY: THE AESTHETICS OF PESSIMISM

Perhaps the most unusual Russian translations of Baudelaire were written by Innokenty Fyodorovich Annensky (1856–1909). Although a contemporary of the symbolists, Annensky spent his entire life outside the limelight in a self-chosen seclusion. His "aesthetic mysticism"[93] differs greatly from the theurgic mysticism of the Russian religious symbolists. Rather than with metaphysical essence, he was concerned with the hidden beauty of the seemingly trivial, which, as he saw it, could be revealed in the creative process of poetry—and in its reception. Anticipating certain postulates of modern reader response criticism, Annensky asserted that "the *very reading* of a poet is already creation."[94] With his rejection of transcendentalist mysticism, Annensky's position seems akin to Bryusov's, with whom he also shares an intense interest in French modernist poetry. However, Bryusov's grandiose posturing and flair for exoticism were totally alien to Annensky. His poetry is one of subdued half-tones and nu-ances, a sort of "chamber music" well caught in the title of his first collection of poetry (and the only one ever to appear in his lifetime): *Tikhie pesni* (Silent Songs, 1904). With his unabashed impressionism, Annensky seems closer to Balmont, to whom he devoted a sympathetic essay.[95] His focus on spiritual an-guish, the banality, ugliness, and decay of modern urban life, his musical lan-guage, and his highly crafted poetic style replete with unusual conceits make his poetry appear similar to Baudelaire's.[96]

Subjective impressionism is the predominant feature not only of Annen-sky's poetry but also of his literary criticism—in his own terminology a "reflec-tion" (*otrazhenie*) of the work of art in the mind of the critic. Annensky's con-cept seems close to that of Baudelaire, who stated in his "Salon de 1846": "I believe sincerely that the best critique is one which is amusing and poetic, not the one which, cold and algebraic, under the pretext of explaining everything, has neither hate nor love, and rids itself voluntarily of all temperament, but—a beautiful painting being nature *reflected* by an artist—the one which is a *reflection* of this painting by an intelligent and sensitive mind. Thus the best ac-count of a painting could be a sonnet or an elegy."[97] It is probable that Annen-sky was familiar not only with the poetic but also with the critical work of Baudelaire. Although he never devoted a special essay to Baudelaire, references to the French poet appear repeatedly in his criticism. The brief discussion of "Spleen [I]" included in the article "What Is Poetry?," which was published posthumously in the journal *Apollon*, provides a good example of Annensky's impressionist approach:

I don't know what you think of, reader, when you are reading this sonnet. For me, it was overheard by the poet in an autumn dripping. . . .Baudelaire's sonnet is the echo in the soul of the poet to this sadness of being, which opens in the dripping another, mystical sadness consonant with it. The sym-bols of Baudelaire's fourteen lines are like masks, or clothes hastily thrown over, under which the yearning soul of the poet is glimpsed fleetingly, wish-ing, and fearing to be discovered (*razgadannoi*), seeking unity with the whole world and at the same time involuntarily longing for its interrupted soli-tude.[98]

The passage sheds more light on Annensky than on Baudelaire. The critic seems only indirectly concerned with the concrete text of Baudelaire's "Spleen."

The magnified "dripping," for example, of which Annensky makes so much, is nowhere to be found in Baudelaire's poem, which only contains general allusions to a rainstorm. Annensky's discussion is permeated with key terms that are central to his own thinking and poetry. The idea of "reflection," translated into acoustic terms, reverberates through the text with expressions like *otzvuk* (echo) and *sozvuchnyi* (consonant). Although Annensky does not use the term, his understanding of "Spleen" seems to be another application of the famous Baudelairean "correspondences." The "sadness of being" finds a corresponding "mystical sadness" in raindrops, which in its turn find a corresponding element of sadness in the "soul of the poet," which is reflected in the poetic text of the sonnet. The word *mystical* carries a more emotional than metaphysical significance for Annensky. His "symbols" do not refer to a metaphysical all-unity but only to the isolated "anguished soul" of the poet, longing in vain for connectedness. "Being" (*bytie*) does not signify here an abstract ontological essence but simply refers to the triviality of everyday life. Annensky's lyrical persona is caught in this reality without a transcendentalist escape hatch. The result is "sadness" (*pechal'*) and "anguish" (*toska*). The word *toska* plays a key role in Annensky's poetry. It appears in the title of numerous poems, including his last one, which is entitled "Moia Toska" (My Anguish). In a certain sense, Annensky's "Toska" is nothing but the Russian equivalent of Baudelaire's "Spleen."

Annensky's impressionism is characteristic also of his approach to translation. A. V. Fyodorov, the Soviet editor of Annensky's works and a specialist in translation theory, points out that "in his lyric translations, Annensky sometimes picks up only some separate characteristic elements and concentrates his attention on them, rendering them precisely, while he reproduces all the rest only remotely, creating a background from which the more colorful patches have to stand out. It is a method of showing the general through the particular and singular, which plays a typifying role."[99] Unlike Bryusov, who saw the selection of the elements rendered by the translator as the result of a rational, analytical process, Annensky's selection is based on pure intuition. His aim is to reproduce the "impression" of the translated poem rather than to reconstruct it as a sum of constitutive elements. As a consequence, he tended to be rather free in his approach. As Efim Etkind noted, Annensky displays a similar attitude toward the texts he translated to that which the modernist poets Annensky translated display toward "reality."[100] Modernist poetry is never a simple mimetic reproduction of "life." It transforms and deforms reality in order to create something new and original. Similarly, the process of translation is for Annensky not the simple reproduction of an original. He willfully distorts the original in order to convey to his text the status of an independent work of art.

Translations are an important part of Annensky's poetic oeuvre. A classicist by training, he undertook the monumental task of translating all of Euripides' tragedies into Russian. But his special predilection belonged to French modernism. His collection *Tikhie peshi* (Silent Songs) contains, in addition to fifty-three poems of his own, no fewer than forty-seven translations mostly of French poetry. Leconte de Lisle, Verlaine, and Sully Prudhomme are represented most fully, along with works by Baudelaire, Rimbaud, Mallarmé, Francis Jammes, and the "décadents" Charles Cros, Maurice Rollinat, and Tristan Corbière. It is significant that Annensky chose to publish his translations together with his own poetry (unlike Bryusov, who issued his *Frantsuzskie liriki* as a separate volume). The boundaries of the genre "translation" become permeable for Annensky. His prose translations of the Italian poet Ada Negri, for example, were for a long time believed to be original prose poems, since he failed to identify his source. In a way, all of Annensky's translations belong to the corpus of his own poetry.

Baudelaire is represented with seven poems in Annensky's oeuvre— "Réversibilité," "Le Revenant," "Les Hiboux," "Sépulture," "La Cloche fêlée," "Spleen [IV]," and "Les Aveugles." With the exception of "La Cloche fêlée," they were all included in the collection *Tikhie peshi* (1904). Annensky's selection shows a clear preference for the pessimistic side of Baudelaire. The importance of Baudelaire's "Spleen" for Annensky has been mentioned, and of all four poems with this title, the fourth one, selected by Annensky, is probably the darkest expression of despair. A mood of morbid agony and *taedium vitae* also permeates all the other poems. Only "Réversibilité," which belongs to the cycle of love poems devoted to Madame de Sabatier, offers a faint glimmer of hope. The sequential arrangement of the texts follows the order in which they appear in *Les Fleurs du Mal*. Read as a coherent "cycle," the poems offer a message of gloom. The series starts with the tentative spirituality of "Réversibilité," where the persona implores the female adressee of the poem to pray for him. It ends with "Les Aveugles," which, as we will see, becomes in Annensky's interpretation an expression of agnostic nihilism.

In some instances, Annensky strays so far from Baudelaire's text that the original seems hardly recognizable. This is particularly true for the sonnet "Le Revenant," as the example of the two tercets will demonstrate:

Quand viendra le matin livide,
Tu trouveras ma place vide,
Où jusqu'au soir il fera froid.

Comme d'autres par la tendresse,
Sur ta vie et sur ta jeunesse,
Moi, je veux régner par l'effroi.

When the livid morning will come,
You will find my place empty,
Where until the evening it will be cold.

Like others with tenderness,
Over your life and your youth,
I want to reign with horror.

А заря заселенеет,
Ложе ласк обледенеет,
Где твой мертвый гость лежал,

И, еще полна любовью,
Прислоненный k изголовью
Ты увидишь там—кинжал.[101]

And dawn will settle in,
The couch of caresses will become covered with ice,
Where your dead guest was lying,

And, still full of love,
Leaning against the head of the bed
You will see there—a dagger.

One hesitates even to call Annensky's text a translation, unless we accept it as a "translation" in a wider sense—an independent work partially inspired by Baudelaire. With its sense of decadent melodrama, "Le Revenant" hardly ranks among Baudelaire's best poems. Annensky's translation emphasizes almost parodistically the tackiness of the imagery. The translation is visibly "taking off" from the original in the second tercet, where any semantic connection with Baudelaire's text seems to disappear. The theatrical "dagger," which is so prominently displayed in the last line, is entirely Annensky's invention. It reveals Baudelaire's "effroi" to be an item from a decadent horror show. The literary instrumentarium of decadence turns with Annensky's translation into a self-parody.[102]

More faithful to Baudelaire's original, although still far from exact, is Annensky's translation of "Spleen [IV]." As an example, here is the last stanza (already discussed in the translation of N. S. Kurochkin and S. A. Andreyevsky):

—Et de longs corbillards, sans tambours ni musique,
Défilent lentement dans mon âme; l'Espoir,
    Vaincu, pleure, et l'Angoisse atroce, despotique,
    Sur mon crâne incliné plante son drapeau noir.

И вот . . . без музыки за серой пеленой
Ряды задвигались . . . Надежда унывает,
    И над ее поникшей головой
    Свой черный флаг Мученье развивает . . . [103]

And see . . . without music behind the grey shroud
Processions began to move . . . Hope is depressed,
    And over her bent head
    Torment is unfolding its black flag . . .

Annensky's vision is an impressionist "snapshot"—patches of indistinct figures vaguely emerging and disappearing behind a "grey shroud" (nonexistent in Baudelaire's text). The vagueness of vision is reflected in the syntax, consisting of aimlessly floating fragments of sentences, introduced by the conversational "*I vot*" and frequently ending in suspension points. The meter too is strangely fluid and inconsistent, changing midway from hexameter to pentameter. The depersonalization of the persona, already observable in Baudelaire's original, is taken a step farther in the Russian translation. There is no reference to the first person in Annensky's text. In the last line, Anguish plants her black flag not in the persona's skull but over the lowered head of Hope.[104]

It is interesting to compare Annensky's version with that of the symbolist poet Vyacheslav Ivanov:

—И дрог без пения влачится вереница
В душе:—вотще тогда Надежда слезы льет,
Как знамя черное свое Тоска-царица
Над никнущим челом победно разовьет.[105]

And a file of hearses without singing drags along
In the soul: in vain then Hope sheds tears,
As Queen Anguish unfolds her black banner
Triumphantly over the bent forehead.

Ivanov's translation, besides being more exact than Annensky's, also renders more closely Baudelaire's tone of somber sublimity. His vision, like Baudelaire's, is remorseless in its clarity. The slow procession unfolds before our eyes with the heavy steps of its regular rhythm. Gravity is achieved both by lexical means (archaisms like *votshche* [in vain], *chelo* [forehead], and the rendition of "despotique" with *tsaritsa*) and the metric structure, featuring a significantly higher number of stressed beats than Annensky's fleeting verses.

An example of an Annenskian but nevertheless successful Russian version of Baudelaire is provided by Annensky's translation of "La Cloche fêlée":

La Cloche fêlée

Il est amer est doux, pendant les nuits d'hiver,
D'écouter, près du feu qui palpite et qui fume,
Les souvenirs lointains lentement s'élever
Au bruit des carillons qui chantent dans la brume.

Bienheureuse la cloche au gosier vigoureux
Qui, malgré sa vieillesse, alerte et bien portante,
Jette fidèlement son cri religieux,
Ainsi qu'un vieux soldat qui veille sous la tente.

Moi, mon âme est fêlée, et lorsqu'en ses ennuis
Elle veut de ses chants peupler l'air froid des nuits,
Il arrive souvent que sa voix affaiblie

Semble le râle épais d'un blessé qu'on oublie
Au bord d'un lac de sang, sous un grand tas de morts,
Et qui meurt, sans bouger, dans d'immenses efforts.

The Cracked Bell

It is bitter and sweet, during winter nights,
To listen, at the fire which palpitates and smokes,
How distant memories rise slowly
At the sound of the chimes which sing in the mist.

Blessed the bell with the vigorous throat
Which, despite its old age, alert and in good health,
Utters faithfully its religious cry,
Like an old soldier who stands guard at the tent.

I, my soul is cracked, and when in its boredom,
It wants to populate with its songs the cold air of the nights,
It happens frequently that its enfeebled voice

Seems the heavy rattle of a injured one, forgotten
At the shore of a lake of blood, under a big heap of corpses,
And who is dying, without moving, with immense efforts.

Старый колокол

Я знаю сладкий яд, когда мгновенья тают
И пламя синее узор из дыма вьет,
А тени прошлого так тихо пролетают
Под вальс томительный, что вьюга им поет.

О, я не тот, увы! над кем бессильны годы,
Чье горло медное хранит могучий вой
И рассекая им безмолвие природы,
Тревожит сон бойцов, как старый часовой.

В моей груди давно есть трещина, я знаю,
И если мрак меня порой не усыпит
И песни нежные слагать я начинаю—

Все, насмерть раненый, там будто кто хрипит,
Гора кровавая над ним все вырастает,
А он в сознании недвижно умирает.[106]

The Old Bell

I know a sweet poison, when the moments melt
And the blue flame weaves a pattern of smoke,
And the shadows of the past fly by so silently
Under the wearisome waltz which the blizzard sings to them.

Oh, I am not the one, alas! over whom the years have no power,
Whose copper throat preserves a mighty howl
And cutting through the silence of nature
Alarms the sleep of the fighters, like an old sentry.

In my breast has been a crack for a long time, I know,
And if darkness at times does not put me to sleep,
And I begin to compose tender songs—

Always, fatally wounded, somebody seems to wheeze there,
The bloody mountain over him keeps growing,
And consciously, without moving, he dies.

Baudelaire's sonnet is characterized by a certain logical consistency. The poem systematically develops the theme of the "cracked bell" announced in the title, first in the first quatrain with the allusion to the "carillons", which is picked up by the "cloche au gosier vigoureux" in the second. Whereas the quatrains elaborate thus on the word *cloche*, ending with a military comparison, the tercets are devoted to the second title word, *fêlée*. The crack in the bell corresponds metaphorically to the "cracked soul" of the poet, and at the end of the poem the military image recurs, only this time with negative connotations. This logical symmetry is lost in Annensky's translation. The word *bell* never occurs in his poem, except in the title. The carillon of the first quatrain is replaced by a snowstorm, and in the second quatrain all that remains of Baudelaire's bell is a rather enigmatic "copper throat" (*gorlo mednoe*). The "crack" (*treshchina*) appearing in the tercets bears no direct relation to the title, since the "cloche fêlée" becomes in Annensky's translation an "*old* bell." Whereas Baudelaire's poem puts the classical sonnet structure to traditional use, featuring a change of mood between the quatrains and the tercets, Annensky anticipates the negative ending with his resigned fifth line. His *uvy!* (alas!) seems directly opposed to Baudelaire's "Bienheureuse . . . cloche."

Annensky's free transformation manifests itself not only in the overall structure but also in many details. Baudelaire's observation "il est amer et doux" turns into a strange "sweet poison," and the fireplace is reduced to a mysterious "blue flame." The second stanza seems even more elusive with its avoidance of the word *bell*. With its suggestive technique of indirect allusion, Annensky's text looks more like a translation of a poem by Mallarmé than by Baudelaire. At the same time, we can observe a certain "Russification" of the French original. The grey mist of Baudelaire's wintry Paris disappears in the "wearisome waltz" of the St. Petersburg snow flurry (incidentally, a similar fate also befalls Baudelaire's "Hiboux," which in Annensky's translation sit not in ivy but on "dark birch trees"). Annensky pays special attention to the euphonic qualities of the original. His poem opens with a line containing no less than five stressed *a*'s, conveying to his translation an air of refined musicality. Frequently he attempts to reconstruct the Baudelairean sound effects by similar means. Line three, for example ("Les souvenirs lointains lentement s'élever"), with its symphony of nasal vowels in the center and symmetric alliteration of *l* and *s*, is rendered by Annensky with an alliteration of alternate *t* and "pro" ("*A teni proshlogo tak tikho proletaiut*"). While Annensky's translation may seem inexact in many respects, it nevertheless manages to convey successfully the aesthetic *frisson* of Baudelaire's original.

As a last example of Annensky's art of translation, which will also allow certain conclusions about his worldview, here is his version of "Les Aveugles":

Les Aveugles

Contemple-les, mon âme; ils sont vraiment affreux!
Pareils aux mannequins; vaguement ridicules;
Terribles, singuliers comme les somnambules;
Dardant on ne sait où leurs globes ténébreux.

Leurs yeux, d'où la divine étincelle est partie,
Comme s'ils regardaient au loin, restent levés
Au ciel; on ne les voit jamais vers les pavés
Pencher rêveusement leur tête appesantie.

Ils traversent ainsi le noir illimité,
Ce frère du silence éternel. O cité!
Pendant qu'autour de nous tu chantes, ris et beugles,

Eprise du plaisir jusqu'à l'atrocité,
Vois! je me traîne aussi! mais, plus qu'eux hébété,
Je dis: Que cherchent-ils au Ciel, tous ces aveugles?

The Blind

Look at them, my soul; they are really hideous!
Similar to dummies; vaguely ridiculous;
Terrible, odd like sleepwalkers;
Flashing who knows where their gloomy globes.

Their eyes, from which the divine spark has departed,
As if they were looking in the distance, remain lifted up
To the sky. One never sees them bend to the pavement
Dreamingly their heavy head.

So they walk through the boundless black,
This brother of the eternal silence. Oh city!
While around us you sing, laugh and bellow,

Taken with pleasure to the point of atrocity,
See! I too am dragging along! but, dazed more than them,
I say: What are they looking for in the Sky [or: in Heaven], all these blind?

Слепые

О, созерцай, душа: весь ужас жизни тут
Разыгран kуkлами, но в настоящей драме.
Они, kak бледные лунатиkи, идут
И целят в пустоту померkшими шарами.

И странно: впадины, где исkры жизни нет,
Всегда глядят наверх, и будто не проронит
Луча небесного внимательный лорнет,
Иль и раздумие слепцу чела не kлонит?

А мне, kогда их та ж сегодня, что вчера,
Молчанья вечного печальная сестра,
Немая ночь ведет по нашим стогнам шумным

С их похотливою и наглой суетой,
Мне kриkнуть хочется—безумному безумным:
«то может дать, слепцы, вам этот свод пустой?»[107]

The Blind

Oh look, my soul: all the horror of life
Is played out here with puppets, but in a real drama.
They are walking like pale lunatics
And aim into emptiness with globes that have grown dark.

And strange: the cavities, where there is no spark of life,
Look always upward, and the attentive lorgnette
Seems not to let through a ray from the sky,
Or does thought not nod to the blind either?

And I, when, the same today as yesterday,
Eternal silences's sad sister,
Mute night, leads them through our noisy squares

With their lewd and impudent bustle,
I want to shout—from madman to madman:
"What can give you, blind, this empty vault?"

The allegorical nature of Baudelaire's poem is made explicit in Annensky's translation at the beginning. He reveals from the outset that we are dealing not just with a description of blind people but that "the whole horror of life is played out here with puppets, but in a real-life drama." While Baudelaire probably would not have disagreed with this interpretation, Annensky seems nevertheless much more categorical and relentless in his statement about the "horror of life." Whereas the eyes of Baudelaire's blind turn "on ne sait où," in Annensky's text they stare into "emptiness." This seemingly minor detail contains the entire difference between Baudelaire's and Annensky's approaches. Baudelaire's poem can be read as an allegory of religious doubt. Annensky's goes beyond mere doubt and sounds more like a straightforward statement of atheism. All religious connotations are carefully avoided: the "divine spark" becomes a mere "spark of life" in his translation, and, more importantly, Baudelaire's capitalized "Ciel" (Heaven) in the last line turns into an "empty vault," echoing the "emptiness" of line four.

Baudelaire's poem contains as a subtext the old myth of physical blindness and prophetic insight, as it appears in the popular image of Homer as a blind bard, or Oedipus's and King Lear's gaining of knowledge after losing their eyes. The question uttered in the last line is therefore not merely rhetorical. Could it be that these pathetic, horrible, and vaguely ridiculous blind "mannequins" partake of some mystic secret of which the poet is deprived? Do they know something we don't know? Annensky's text dismisses this possibility. His final line is not really a question but rather a sort of disillusioning piece of advice that the persona "would like to shout" to the blind: "What, blind people, can this empty vault give you?" There is only one possible answer: nothing. Interestingly enough, Annensky qualifies not only the blind but also the persona of the poem as "insane" (*bezumnyi*). The double dative case *bezumnomu bezumnym* creates a direct connection between the poet and the blind, based on a shared insanity. With this, Annensky provided perhaps an indirect commentary on Russian symbolism. The insanity of the poet lies in expecting a mystic revelation where there can be none. His discontent with materialism and longing for a transcendent meaning is something that connects Annensky with his fellow symbolists of the mystic school. Unlike the later postsymbolists, he was not ready to accept calmly the absence of a communication with the beyond and joyfully turn to the immanent world. He kept yearning for something more. Unlike the mystic symbolists, however (but perhaps not unlike Baudelaire), he could find in his quest nothing but an "empty ideality."

THE BACKLASH: BAUDELAIRE AS A TARGET
OF ANTI-DECADENT ATTACKS

Baudelaire's appropriation by the Russian decadents undoubtedly set the tone for the way he was perceived by the Russian public. It is true that some clear-sighted critics pointed to the artificial nature of the decadent Baudelairism. Viktor Chernov, for example, contrasted the spontaneity and intensity of Baudelaire's poetry with the "cerebral pessimism" of Bryusov.[108] P. F. Yaku-bovich, as we have seen, attempted to clear Baudelaire of his decadent image. Nevertheless, the image of Baudelaire as a poet of cheap frisson, blasphemous diabolism, and perverse sensuality became ingrained as a powerful cliché for a long time to come.

The new decadent literary tendencies met with fierce resistance by a large part of the Russian cultural and political establishment. The anti-decadent re-action in Russia was perhaps even more violent and far-reaching than in the West. In addition to reactionary functionaries of the tsarist government such as the procuror of the Holy Synod, K. P. Pobedonostsev, who tried to stifle any subversive stir by tightening the screw of censorship, the unholy alliance of Russian anti-modernists went far beyond conservative circles to include such diverse figures as Lev Tolstoy and most radical critics of the left.

The radical critics, who at the end of the nineteenth century still dominated the literary scene, were enraged by what they perceived as a lack of social con-cern and sanity in the new literary trends. A typical example is N. K. Mikhail-ovsky, the leading populist critic of the time, already mentioned in his role as P. F. Yakubovich's mentor at the editorial board of *Russkoe bogatstvo*. It seems doubtful that Yakubovich actually succeeded in converting Mikhailovsky to his pro-Baudelairean attitude, at least to judge from his scathing condemnation of the symbolist movement in his article "A Russian Reflection of French Symbol-ism," written in reply to Merezhkovsky's essay on the decline of Russian litera-ture. Mikhailovsky declared there that "Symbolism consists of mental and moral decrepitude, going as far in the opinion of some as psychic disorder, as well as of charlatanism, excessive pretensions, and what the French call *blague*."[109]

The rejection of decadence was probably one of the few points where the radical left and the tsarist government were in agreement. Characteristically, one of the earliest institutions in Russia to take notice of Baudelaire was the office of the censor, which, shortly after the publication of *Les Fleurs du Mal* in

1857, issued the following report about the book: "The examined poems can only arouse feelings of disgust. The author displays in almost all of them his poisoned soul and tries with disgusting comparisons, taken from debauchery and crime, to instill in the reader a deep contempt for human nature. . . . The examined poems, due to their immorality, should be subject to prohibition from the public."[110] The censorship committee heeded this advice and officially banned *Les Fleurs du Mal* because of its"pornographic character." The prohibition was not revoked until 1906, and even two years later Arseny Alving, the translator of a complete edition of the book, was accused of blasphemy.[111] As it turned out, however, the banishment of Baudelaire by the tsarist censorship did not prove watertight. The only practical consequence was that up to 1906, the title *Tsvety Zla* (Flowers of Evil) had to be avoided. Russian translations of individual poems, however, started to appear uncensored in the periodical press in 1869, perhaps simply because the censors ignored or chose to overlook the fact that they were taken from a forbidden book.

Baudelaire was not only criticized by the government. The first anti-decadent attack in the Russian press specifically directed against him occurred as early as 1875—a time when decadence per se was not even born yet in Russia. In a review of Gautier's *Portraits contemporains* and Champfleury's *Souvenirs et portraits de jeunesse*, the novelist and journalist Pyotr Dmitrievich Boborykin (1836–1921) expressed his condemnation of Baudelaire in terms that anticipate much of the rhetoric that would later become customary. Boborykin criticizes the French poet for his lack of realism, his mental disarray (*umvstvennoe besputstvo*), and the absence of healthy elements in his work: "'Let's be strange!' [Baudelaire] always said, and he flavored his work with the most pungent spices. Healthy people let out a squeamish 'pouah,' and this 'pouah' removed Baudelaire even more from healthy motifs: youth, the joys of family, love, motherly tenderness." Boborykin lays the blame for this on a lack of educational guidance and of peer monitoring: "It seems to us that if the friends and colleagues of such Baudelaires took a sterner attitude toward their queer behavior and pitiful squandering of their life forces, these fops of intelligence and talent would in time bid farewell to their poetic cynicisms, their wigs of heavenly blue color, and to the conduct of experiments on their sinful body by means of opium and debauchery."[112]

Boborykin's incrimination of Baudelaire contains all the major points that were to be raised seventeen years later by a more formidable adversary, Max Nordau. Nordau's book *Entartung*, a voluminous "scientific" study devoted to the degeneration of European culture, caused a sensation when it appeared in 1892, and it soon turned into an international best-seller. A Russian translation came out in 1894. Nordau, a psychiatrist by training, saw much of contemporary art, music, and literature as a psychopathological aberration which should be analyzed. He took on this task in a style peppered with aggressive attacks and invective. It goes without saying that he treated Baudelaire with contempt. He characterized him as a "Mystiker und Erotomane" worthy of attention only because of his nefarious influence on contemporary European literature. Nordau expatiated mainly on Baudelaire's various "perversities," including his predilection for the olfactory sense, which in Nordau's distorted representation becomes an obsession with "rot, decay, and pestilence."[113] Nordau's book provided the adversaries of modernism in all of Europe with a convenient arsenal of pseudoscientific arguments for years to come. In the 1930s, the Nazi government in Germany borrowed the term *entartete Kunst* to justify its crackdown on modernist art. To be sure, Nordau himself was disqualified from playing a more prominent role in the Nazis' ideology because he was a Jew (the fact that he placed Nietzsche and Wagner among the degenerate was not likely to endear him to Hitler either). In Russia, K. P. Pobedonostsev, the reactionary procuror of the Holy Synod, quoted entire passages from the atheist Jew Nordau in his *Moskovskii sbornik* (1896), although without identifying his source.[114] Nordau's fuming invective against modern art inspired Andrey Bely to use him as a character in his "Second Symphony."[115]

In the wake of Nordau, psychiatric investigations of art and literature began to multiply in Russia. The psychiatrist N. N. Bazhenov (1857–1925) devoted several pages of his study *Simvolisty i dekadenty* (1899) to Baudelaire. Bazhenov was the medical superintendent of the first psychiatric hospital in Moscow. Andrey Bely describes him in his memoirs as an "epicurean and cynic." According to Bely, he considered the Moscow symbolists his "patients."[116] Less radical than Nordau, Bazhenov readily acknowledged Baudelaire's poetic talent, but he used the poems "Une Charogne" and "Correspondances" to analyze the author's disturbed mind. Baudelaire's synaesthetic association of perfumes, colors, and sounds is treated in Bazhenov's interpretation as a pathological anomaly. In order to make his point, the Russian psychiatrist quoted "Correspondances" in his own verse translation, which, strangely enough, turned out to be more successful than Yakubovich's earlier attempts. Bazhenov's unusual title, *Sochetan'ia* ("Combinations," instead of *Sootvetstviia*—"Correspondences"), hints at his understanding of the phenomenon of correspondences as a mental activity rather than as a revelation of mystical unity. Baudelaire's "forêt de symboles" becomes in his translation a "forest of vague dreams, symbols, and fantasies" (*les neiasnykh snov, i simvolov, i grez*).[117]

Ironically enough, one of Nordau's targets, Lev Tolstoy, who figures prominently as a Russian "mystic" degenerate in *Entartung*, himself launched a vigorous attack against modernism in terms that seem rather reminiscent of Nordau. We know in fact that Tolstoy was familiar with at least some of Nordau's ideas and agreed with them. In a diary entry on June 5, 1893, commenting on a book review of *Entartung*, Tolstoy noted with approval Nordau's prediction that "literary fiction has to become soon a mere amusement for women and children, like dancing."[118] In the tenth chapter of *What Is Art?* (1898), Tolstoy delivered a devastating indictment against Baudelaire. He calls Baudelaire's poetry "clumsy in its form and exceedingly low and vulgar in its content" and characterizes his worldview as a theory of "coarse egoism" which replaces morality with a "vague notion of beauty." Like Nordau, Tolstoy was displeased by Baudelaire's cult of the artificial and accused him, among other things, of preferring "metallic trees" to real ones. Baudelaire's decadent art, in Tolstoy's opinion, serves only as entertainment for the idle upper classes, which are in need of more and more refined and bizarre pleasures for their corrupted taste: "Baudelaire and Verlaine think up a new form, renovating it with hitherto unseen pornographic details. And the critics and the public of the higher classes applaud them as great writers. Only with this can we explain the success not only of Baudelaire and Verlaine, but of the whole decadence."[119] What seems to distress Tolstoy most of all is simply the fact that he *cannot understand* Baudelaire's poems. He quotes five entire texts in the French original ("Je t'adore à l'égal de la voûte nocturne," "Duellum," and the prose poems "L'Etranger," "La Soupe et les nuages," and "Le Galant tireur")—only to demonstrate that they do not make sense. He seems particularly vexed by the prose poems because in prose, he notes, "the author could have talked simply, if he wanted to." Instead, according to Tolstoy, Baudelaire wrote in a deliberately obscure style that requires a special effort of the reader, "an effort rarely rewarded, since the feelings expressed by the poet are unpleasant (*nekhoroshie*) and very base."[120]

Of course, Baudelaire is not the only author denounced by Tolstoy for producing bad art. He shares this honor with many classics of world literature, including the author of *War and Peace* and *Anna Karenina*. The condemnation of Baudelaire is one of the many egregious misjudgments in *What Is Art?* which leave even Tolstoy's admirers in consternation. One wonders how well the Russian novelist really read the French poet. The choice of texts on which he bases his attack is puzzling. The two poems that he quotes are taken from the first section of *Les Fleurs du Mal* (numbers 24 and 35). Did he ever get as far as the "Tableaux parisiens"? His reading of the prose poems seems to have been rather cursory too. Obviously he approached Baudelaire with preconceived ideas and the firm intention to deal a blow to the spirit of the fin de siècle. We know that Tolstoy became aware of Baudelaire in 1892 through a letter from N. N. Strakhov, who drew his attention to the new decadent literature. Tolstoy asked his wife to get him a copy of Baudelaire's works from Moscow, and, having received it, he wrote to her on November 15: "I received Baudelaire. It wasn't worth it. It was only in order to have an idea about the degree of depravity of the fin de siècle. I love this word and this notion."[121]

Tolstoy himself recognized the problematic character of his main charge against Baudelaire, namely that his poetry is "unintelligible." He mitigated this accusation somewhat by stating, "I do not have the right and cannot condemn the new art simply for the reason that I, a man educated in the first half of the century, do not understand it; all I can say is that is unintelligible to me."[122] After all, couldn't Tolstoy simply have failed to understand something that might be clear to others? This objection seemingly only weakens Tolstoy's argument. Even if some sophisticated critic could come up with a plausible interpretation for Baudelaire's poems, this would be irrelevant to Tolstoy. Great art, according to the theory put forth in *What Is Art?*, has to be directly and immediately accessible. It has to "infect" *all* people, or it has no right to exist. If Tolstoy, an educated member of society, has trouble understanding Baudelaire, his poetry must be *a fortiori* inaccessible to simple folks. Tolstoy's rejection of Baudelaire, whatever one might think of it, is thus at least consistent on his own terms.

Rather than blaming Tolstoy for his lack of understanding, it might be more interesting to look at the reasons for his negative attitude. Why did Baudelaire fail to "infect" Tolstoy? The Swiss writer Georges Haldas, who tried to find an answer to this question in his 1967 article "Tolstoï juge de Baudelaire," points to the enormous differences between Tolstoy and Baudelaire in almost every respect: they were antipodes with regard to fortune, social position, creative energy, sexual potency, longevity, and health. Tolstoy's exceedingly vital personality enabled him to embrace and understand almost any point of view, except, perhaps, sickness and its specific worldview and creativity. One could add to this that Tolstoy's emphasis on the transmission of "feelings" as the main purpose of art lead him to postulate an aesthetic of simplicity that looked askance at any formal virtuosity. Baudelaire's mastery of the poetic form had to provoke his suspicion. Interestingly enough, instead of confronting this problem, Tolstoy chose to ignore it by declaring, against all evidence, that Baudelaire's form was "clumsy" (*neiskusno*).[123] This deliberate blindness to the formal beauty of Baudelaire's poetry is revealing of Tolstoy's postconversion attempt to repress his own aesthetic creative impulse. Was Baudelaire perhaps a dangerous temptation for him?

Had Tolstoy studied Baudelaire more attentively and without prejudice, he might have discovered a worldview that was not totally alien to his own. The notion of universal brotherhood, postulated by Tolstoy as the ultimate goal of art, is certainly not absent from Baudelaire when one thinks of his solidarity with the downtrodden victims of society, as highlighted by P. F. Yakubovich. Tolstoy might have recognized too that Baudelaire's obsession with evil was more than a provocative pose and had perhaps even some uncanny resemblance to his own preoccupations. On November 6, 1892, after N. N. Strakhov told him in a letter about the new decadent literature, and *before* he actually read anything by Baudelaire, Tolstoy hastened to refute the decadents and Baudelaire in a diary entry that sounds strangely Baudelairean in its categorical formulations of existential horror and almost manichean dualism of good and evil: "Today's decadents, [including] Baudelaire, say that for poetry one needs extremes of good and extremes of evil. That without that there is no poetry. That the striving only for the good destroys the contrasts and therefore poetry. They worry in vain. Evil is so strong—it is the whole background—that it is always there for contrast. If we admit it, then it will drag in everything, there will be only evil and no contrast. In order to have contrast and evil, one has to strive with all forces for the good."[124]

Although Tolstoy's philosophy significantly differed from that of the left-wing radicals, in his rejection of modernism he took a position that paralleled their views in many respects. It comes as no surprise then that in the ninety-volume Soviet edition of Tolstoy's complete works, the author, while being criticized for his "religious mysticism" and emphasis on feeling instead of thought, reaps praise for his attacks on Baudelaire and the French symbolists. As the commentator points out, Tolstoy's polemic sallies against modernism "will help our writers and artists in their own struggle with contemporary decadent bourgeois art."[125] In many respects, the nineteenth-century attacks on Baudelaire indeed helped to prepare the ground for the later Stalinist crackdown on modern art with its charges of "bourgeois depravity" and "formalism." Kogan's indictment of Baudelaire in the first edition of the *Great Soviet Encyclopedia* looks like a warmed up version of nineteenth-century anti-decadent criticism, with the added "vulgar sociologist" ingredient of class determinism.

The discovery of Baudelaire by the Russian decadents thus left a twofold legacy. If, on the one hand, it helped to focus attention on the aesthetic qualities of Baudelaire's modernity and to win him recognition as a major figure in the history of European poetry, it also burdened his reputation with a stain of immorality. Frequently, the moral condemnation of Baudelaire was not based on an informed judgment but seemed more to stem from hearsay. The proliferation of translations after the turn of the century did not help the situation either, since many of them were of questionable quality and rather reinforced than dispelled the notion of Baudelaire as a decadent. The following excerpt from "Une martyre" in the translation of Arseny Alving provides an example:

> Рядом, на столе, валяются браслеты,
>> Кольца, серьги,—всюду жемчуга
> Тело чудное лежит совсем раздето,
>> Кровью залита одна ее нога . . .

> Close by, on the table, bracelets, rings,
>> Earrings are lying about—pearls everywhere;
> A gorgeous body lies completely undressed,
>> Only her foot is covered with blood . . .

This lubricious tableau is entirely Alving's invention. He manages to render the complete stanza without translating *one single word* of the original, except for "table":

> Sur la table de nuit, comme une renoncule,
>> Repose; et, vide de pensers,
> Un regard vague et blanc comme le crépuscule
>> S'échappe des yeux révulsés.

> On the night table, like a ranunculus
>> Rests [her head]; and, empty of thoughts,
> A vague and blank stare like dawn
>> Escapes from the turned up eyes.

One cannot disagree with the critic Semyon Rubanovich, who quoted this stanza in his review of Alving's edition with this comment: "Is this the aroma of *Les Fleurs du Mal*? Is this Baudelaire? . . . No, this is the smell of 'cheap wine,' this is the spirit of vulgarity 'hidden everywhere,' this is the visitor of private rooms, noisy and cheerful,—this is Alving, having defiled one of our most sacred treasures."[126]

Baudelaire's decadent image became so widespread in popular culture after the turn of the century that a journalist of the newspaper *Russkoe slovo* could venture to enrich the Russian vocabulary with two new verbs derived from the names of Richepin and Baudelaire: "*rishpenit'sia*" ("to richepinize oneself") and "*bodlernichat'*" ("to baudelairize"). These expressions appear in a review of a 1903 poetry reading by Balmont devoted to the memory of Prince Urusov. Launching a scathing attack on Balmont and Bryusov, who are accused of producing "erotomantic gibberish," the reviewer contributes a quatrain of his own making:

Наклонись ко мне главою,
Слушай, что тебе шепчу;
Наришпенившись с тобою,
Пободлерничать хочу . . . [127]

Bend your head down to me,
Listen to what I whisper:
Having richepinized enough with you,
I want to baudelairize a little . . .

This quote is actually from an article written in defense of Baudelaire. The reviewer points out that "Baudelaire's poems draw real beautiful pictures" and that "erotic affectations à la Baudelaire are not the same as Baudelaire." He adds that "Prince Urusov would have condemned the trick riding (*dzhigit*) of Mr. Bryusov and Balmont, as we condemn it." However, even if Baudelaire was largely rehabilitated as a "serious" writer after the turn of the century, the decadent concept never completely disappeared. It was to come back with a vengeance during the Soviet period, when the mere suspicion of decadence was considered reason enough to obliterate a writer from the literary world and from public memory.

The "Younger Symbolists"

After the turn of the century, a new generation of Russian poets entered the literary arena. They are frequently referred to as the "younger symbolists" (*mladshie simvolisty*), although some of them were in fact born before the older generation. With the decadents they shared a common predilection for poetry and poetic craftsmanship over realistic socially committed prose. However, their claims went beyond the pursuit of pure literature and encompassed philosophy, religion, and the whole realm of being. The frivolous provocativeness of the decadents gave way to a rather solemn, hieratic approach: the poet became a high priest of "theurgy" and poetic language the vehicle for revealing the ultimate secrets of the universe. The flourishing of mystic symbolism went hand in hand with a renewed interest in religious thought. The eschatological philosophy of Vladimir Solovyov (1853–1900) became a main source of inspiration for the new generation of Russian symbolists.

Baudelaire was virtually the only French poet who played a significant role in the Russian decadence of the 1890s and also in the symbolist movement of the 1900s. The members of the mystical school that had come to dominate the literary scene in the beginning of the twentieth century did not share the Francophile leanings of their predecessors and even showed contempt for Western decadence. Nevertheless, although more interested in the indigenous Russian tradition and in the Germanic and classical world than in contemporary French civilization, the younger Russian symbolists held Baudelaire in high esteem.

To be sure, there was no unanimity in the reception of Baudelaire among the symbolists. This is not amazing inasmuch as Russian symbolism presented itself as a multifaceted and rather heterogeneous movement that cannot be easily reduced to a coherent and uniform doctrine. In some cases, the proclaimed mysticism of the new poets amounted to no more that sloganeering and hardly expressed any deeply felt metaphysical concerns. Moreover, the question of Baudelaire's own attitude toward religion remains a controversial issue. It is not my intention to delve into this protracted debate.[1] The most eminent spokesman for a "Catholic" Baudelaire in France was M. A. Ruff (see his books *L'esprit du mal et l'esthétique baudelairienne* and *Baudelaire. L'homme et l'oeuvre*). The opposite position was taken by L. J. Austin, among many others, who wrote: "It is evident that Baudelaire, if he was a Catholic, was neither believing nor practicing."[2] In any event, Baudelaire's Roman Catholic background was different from the Orthodox tradition prevalent in Russia. It is interesting to note that the Russian religious symbolists who were most interested in him (Ellis and Vyacheslav Ivanov) both converted to Catholicism. Even so, their approaches to Baudelaire varied considerably. It is also noteworthy that neither of the two most famous younger Russian symbolists, Aleksandr Blok and Andrey Bely, favored a mystic reading of Baudelaire. Blok turned him into the butt of a parody, and Bely, as will be shown, subjected Baudelaire to a formalist rather than a symbolist interpretation.

The theurgic reading of any poet remains a problematic enterprise, and it proves to be particularly problematic with a poet like Baudelaire, who on the one hand seems to ask for a religious interpretation of his "vertical," platonic correspondences, and on the other hand keeps ironically subverting his own position. Unlike in France, where the "Catholic" Baudelaire has become a mainstay of twentieth-century criticism, in Russia the religious images of the poet remained on the whole a transitory and unstable phenomenon.

THE TRIUMPH OF "CORRESPONDANCES"

Correspondances

La Nature est un temple où de vivants piliers
Laissent parfois sortir de confuses paroles;
L'homme y passe à travers des forêts de symboles
Qui l'observent avec des regards familiers.

Comme de longs échos qui de loin se confondent
Dans une ténébreuse et profonde unité,

Vaste comme la nuit et comme la clarté,
Les parfums, les couleurs et les sons se répondent.

Il est des parfums frais comme des chairs d'enfants,
Doux comme les hautbois, verts comme les prairies,
-Et d'autres, corrompus, riches et triomphants,

Ayant l'expansion des choses infinies,
Comme l'ambre, le musc, le benjoin et l'encens,
Qui chantent les transports de l'esprit et des sens.

Baudelaire's sonnet "Correspondances" was of particular importance for the new generation of Russian symbolists. Once denounced by psychiatrists like Bazhenov as a pathological aberration, and purged of decadent elements by the populist translator Yakubovich, who tried to familiarize the strange imagery by transposing it into realistic urban and romantic mountain settings, "Correspondances" became a cornerstone of the symbolist creed. The very mysteriousness of the text, which had been so unsettling to former readers, emerged as its main source of attraction.

To be sure, "Correspondances" hardly expresses any new and groundbreaking ideas that had not been uttered before. The concept of the material world as a symbol participating in a transcendental beyond has been a philosophical commonplace at least since Plato. Possible sources for the treatment of synaesthesia in Baudelaire's text have been located in E. T. A. Hoffmann and Balzac. The extraordinary appeal of Baudelaire's poem lies less in its philosophical content than in its aesthetic qualities. With its dreamlike, surrealistic imagery, musical expressiveness, and solemn, "oracular" tone, the text has exerted a continuous fascination on generations of readers. Although considerable critical attention has been lavished on the enigmatic sonnet over the years, no consensus has ever been reached on its ultimate "meaning." It has been interpreted in turn as a neo-platonic or Swedenborgian assertion of mystical transcendence, a psychological investigation on synaesthesia, or a poetological inquiry on the nature of figural speech. As Paul de Man put it, "Like the oracle of Delphi, it has been made to answer a considerable number and variety of questions put to it by various readers. . . . In all cases, the poem has never failed to answer to the satisfaction of its questioner."[3]

In the literary environment of Russian symbolism, *sootvetstviia* (correspondences) became an omnipresent slogan and catchword. Ellis, the most zealous of all Russian Baudelaireans, hailed "Correspondances" as the "quintessence of Baudelairism, the program of all contemporary symbolism."[4] Georgy Chulkov (1879–1939), the symbolist writer, poet, and theoretician of so-called mystical anarchism, repeatedly referred to Baudelaire's "Correspondances" in his critical writings. Some of his "manifestos," with their insistence on communication with the "Mystery" through the synaesthetic confusion of sensual impressions, read like a commentary on Baudelaire's sonnet: "There are moments when the human soul, throwing off the fetters of rational consciousness, enters into direct communication with the Mystery. Then all earthly sounds, colors, and smells receive another meaning; the objects become illuminated from within; their shining is reflected in our soul in a many-colored rainbow . . . We make one more effort—and before us another world opens up: We can hear how the colors sound, we can see sounds. . . ."[5]

As time went by, Baudelaire's "Correspondances" took on a life of its own, independent of the original poem. Despite the manifold occurrence of various forms of synaesthesia and mystical "forests of symbols" in Russian symbolism, this Baudelairism was on the whole a rather superficial phenomenon. Few Russian symbolists bothered to dig up corroborating evidence for their theories in Baudelaire's critical and theoretical writings or even to put the concrete text of "Correspondances" under closer scrutiny. Surprisingly, among the many Russian translators of the poem, there is only one symbolist (Ellis).[6] To be sure, Baudelaire himself probably would have been astonished to learn that he had become the father of symbolist poetry. As Claude Pichois and others have pointed out, the appropriation of "Correspondances" as a manifesto of symbolism was ultimately based on a creative misreading.[7]

The triumph of symbolism in Russia had an important bearing on Baudelaire's reception. In the first decade of the twentieth century, he enjoyed an unprecedented boom in the Russian book market. Nina Petrovskaya, the wife of the symbolist publisher S. A. Sokolov and the lover of Andrey Bely and Valery Bryusov, describes in her memoirs the "furious demand" for Baudelaire's works as a "sign of the time": "The public literally demanded (*potrebovalos' bukval'no rynkom*) the new edition of *Les Fleurs du Mal* and every last line of Baudelaire."[8] After the ban on *Les Fleurs du Mal* was lifted by the tsarist censors in 1906, the book could finally be published under its original title. Between 1907 and 1909, there appeared no fewer than four different Russian editions (A. Panov, 1907; A. Alving and Ellis, both 1908; and P. Yakubovich, 1909). In addition, four complete translations of the prose poems were available

(A. Aleksandrovich, 1902; L. Gurevich and S. Parnok, 1909; M. Volkov, 1909; Ellis, 1910), and also Russian editions of *Mon coeur mis à nu* (Ellis, 1907), of *Les Paradis artificiels* (V. Likhtenshtadt, 1908), and of Baudelaire's writings on Edgar Allan Poe (L. Kogan, 1910). Baudelairean poems became a mainstay of literary journals and almanacs and surfaced in various anthologies and "declamation-readers" (*Chtets-Deklamatory*). Thanks to the widely circulated editions of the popular Vseobshchaia Biblioteka (Universal Library), the poet also became accessible to the budget-minded reader.

Baudelaire's "rehabilitation" in Russia occurred around the same time as in France.[9] From a controversial *poète maudit,* he had turned into a respected and celebrated "classic." Perhaps the best Russian illustration for this metamorphosis is provided by the impressionist critic Yuly Aikhenvald (1872–1928). In a critical essay published in 1910, the same year in which the municipality of Paris inaugurated the "rue Charles Baudelaire,"[10] Aikhenvald hailed Baudelaire as a "highly cultivated, refined and charming" human being, whose idealism put him in the same company as Friedrich Schiller. As Aikhenvald wrote, "Baudelaire has not less of an affirmative attitude to the eternal values of life, lyricism, and respectfulness than the German singer with his beautiful soul." Perhaps the most curious compliment that Aikhenvald paid to Baudelaire is that he commended the poet for being a *meshchanin* (bourgeois), a term normally used with a derogatory rather than a complimentary intention. Commenting on "Les Phares" and the prose poem "Le Thyrse," Aikhenvald remarked: "What can be more bourgeois than thoughtfully adding up rhymes and putting the finishing touches on one's style? Is the devil really going to write sonnets? And will he, like Baudelaire, appreciate the paintings of great masters as shining beacons, as a testimony of human greatness, will he go into raptures over Liszt, to whom in all cities of the world 'the pianos sing glory,' will he in general listen rapturously to the 'music of life?' No, the singer and botanist of evil flowers did not leave the 'bourgeoisie,' and in this lies his main dignity."[11] With regard to the Devil, one wishes to remind Aikhenvald of the polite bourgeois "gentleman" in Dostoyevsky's *Brothers Karamazov* or Baudelaire's own cigar-smoking, jovial, and well-spoken "Joueur généreux." In light of Baudelaire's own scornful attitude toward bourgeois values, it seems doubtful whether he would have been flattered to be called a *meshchanin.* It is true that he expressed a positive attitude toward the bourgeoisie in his early "Salon de 1845", but this was not his later opinion. In any event, Aikenvald makes no reference to this text. One wonders what Baudelaire would have thought of his characterization as a laborious and meticulous "botanist of evil flowers." Since he was now cleared from his dubious reputation and pronounced a *meshchanin*, there were no more obstacles for welcoming him into polite society, where his herbarium of evil flowers provided enjoyment to the literary gourmet and also served as edifying reading for the young.

Unfortunately, Baudelaire's new popularity proved in fact to be a mixed blessing. If earlier he had been translated mainly by "disciples" who genuinely identified with his work, he now became the prey of professional translators who were hired with purely commercial motives. The results are rather sobering, if we look at the first Russian edition with the title *Flowers of Evil*, A. A. Panov's translation of 1907. Despite the subtitle promising a "complete edition," the book contains only the 107 poems forming the section "Spleen et idéal" in the 1868 edition of *Les Fleurs du Mal*. Even before reaching the actual translations, the reader gets an unfavorable first impression from A. A. Panov's fifty-page introduction, which shows evidence of shoddy research and hasty composition. Panov's rendering of Baudelaire's poetry is as inexact and distorting as his Russian verses are clumsy. The publisher must have simply disregarded the fact that many poems of Baudelaire were already available in Russian translations of a much higher quality. Ellis, the chief symbolist Baudelairean and translator, accused Panov of "literary hooliganism."[12] Arseny Alving's translation, which came out a year later, was no improvement and received equally harsh treatment in the symbolist press. Semyon Rubanovich wrote in *Vesy* that "a total unfamiliarity with the simplest devices of versification, ignorance of the French language, and a clumsy use of Russian place [Alving] outside the limits of any serious critical attention."[13]

Besides the boom of editions of questionable quality, Baudelaire's new popularity also encouraged an outpouring of not always distinguished critical praise. A good example is A. S. Kachorovskaya's book *Zametki o modernizme. Sharl' Bodler* (Notes about Modernism. Charles Baudelaire), published in 1910 in Tomsk—proof that Baudelaire's glory not only affected the capital cities but penetrated far into the Siberian province. Kachorovskaya compares Baudelaire with none other than Socrates, whom she sees in a complementary position to the French poet: if the Greek philosopher represents logical thought, Baudelaire stands for the "wisdom of art." His style is defined as "neorealism," a mixture of realism and impressionism. In her explanation of neorealism, Kachorovskaya reveals herself as an impressionist of no mean stature: "The images of reality acquire a soft lightness, they seem almost spectral, as if ready to disappear. At the same time they have many meanings. Neorealism recalls an early morning in the mountains; down in the valley damp shadows are scattered, and over them a formless light, young and fresh, not yet tired and callous . . . With its caress it covers the mountain peaks and trees; with its tone, only with its tone, how strangely, how mysteriously live now the shadows." [14] Kachorovskaya's idyllic sunrise in the mountains seems the exact opposite of Baudelaire's gloomy urban squalor. It becomes clear that the Russian critic is not interested in thematic analysis; like K. D. Balmont, she is enthralled by Baudelaire's vague mysticism and languorous musicality, which she tries to imitate herself. Her last sentence features an impressive series of [t]alliterations and a vocalic instrumenation shifting from o over a to e (*ego tonom, tol'ko tonom, tak stranno, tak tainstvenno zhivut teper' teni*). In Kachorovskaya's prose poem, Baudelaire's nightmares dissolve and disappear in a harmonic merging with Nature, "in one common melody of All-Being." While her impressionist approach places Kacharovskaya in the company of Balmont and Annensky, her vocabulary shows the influence of the new "mystic" wave. The notion of "correspondences" proved to be flexible and vague enough to fit into almost any sort of metaphysical speculation or sentimentalist "mood piece."

To be sure, Baudelaire's triumph after the turn of the century manifested itself not only in impressive sales figures, critical praise, and acknowledgment as a serious author but also in his continuous impact on Russian poetry. Rather than Baudelaire's enshrinement in the bourgeois pantheon of classics and his appropriation and dissemination by enterprising publishers, it was this creative response that guaranteed his continuous presence in Russia as a living source of poetic inspiration.

ELLIS: THE PRIEST OF BAUDELAIRISM

Although a poet of little distinction, Ellis (the pseudonym of Lev Lvovich Kobylinsky, 1870–1947) is remembered as one of the more zealous theoreticians of the symbolist movement in Russia. He also deserves attention as perhaps the most fanatic Baudelairean of all time. His veneration of Baudelaire went far beyond simple literary interest and took on the character of a rather peculiar religious worship. At the same time, Ellis was also the most prolific, if hardly the most distinguished, Russian translator of Baudelaire.

As a Russian symbolist, Ellis falls somewhere between the decadent and the mystic camps. Like the decadents of the 1890s, he was a "westernizer" with a special interest in French poetry. He maintained that Russian symbolism was nothing but the product of the "great renewal of art in the West."[15] However, he did not share the agnosticism and the aestheticist philosophy of other westernizers like Bryusov. With his strong religious and mystic bent, Ellis belongs to the generation of Russian symbolists who favored a "vertical" reading of literature. Thus he agreed with Vyacheslav Ivanov, the great theoretician of theurgic mysticism, that art should strive toward the *ens realissimum* as its ultimate goal.[16] Like Ivanov, he eventually converted to Catholicism.

Ellis's significance lies less in his literary talent than in his unusual, "demonic" personality, with which he exerted a strange fascination on his contemporaries. A similar portrait of his eccentric behavior and personal magnetism emerges from the memoirs of Andrey Bely, N. Valentinov, and Anastasiya Tsvetayeva, Marina Tsvetayeva's's sister.[17] Marina Tsvetayeva called Ellis a "disorganized poet, but a man of genius."[18] Several of her early poems, among them the poema "Charodei" (The Enchanter, 1914), are devoted to Ellis, with whom she was entangled in a curious *affaire à trois* together with her sister Anastasiya in 1909.[19] Ellis's outlandish external appearance evoked associations with a "medieval magician" (A. Tsvetayeva), with "Savonarola" or even the "Grand Inquisitor" (Bely). Valentinov gives the following description: "This strange man with sharply green eyes, a white marble-like face, an unnaturally black, as if lacquered, little beard, and shiningly red 'vampire'-lips, turning night into day and day into night, living in an always dark room with lowered blinds and candles in front of the portrait of Baudelaire, and later the bust of Dante, had the temperament of a furious agitator, invented extraordinary myths and fantasies, was the creator of parodies of all sorts and was an astonishing mime."[20]

Ellis's intellectual biography is characterized by restlessness and strangely erratic leaps and bounds. In the course of his life, he identified himself with the most diverse positions and philosophies, each of which he defended with equal missionary zeal. He began his career as a Marxist and a student of economics at Moscow University, where he graduated in 1903 from the Faculty of Law. However, to the astonishment of his professors, who foresaw an academic teaching position for the brilliant and flamboyant Kobylinsky, he declared one day to his mentor I. Kh. Ozerov that all economic theory was nothing but "trash" (*khlam*), and worth less than the smallest poem of Baudelaire.[21]

Giving up his academic pursuits, Ellis became a full-time *homme de lettres*. Together with Andrey Bely, he was the chief inspirer of the Argonaut group, an association of Moscow symbolists propagating a spiritual renewal of being in the face of an apocalyptic view of history.[22] As an alternative to the aesthetic-literary program of contemporary decadence, which was championed by Bryusov, Ellis promoted Dante, Baudelaire, and Nietzsche as the "true symbolists." According to Bely's testimony, Ellis was the only Argonaut to have serious interest in French symbolist poetry.[23]

Between 1907 and 1909, Ellis contributed together with Bely to Bryusov's journal *Vesy* (Libra). In this period, we can observe a certain rapprochement with Bryusov's position. Ellis's articles and book reviews in *Vesy* are mostly of a polemical character. He defends the sacred autonomy of art against populist heresies like Chulkov's and Ivanov's "mystical anarchism," and attacks Berdyaev's notion of theurgic art as a "sort of oatmeal for the breeding of mystics."[24] He shows particular scorn for the almanacs of the Shipovnik publishing house and writers like Leonid Andreyev and Boris Zaitsev, whom he accuses of vulgarizing the ideals of symbolism. At the same time, Ellis heaps praise on his new idol Bryusov, congratulating him for having developed the "catechism of a new faith, a new cult."[25] The only objection he ventures to Bryusov's book *Frantsuzskie liriki XIX veka* (1909) is the minimal number of poems by Baudelaire that Bryusov included in his collection and the fact that he presented Baudelaire as a poet *sui generis* instead of proclaiming him the leader of symbolism.[26]

Ellis's tactical alliance with Bryusov was probably based more on hostility toward common enemies than on truly shared beliefs, although he was genuinely enthralled for a while with Bryusov's personality. As we learn from a letter to his fellow Argonaut E. K. Medtner in May 1907, the reasons for his infatuation were rather peculiar and typical for Ellis's frame of mind: "Don't be amazed, but I have now definitely become good friends with Bryusov and see him every day. . . . A shadow from Baudelaire's soul has fallen on him, and this means everything to me, absolutely everything! . . . '*The heroic in demonism*'— this is his essence, and for me this is the most important. I deeply believe in the providentiality of our former enmity and I believe in the eternity of our friendship."[27]

Of course, Ellis's prediction turned out be be untrue. The breakup between the two poets is illustrated in a satirical poem that Bryusov dedicated to Ellis in 1914, declaring that he prefers sensual earthly love to the knightly cult of mystical ladies.[28] Even during his tenure as a contributor to *Vesy*, Ellis seemed to drift slowly back toward his temporarily repressed mysticism. His review of Vyacheslav Ivanov's essay collection *Po zvezdam* (By the Stars) was surprisingly sympathetic, except for the fact that he took issue with Ivanov's dualistic interpretation of Baudelaire's "Correspondances."[29] Ellis's last contribution to *Vesy*, an essay entitled "Kul'tura i simvolizm," ends with a call for religious myth building that seems to have more in common with Ivanov than with Bryusov.[30]

The establishment in 1909 of the publishing house Musaget, together with Bely and Medtner, signified in a certain sense a return to the "argonautic" program. In his book *Russkie simvolisty*, published in 1910, Ellis gives a survey of the development of symbolism and discusses the work of Balmont, Bryusov, and Bely. In the present crisis of symbolism, caused, according to Ellis, by the predominance of "pure art" with its solipsism, formalism, and amoralism, he sees as the only solution the total subordination to the spirit of Christianity and the return to the *ens realissimum*. He proclaims that "this Arch-Symbol, this highest Face, is the face of the Eternal Feminine, the *Face of the Madonna!*"[31] Ellis's contempt for positivism and decadence prompted him eventually to reject modern civilization entirely and retreat to the Middle Ages. In 1912, he declared in a letter to Medtner, "I am a man of the thirteenth century, and my whole life I will fight against the six centuries that followed."[32]

Ellis's two volumes of poetry published by Musaget, *Stigmata* (1911) and *Argo* (1914), show evidence of this medieval Catholic spirit. The term *stigmata* also occurs in his literary criticism: he refers to Baudelaire's diaries as the "stigmata of his soul" and asserts that in Baudelaire's prose "every word is a fiery stigma."[33] In his poetry, the religious themes (struggle with Satan's temptations, Apocalypse and *Dies Irae*, redemption through prayers to the Virgin Mary) are presented in the rather stiff style of a *poeta doctus* and garnished with quotes in Latin and Italian. At the same time, traces of a decadent Baudelairism become evident. The collection *Stigmata* contains the poem "Ekzoticheskii zakat" (Exotic Sunset), which, as the subtitle reveals, was written "while translating Ch. Baudelaire's 'Fleurs du Mal.'"[34] The title seems to be an amalgamation of Baudelaire's "Parfum exotique" and "Le Coucher du soleil romantique." Ellis tries to combine the exotic dreamworld of the first poem with the decadent gloom of the second. The creation of an image of transfigured beauty based on a repulsive picture of decay is reminiscent of "Une Charogne":

В небо простерлось из гнилости склепной
все, что кишело и тлело в золе,—
сад сверхестественный, великолепный
призрачно вырос, качаясь во мгле.

Out of the rottenness of the burial vault,
everything that teemed and decayed in the ashes stretched into the sky—
a supernatural, grandiose garden
grew up like a phantom, rocking in the haze.

The eerie atmosphere reaches its culmination in the last stanza, when Baudelaire's face looms for a moment as a sort of fata morgana on the evening sky:

И на меня, как живая химера,
в сердце вонзая магический глаз,
глянул вдруг лик исполиский Бодлэра
и, опрокинут, как солнце погас.

And, like a living chimera,
thrusting its magic eye into my heart,
suddenly the gigantic face of Baudelaire stared at me,
and, toppling over, went out like the sun.

Ellis temporarily abandoned his newly found Catholic faith in 1910, when he was the first Russian symbolist to come under the spell of Rudolf Steiner. He followed Steiner for a while on a lecture circuit through Europe, but his enthusiasm for anthroposophy proved to be short lived. In the book *Vigilemus!* (published 1914), which caused considerable controversy in the Musaget publishing house and was responsible for Bely's final breakup with Ellis, he denounced anthroposophy and drew up the balance sheet of his spiritual tribulations and peregrinations. In 1913, Ellis left Russia forever. He moved first to Italy and later to Switzerland, where, having cut off all links with his past, he lived as a Jesuit priest until his death in 1947. Despite his conversion to Catholicism, Ellis seems to have become more of a Slavophile in his later years. His new guiding star became Vladimir Solovyov, whom he translated into German and to whom he dedicated his monumental biography of Zhukovsky.[35] In his last book, a study of Pushkin as the "religious genius of Russia," published in Switzerland, Ellis makes frequent references to Solovyov and also commends Vyacheslav Ivanov, Merezhkovsky, Rozanov, Berdyaev, and Lossky for serving the ideal of "Holy Russia."[36] His former colleagues Bryusov and Bely and his idol Baudelaire are not mentioned even once in the book.

Bely's judgment of Ellis is rather harsh. He dismisses Ellis in his memoirs as an "economist-pessimist-Baudelairean-Bryusovian-Dantean-occultist-Steinerian-Catholic," whose only talent was that of an actor: "He could have been a great artist, and became—a bad translator, a talentless poet and a mediocre publicist and 'ex' (ex-symbolist, ex-Marxist, etc.); a 'man of the past' (*byvshii chelovek*) for all movements in which he wanted to play an important role, he slept through his role: to open a new era of mimetic art."[37] Valentinov, while more benevolent toward Ellis and interpreting his erratic spiritual development and ultimate conversion to Catholicism as the logical consequence of his Baudelairism, also expresses admiration for Ellis's mimetic talent, in particular his almost uncanny ability to imitate people. Ellis's clowning productions à la Charlie Chaplin, mentioned by all memoirists, seem to have had an irresistible comic appeal. As we know from Valentinov, "[Ellis's] parodies of the manner in which a Bolshevik, Menshevik, Social Revolutionary, Constitutional Democrat, cadet, page, Jew, and Armenian waltz, were so expressive, so comical, that the spectators split their sides with laughter."[38]

Perhaps Ellis would indeed have been more successful as a comedian or a movie star than as a poet and critic. His poetic oeuvre has largely sunk into oblivion,[39] and his literary criticism is remembered by historians of Russian symbolism only for its rather extreme statements. James West has called Ellis "perhaps the most naïvely dogmatic theorist of the Russian symbolist movement."[40] With their shrillness and tendency toward apodictic statements and hyperbole, Ellis's articles inform us better about his own views than about the objects of his criticism. It is true that his later work, written in German, gives a more balanced impression, but that did not save it from being ignored by the scholarly world.

One salient feature in Ellis's thinking that seems to have survived all his changing allegiances, at least up to his emigration, was the plea for an "aristocratic" elitism and contempt for the *profanum vulgus*. As he made clear many times, "art is essentially a concern of the few and for the few."[41] He therefore rejected the collectivist concept of *sobornost'* (ecumenicity) propagated by Vyacheslav Ivanov and the "mystical anarchists," and although still a a card-carrying member of the Social Democratic Party in 1908, he denied any connection between literature and social activism.[42] Ellis was well aware that his opposition to any societal involvement of art went against the grain of most Russian literature. In a polemic attack against Professor S. A. Vengerov, he denounced the social engagement of Russian authors (which had been praised by Vengerov) as a sign of the "backwardness" and "primitivism" of aesthetics and politics in Russia.[43] Ellis's philosophical position was grounded in a relentless dualism. He rejected the visible reality in the name of an abstract and unattainable "beauty," which was not contained in the material world. Ellis therefore opposed Vyacheslav Ivanov's theory that art should reveal the transcendental essence immanent in the visible phenomena. Art, according to Ellis, had necessarily to express a negative attitude to the world: "The ideal image is always inevitably hostile to the primary, external reality that once brought it forth. From this comes the tragic wavering of the creative spirit between the two poles of being."[44]

While it is comparatively easy, looking at his tireless polemical fights, to state what Ellis was *against*, it is more difficult to establish what he was *for*, since his positive theoretical statements are not characterized by clarity and coherence. In one of his articles, Ellis even explicitly rejected the notion of coherence, which he denounced as "epic thinking," and pleaded instead for an aphoristic "lyric thinking."[45] There can be no doubt on one issue, however: Baudelaire was the most important author for Ellis, his perennial source of inspiration and point of reference. The French poet is mentioned throughout all of Ellis's critical writings up to 1914. Unfortunately, however, Ellis never explained in an extensive manner what exactly Baudelaire meant to him. Neither his article with the title "Bodler i bodleristy," promised for *Vesy* in 1909, nor his book on French symbolism, announced by Musaget in 1910, ever materialized.[46] Ellis's view of Baudelaire has to be stitched together from his numerous allusions in poems, book reviews, essays, and introductions. Whether all these fragments really add up to a coherent whole is another question. It is true that his fascination with Baudelaire did provide an element of stability in an otherwise shaky intellectual biography. Aside from the final period in Switzerland, the only possible defection from the cause of Baudelairism occurred during the short-lived involvement with anthroposophy, when Ellis momentarily acknowledged to Medtner the "supremacy of the Germans over the French" and in particular the "supremacy of R. Wagner over all Symbolism, with Baudelaire at the head," and he even declared to have "abandoned [the French] once and for all." However, this was not his final word. Shortly after this statement, Ellis suggested to Medtner an article on "Baudelaire and Wagner" and proposed "to do a decent monograph on Wagner *in a year* and then go on to Baudelaire."[47] Remaining the guiding star for Ellis throughout the various stages of his career, Baudelaire proved flexible enough to fit into different creeds, from argonautism to "Bryusovism" to Catholicism. Ellis's view of Baudelaire, not surprisingly, if we consider his frequent conversions, seems to have evolved over the years, but in light of the rather grandiose and opaque character of his critical statements it becomes difficult to give an exact account of this evolution. The outline that follows is therefore somewhat conjectural.

Baudelaire's sonnet "Correspondances" (curiously misspelled as "Correspondences" by Ellis)[48] represented for him the "quintessence" of Baudelairism and symbolism at large. From Ellis's explanations, we can gather that the emphasis seems to lie for him on "exclusiveness" more than on anything else:

> The essence of symbolism is the ability to capture the most subtle overtones of things . . . to understand the persistent "regards familiers" of anything in the great temple of Nature.
>
> The essence of symbolism are "correspondences" [*sic* in the Russian text], the innumerable, elusive "correspondences," barely and only partially embodied and never coinciding with the world of appearances, and the only means of rendering them always were and always will be the "confuses paroles" of the lyric poet. As their most essential quality, one has to acknowledge their inaccessibility to the average person immersed in the bustle of life, their aristocratic exclusiveness, and their absolute unfitness for any kind of social experiment.[49]

While it is true that Baudelaire expressed in his diaries contempt for the "herd" and for democratic values, the linkage of the theory of correspondences with aristocratic aloofness seems to be Ellis's own doing. Incidentally, the belief that true art was accessible only to a few "initiated" did not prevent Ellis from proselytizing. Valentinov, the positivist and social democrat, gives a rather amusing account of the nightly sessions in which Ellis tried to convert him to Baudelairism. Having assured Valentinov that Baudelaire was a greater revolutionary than Marx, Engels, and Bakunin, he carried off his skeptical guest into a mystical phantasmagoria: "Combining the propaganda of Baudelairism with a striving toward the 'infinite,' his 'aspiration à l'infini' with occultism, he began to entertain me with grandiose inventions, in which, in a fantastic attire, appearances of other worlds chaotically interlaced with demonic flights into the abyss, various 'paradis artificiels,' Death and Love, Sin and Beauty."[50]

Ellis's emphasis on Baudelaire's individualism contains a heavy dose of decadent Nietzscheanism. The earliest document of his interest in Baudelaire, three poems in his 1904 edition of translations from *Les Fleurs du Mal*,[51] evokes the lurid horror-cabinet of Balmont's and Bryusov's Baudelairean poems of the 1890s. The startled reader is immersed in an eerie procession of "horrible ghosts," such as "swarms of nude women with a smile of voluptuousness on their lips," "Titans, marching with heavy footsteps and gloomy anger, wreaking terrible havoc everywhere, like hurricanes," as well as "throngs of black snakes, curling and gliding rapidly." Baudelaire himself appears as an outcast and fallen angel of sinister pride. Using Baudelaire's own imagery, Ellis compares him to Icarus and to an "Albatross, thrown down from the kingdom of dreams into the crowd of supercilious and soulless fools." The victim seeks revenge by weaving for his henchmen a "wreath of poisoned flowers" so terrible that "Dante himself probably would have paled." Only he who, like Ellis, "has heard the call of Zarathustra," is not frightened by this spectacle.

Ellis proclaims that he identifies with Baudelaire because of his own analogous experience with the "fall":

Тебя люблю я потому,
Что знаю ужасы паденья,
Что сам порой любил я тьму
Сильней, чем свет и возрожденье . . .

I love you, because I know myself
The horrors of the fall,
Because I myself at times loved
Darkness more than light and revival . . .

However, the poet resists the temptation of embracing evil for its own sake. Baudelaire's main preoccupation, Ellis assures us, is the pursuit of beauty and truth:

Пусть гордый дух враждует с небесами,
В нем—жажда правды, жажда красоты! . . .

May the proud spirit be at enmity with the heavens,
In him there is thirst for truth, thirst for beauty! . . .

Beauty becomes a key term in Ellis's understanding of Baudelaire. The word has the advantage of being sufficiently ambiguous to fit into various philosophies of artistic creation. In the passage cited, it is used in conjunction with "truth," that is, it seems to suggest a sort of platonic *kalokagathia*, rather than a purely aesthetic category. This impression is confirmed when we look at the most extensive critical discussion Ellis ever devoted to Baudelaire, the foreword to his 1907 edition of *Mon coeur mis à nu*. The text begins like a manifesto of Ellis's own philosophy of art. Artistic creation is defined as a "struggle of the spirit with the world of matter in the name of the idea," and the artist himself appears as a "deity," "magician," "prophet," "theurgist," and "lawgiver of being." As the most prominent examples, Ellis names Dante, Lermontov, Schopenhauer, Nietzsche, and, as the absolute culmination, Baudelaire. Baudelaire's "amoralism," which was so dear to the Russian decadents, appears here as the result of a particular spiritual aspiration:

> The poetry of Ch. Baudelaire is a titanic upsurge toward perfect and immense beauty, its internal essence an unconsciously religious quest, the immutable motto—"Et eritis sicut dii" [*sic*], the ultimate ideal "l'homme-Dieu!" From here comes the inevitability of the fall (*nizverzhenie*) and the great horror of duality (*razdvoenie*)! . . . From here comes the transformation of the path of theurgy into the path of theomachy, the conversion of the service to a beauty impossible on earth to the theory of the artificial and monstrous, of the impulse toward reincarnation to the cult of destruction, from here comes the transformation of the servant of a perfect world into a knight of evil, of the prophet of immortality into a teacher of non-being! . . . The mad attempt to return the lost paradise did not succeed![52]

In his *Vesy* articles, Ellis also emphasizes Baudelaire's amoral side, his fascination with the "beauty of evil," while downplaying the "theurgic" component. In the review of Panov's translation of *Les Fleurs du Mal*, he describes Baudelaire's collection of poetry, "a book that appears once per millennium," as "the poetic confession of a soul that subdued in itself the 'good' in the name of the 'beautiful,' sacrificing to its only idol, *Beauty*, the whole universe and itself."[53] His aristocratic distaste for mediocrity led Ellis to indulge himself sometimes in a sort of immoralist satanism. In the conclusion of an essay on contemporary symbolism, he declares, "Besides, is not *Satan* better than a good part of the human race whom we save from him, is he not the enemy of those low forms of tepid evil-good, which are worse than absolute evil?"[54]

In the Musaget period, Ellis reverted to a more mainstream religious and moralist understanding of Baudelaire. In his book on the Russian symbolists he expressed a clear rejection of the decadent view: "Whatever the superficial connoisseurs of the 'new, all too new' may say of Ch. Baudelaire's amoralism and 'aesthetism,' for us it remains indubitable that the essence of his work, of his madness, of his whole life path and teaching lies in the tragic search of another, new reconciliation of the fatal antinomy between Beauty and Goodness, in the craving for a new form of perfection, in the attempt to find a different mystical interpretation of the fundamental antinomy between God and Satan, in one word—in the pathos of the conscious fall and in the inevitable return to the problem of mystic redemption."[55]

Ellis espoused an openly Catholic view of Baudelaire in the book *Vigilemus!*, where he refers to the "ritual style" of *Les Fleurs du Mal* as an "inverted Catholic mass" and "gothic à rebours." He asserts that Baudelaire's "modernism" was only a "mask" and that his real concern was always the metaphysical. Baudelaire, according to Ellis, was "dogmatic, and frequently even theological." The only solution that Ellis sees for Baudelaire's conflict is also the one he adopted for himself—to join the Catholic church: "Baudelaire's tragic mission was the disclosure of the mystery of dualism. No one of the symbolists penetrated deeper in this mystery than he. Like Huysmans, he could have found tranquillity and a metaphysical way out from dualism only on the stern path in the interior of the Catholic church."[56]

As one can see, Ellis's view of Baudelaire has certain invariables that remained constant over the years, such as his insistence on the fall and the dualism between Good and Evil. However, the emphasis given to these elements seems to have shifted with time. Whereas in his earlier period, Ellis had stressed the confrontational, rebellious, and amoral aspect of Baudelaire, he now gravitated toward "reconciliation." From his flirtation with Satan he had come around to the acceptance of God. It is worth noting, however, that, unlike other Catholic interpreters of Baudelaire, Ellis never claimed explicitly that Baudelaire himself was or became a Christian believer. Using the subjunctive mood, he merely observed that Baudelaire "would have found" rest in the Catholic church. Whether he actually did it is not stated. Perhaps we could compare Ellis's view with that of another neo-Catholic follower of Baudelaire, T. S. Eliot, who wrote of Baudelaire's religion, "His business was not to practise Christianity, but—what was much more important for his time—to assert its *necessity*."[57]

The most durable legacy of Ellis was neither his critical writings nor his poetry, both of them largely forgotten nowadays, but his translations. Many of them have survived until this day. The Soviet edition of *Les Fleurs du Mal* published in 1970 contains no fewer than thirty-seven poems in Ellis's translation. Ellis translated not only *Les Fleurs du Mal* in its totality but also *Mon coeur mis à nu* (1907) and *Petits poèmes en prose* (1910). His version of *Les Fleurs du Mal* appeared in two editions. In 1904, he published a first installment of eighty-four poems under the title *Immorteli* ("Immortelles"—the title "Flowers of Evil" was still forbidden at that time). This book also contains texts on Baudelaire by Banville, Bourget, and Sainte-Beuve, as well as the three poems by Ellis mentioned earlier. A complete and entirely refurbished edition of *Les Fleurs du Mal*, introduced by Théophile Gautier's "Notice," appeared in 1908.

In order to get an impression of Ellis's approach to translation, which will allow at the same time a comparison with the method of the other Russian Baudelairean, P. F. Yakubovich, it will be helpful to look at an excerpt from "Le Vin des chiffonniers," which was also translated by Yakubovich:[58]

О вы, уставшие от горя и трудов,
Чьи спины сгорблены под бременем годов
И грудою трапья, чья грудь в изнеможенье—
О вы, огромного Парижа изверженье!

Куда лежит ваш путь?—Вокруг—пары вина;
Их побелевшая в сраженьях седина,
Их пышные усы повисли, как знамены
Им чудятся цветы, и арки, и колонны,

И крики радости, покрытые трубой,
И трепет солнечный, и барабанный бой,
Рев оглушительный и блеск слепящий оргий—
В честь победителей народные восторги.[59]

Oh you, who have grown tired from sorrow and work,
Whose backs are bent under the burden of years
And a heap of rags, whose breast is exhausted—
Oh you, excretion of the enormous Paris!

Where does your path lead to? All around—exhalations of vine;
Their grey hair, whitened in battles,

Their splendid mustaches drooping like banners;
They have a vision of flowers, arches, and columns,

And shouts of joy, drowned in trumpets,
And the quivering of the sun, and the beating of drums,
And deafening roar and the dazzling radiance of orgies—
Popular raptures in honor of the victors.

Whereas Yakubovich had emphasized in his translation the "revolutionary" aspect of the poem, Ellis downplays the element of social criticism. The concrete evocation of urban misery is reduced in his version to rather abstract, general expressions like *gore* (sorrow) and *trudy* (work, trouble). As a propagator of aristocratic individualism with contempt for the rabble, Ellis did not harbor much sympathy for philanthropy. A telling detail, pointed out by Efim Etkind, is the interpretation of the line "vomissement confus de l'énorme Paris." Yakubovich had understood this as a reference to the rags and tatters of the big metropolis. For Ellis, however, it refers to the poor inhabitants of the city—he was not disturbed by a comparison of people with trash (Baudelaire's text allows both readings). Ellis is relatively successful in his rendering of the drunken frenzy of the ragpicker, an impressionist "orgy" of sound and light, which in Yakubovich's version had become a casualty of the revolutionary message. Of course, there is no mention of "freedom" and "resurrection" in Ellis's version. His vision evokes less a revolutionary popular upheaval than the triumphant procession of a commander in chief or emperor basking in the frenzied adulation of the populace after a successful military campaign.

Ellis pays more attention to form than Yakubovich. We find numerous rhetorical figures in his text, such as anaphoras (*O vy—O vy*; *Ikh—Ikh—Im*; *I—I*), alliterations (*trupoi—trepet*) which are partially of an onomatopoetic character ("*barabannyi boi*" [the beating of drums]), "poetic etymologies" (*grudoiu—grud*, suggesting a link between "heap" and "breast"), and corresponding hemistichs with a parallel rhythmic structure and internal rhymes (*Ikh pyshnye usy—Im chudiatsia* tsvety; *rev* oglushitel'nyi—*v chest'* pobe-ditelei). A certain predilection for rare and archaic forms becomes noticeable in the choice of *znameny* (instead of the common *znamena*) to render "drapeaux." Ellis's emotional tonality seems rather aloof and detached: unlike Yakubovich and Baudelaire, he needs no exclamation marks in the third stanza. His intricate parnassian rendering of "Le Vin des chiffonniers" certainly does justice to Baudelaire's perfectionist concern with poetic form but it fails to convey the spontaneity of the original, which is perhaps better preserved in Yakubovich's populist appropriation.

In light of Ellis's claim that "Correpondances" represents the quintessence of Baudelairism, his translation of this sonnet deserves special attention. The first version, published in the 1904 edition, can hardly be called successful. It suffices to quote the first stanza to demonstrate the remoteness from Baudelaire's original:

Природа—дивный храм, и в ней столпы живые
С невятным ропотом сдержали свод небес.
Природа—символов давно известных лес,
Они кивают нам задумчиво-немые . . . [60]

Nature is a marvelous temple, and in it living columns
Were holding with a vague murmur the vault of heaven.
Nature is a forest of long known symbols,
They are nodding to us, thoughtfully mute . . .

Some major components of the text are entirely Ellis's invention, such as the assertion that the columns of the temple are "holding the vault of heaven" or that the symbols, which are "nodding to us thoughtfully mute," have been "known for a long time." Yakubovich's version, which Ellis himself had consulted (he copied not only the *divnyi khram* [marvelous temple] from it but also the mistranslation of "hautbois" with *fleity* [flutes] in the first tercet), certainly gives a more accurate rendering of the stanza, although one wonders whether his "dark forest" is perhaps an unconscious echo of Dante's "selva oscura":

Природа—дивный храм, где ряд живых колонн
О чем-то шепчет нам невнятными словами;
Лес темный символов знакомыми очами
На проходящего глядит со всех сторон.[61]

Nature is a marvelous temple, where a row of living columns
Whisper to us about something in incomprehensible words;
A dark forest of symbols looks with familiar eyes
At the passer-by from all sides.

For the 1908 edition of *Les Fleurs du Mal*, Ellis completely reworked his translation. The ultimate version reads as follows:

Соответствия

Природа—строгий храм, где строй живых колонн
Порой чуть внятный звук украдкою уронит;
Лесами символов бредет, в их чащах тонет
Смущенный человек, их взглядом умилен.

Как эхо отзвуков в один аккорд неясный,
Где все едино, свет и ночи темнота,
Благоухания и звуки и цвета
В ней сочетаются в гармонии согласной.

Есть запах девственный; как луг он чист и свят,
Как тело детское, высокий звук гобоя;
И есть торжественный, развратный аромат—

Слиянье ладана и амбры и бензоя:
В нем бесконечное доступно вдруг для нас,
В нем высших дум восторг и лучших чувств экстаз![62]

Correspondences

Nature is a stern temple, where a formation of living columns
Will emit at times a barely perceptible sound;
Confused man wanders through forests of symbols,
Drowns in their thicket, tenderly touched by their look.

Like an echo of sound reflections in one vague chord,
Where everything is one, light and darkness of the night,

Fragrances and sounds and colors
Combine in it in a concordant harmony.

There is a virginal smell; like a meadow it is pure and holy,
Like a child's body, the high sound of the oboe;
And there is a solemn, depraved aroma—

The blending of incense, amber and benzoin:
In it infinity becomes suddenly accessible to us,
In it there is the delight of highest thoughts and the ecstasy of best feelings!

In Baudelaire's original:[63]

Nature is a temple, where living pillars
Sometimes emit obscure words;
Man passes through forests of symbols
Which observe him with familiar looks.

Like long echoes blending in the distance
In a dark and deep unity,
Vast like the night and like clarity,
Perfumes, colors and sounds respond to each other.

There are perfumes fresh like children's flesh,
Sweet like oboes, green like meadows,
—And others, corrupt, rich and triumphant,

Having the expansion of infinite things,
Like amber, musk, benzoin and incense,
Which sing the raptures of spirit and senses.

Although the second version comes closer to the original than the first, it is still far from convincing. The translation shows evidence of Ellis's inclination to exaggeration and hyperbole. Thus, man not only wanders through a forest of symbols but literally "drowns in their thicket." That he is "tenderly touched" (*umilen*) by their looks seems to have its explanation less in Baudelaire's text than in the fact that Ellis needed a rhyme to *stroi zhivykh kolonn* (which again looks suspiciously similar to Yakubovich's *riad zhivykh kolonn*). Whereas

Baudelaire's meadows are simply "green," they become "pure and holy" for Ellis, and Baudelaire's *esprit* and *sens* turn into "highest thoughts" and "best feelings." The infinite itself becomes "suddenly accessible to us" in Ellis's translation. Aside from its semantic inexactitude, Ellis's version also fails to convince on a purely aesthetic level. Nothing of Baudelaire's subtle musicality and play with sound patterns, with which he applies the principle of "correspondences" to phonetic instrumentation, is preserved in the Russian text.

The shortcomings of Ellis's translations were noticed and criticized by other symbolist poets. Bryusov, in his review of the 1904 edition, called Ellis's translation a step backward from Yakubovich and demonstrated that Ellis had in fact plagiarized many passages from the populist translator. His final verdict was unequivocal: "Mr. Ellis does not have the two most necessary qualifications for the translation of Baudelaire: poetic talent and knowledge of the French language."[64] According to Belyi's testimony, Ellis was so upset about this review that he threatened to kill Bryusov.[65] A similarly negative judgment was expressed by Ellis's fellow Argonaut Bely, who wrote in a letter to Aleksandr Blok on April 8, 1904, "Ellis's translation of Baudelaire has come out. The translation is devastatingly bad (*ubiistvenno plokh*). He insistently asks me to write a review. Alas, alas!"[66] It is true that this harsh condemnation did not prevent Bryusov, after his reconciliation with Ellis, from contributing a benevolent if nebulous foreword to the 1908 edition of Ellis's *Fleurs du Mal*; and Bely, in his review of this edition, blamed the discrepancies between Ellis's translation and Baudelaire's original not on the translator's lack of talent but on the general untranslatability of Baudelaire.[67]

In general, Bely's attitude toward Ellis was strangely inconsistent, wavering between love and hate. He wrote a review of Ellis's edition of *Mon coeur mis à nu*, in which he hailed the translation in the most complimentary terms and commented on the introduction, "Ellis's essay on Baudelaire is amazingly concise. But behind each sentence one feels a real experience (*perezhivanie*). Every sentence is saturated with experience. Ellis *really knows Baudelaire*. We are grateful to the translator for his beautiful, daring description and for the array of deep thoughts about art, handfuls of jewels generously scattered over the article."[68] Two years later, however, Bely tried to prevent the publication by Musaget of Ellis's edition of *Petits poèmes en prose*. His irate letter to the publisher E. K. Medtner, as an unpublished document of Bely's stormy relationship with Ellis, deserves to be quoted more fully:

Dear Emilii Karlovich!

My dear, it is sad that I have to write you, but it is imperative. You know how much I love Ellis, but . . . there are limits to my patience. I see that one needs strong bridles for him or he will straight away get into a mess (*s mesta v kar'er posadit v luzhu*). . . . From the first day, Ellis kept telling everybody that we were going to publish the complete edition of his Baudelaire, his "Garden of the Giant" (a play for children!), and some other book; all this time he has not lifted a finger. . . . But most important—knowing Ellis's translations, I got frightened and asked Petrovsky and Kiselev to "cast an editor's glance" (*proredaktirovat'*). . . . It turned out that these are not translations, but "God knows what." . . . Not before you decide will I give my personal moral sanction to the publication of a work of blatant illiteracy and if he gives it nevertheless to the typesetter (I can't forbid this without encroaching on your rights), then I will understand that his friendship with me is not friendship, but doggish greed and cunning, i.e., something bestial. . . . I became convinced that it is impossible to deal with him on equal terms. He has to be reined in.[69]

In fairness to Ellis, it has to be pointed out that he himself was not uncritical toward the merit of his own translations. In his review of Panov's edition of *Les Fleurs du Mal*, he admitted in 1907, "Among the eighty translations from the 'Flowers of Evil' which I published four years ago, I consider at least fifty absolutely unsuccessful, and somewhat satisfactory no more than three to five."[70]

How then can we summarize Ellis's legacy? In many respects Ellis occupies a unique position in the Russian symbolist reception of Baudelaire, by virtue of the unmatched intensity of his veneration and the unmatched quantity of his translations as well as by his Catholic approach. Ironically, the only other Russian Baudelairean to whom he can really be compared is his antipode P. F. Yakubovich, although Ellis differed from him in almost every respect. Both the populist revolutionary and the anti-populist mystic expressed a love for Baudelaire that went beyond simple literary taste. Both of them personally identified themselves with the French poet and saw him as a guiding star of personal significance. Both of them, like Baudelaire, stylized their role as societal outcasts and their hatred for the bourgeois mainstream, from which they became geographically and sociologically removed as a Siberian convict and an exiled priest. Both of them, although not entirely devoid of talent, wrote poetry of second-rate importance and ultimately left a deeper mark in life than in writing: one as a terrorist, the other as a clown. In their readiness to push their militancy to the ultimate degree, they seem to actualize on a existential level many potentialities inherent in Baudelaire's own personality and literary personae: the revolutionary and the Jesuit, the henchman and the jester, the satanist blasphemer and the saint. In his diaries, Baudelaire declares that there exist only three respectable professions: the priest, the warrior, and the poet.[71] It looks as if Ellis had chosen the first of these, and Yakubovich the second, thus leaving the third to Baudelaire himself.

IVANOV: DISTRUST AND TRANSFIGURATION

Vyacheslav Ivanovich Ivanov (1866–1949), a classical scholar, poet, and renaissance man of formidable learning, was undoubtedly the most outstanding theoretician of the religious strain of Russian poetry, which had become the hallmark of Russian symbolism after the turn of the century. His perception of art as the revelation of a higher, transcendental truth was shaped in part by the theological philosophy of Vladimir Solovyov, whose notion of divine all-unity and the progressive transfiguration of the material world through beauty and art, understood as the eschatological task of reuniting the "world soul" with God, exerted a decisive influence on the new generation of Russian symbolists. Although traces of a decadent aesthetic can be found in Ivanov's early work, and he harbored much sympathy for the refined culture of Alexandrian Hellenism, he condemned the contemporary Western decadence as unsuited for the undeveloped, "barbaric" Russian culture,[72] the task of which he saw as vitalizing the decadent West. Ivanov's propagation of a religiously inspired, theurgic form of art lead him to a rather negative attitude toward French symbolism. In his 1912 essay "Mysli o simvolizme" (Thoughts on Symbolism), he denounced Mallarmé and his school for practicing a "symbolism of poetic rebuses," the essence of which he saw in the illusionism of mere rhetorical "tricks" (*priemy*).[73] Although Ivanov did not extend his condemnation of French symbolism to Baudelaire, whom he respected and translated into Russian, his attitude toward the latter was nevertheless ambiguous and not free of a certain deep-seated mistrust.

It comes as no surprise that Ivanov was attracted by the sonnet "Correspondances," since both the mystic content of the poem and the solemn, hieratic language were congenial to his own poetic style. In fact, many of Ivanov's early poems seem like a reflection of the high-flung, self-assured verbal gesture of Baudelaire's sonnet. Two programmatic texts of the 1902 collection *Kormchie zvezdy* (Lodestars), "Tvorchestvo" (Creation) and "Al'piiskii rog" (The Alphorn), contain definitions of nature that seem to echo Baudelaire's "forêt de symboles," "confuses paroles," and "longues echos":

Природа—знаменье и тень предвечных дел:
Твой замысел—ей символ равный.[74]

Nature is a sign and a shadow of eternal things:
Your design is [to create] a symbol equal to it.

Природа—символ, как сей рог. Она
Звучит для отзвука. И отзвук—Бог.[75]

Nature is a symbol, like this horn. It sounds
For an echo. And the echo is God.

Despite these parallels, Ivanov had an ambiguous attitude toward "Correspondances," as we know from his discussion of this poem in the important essay "Dve stikhii v sovremennom simvolizme" (Two Elements in Contemporary Symbolism), first published in the symbolist journal *Zolotoe runo* (The Golden Fleece) in April and May 1908 and later included in Ivanov's 1909 collection *Po zvezdam* (By the Stars). In this article, Ivanov postulates a dichotomy between "realist" and "idealist" art, which he sees not only reflected in contemporary symbolism but as fundamental paradigms of human creativity in all times. Ivanov's use of *realism* and *idealism* differs from the usual meaning of these words. His understanding of realism comes close to the medieval concept of the term (realism as opposed to nominalism), although it includes also the nineteenth-century literary movement of this name. As for "idealism," Ivanov later recognized himself that the term was misleading. In order to avoid confusion with philosophical idealism (which, after all, was his own position), he later changed the name to *subjectivism*. Ivanov's essay, in a sweeping, extended antithesis, swings back and forth like a gigantic pendulum between the two poles of realism and idealism, piling up definitions and specifications along the way. According to Ivanov, one pole reflects true, objective being, the other free, subjective creation; one is receptive and "female," the other initiative and "male";

one follows the principle of transfiguration (*preobrazhenie*), the other the principle of transformation (*preobrazovanie*); one encourages collective self-abnegation, the other individualistic self-affirmation; one is epistemological, the other psychological; one uses symbols as a means toward a higher goal, the other as a goal in itself.

Interestingly enough, Baudelaire's "Correspondances" serves as a salient example of *both* these tendencies. In fact, the poem, according to Ivanov, is split right in the middle between realism and "idealism." In the quatrains, Ivanov recognizes an expression of realist symbolism: "The poet discloses the real mystery of nature, completely alive and completely founded on secret correspondences, kinships and consonances of something that appears to our dead ignorance as separate and dissonant, accidentally close and lifelessly mute. In nature, for those who can hear, there is the sound of a many-mouthed (*mnogoustoe*) eternal word."[76] Ivanov draws a connection between the quatrains of "Correspondances" and passages from Balzac's "Louis Lambert" and "Séraphîta," and he invokes Novalis and Goethe as masters of realist art. With his reference to Balzac, Ivanov anticipated Jacques Crépet and Georges Blin, who in their 1942 edition of *Les Fleurs du Mal* pointed to passages from Balzac's "Gambara" and "Séraphîta" as possible sources for "Correspondances." Ivanov seems to have noticed these parallels before the French philologists. His distinction between a realist and an idealist half also seems to anticipate the dichotomy between "vertical" and "horizontal" correspondences, which has become a commonplace of French literary criticism. The only difference is that for most critics the hiatus occurs after the first quatrain. The second quatrain, where "Les parfums, les couleurs et les sons se répondent," is already associated to the world of synaesthetic, horizontal correspondences.

According to Ivanov, Baudelaire strays from the path of realism in the tercets of "Correspondances." He abandons the idea of mystical unity in nature and explores instead concrete, psychological associations between different sensual impressions. These parallels, while providing refined pleasures for the individual self, are not contributing toward an understanding of true being. The "psychological experiment" degenerates into decadence: "The mystery of the object, *res*, is almost forgotten, instead, the feasting luxury of the *ego*, all-cognizing and tasting from everything, is royally increased."[77] Ivanov sees the tercets of "Correspondances" as evidence for the "second face of Baudelaire— the parnassian face." He finds the main expression of this parnassianism in the technical, formal perfectionism of Baudelaire's poetry. He points to the "canonically correct and strict verse of marvelous precision," the "balanced, re-strained stanzas," the "rhetorical metaphors" that have not yet become sym-bols, the "lapidarity" and "conservatism in the means of external poetic and musical expressiveness," the "predominance of plasticity over music in lines that seem chiseled in the sculptor's studio of Benvenuto Cellini." Unlike Ver-laine in his "De la musique avant toute chose," Baudelaire demanded for his verse, according to Ivanov, "the weight of metal and the pose of a statue." Ivanov defines Baudelaire's ideal of beauty as an "idol of marble," similar to the one that appears in the sonnet "La Beauté." He points out that the preoccupa-tion with the external form, with the artificial, the rare, and the exotic, that was typical for the parnassian movement later became, in a more exaggerated form, the hallmark of decadence.

Needless to say, Ivanov's sympathies belong not to idealist parnassian deca-dence but to the realist type of art, represented for him by Classical Greece, the religious art of the Middle Ages, Goethe, romanticism, and nineteenth-century realism. However, in light of his own solemn and ornamental language, his reser-vations about Baudelaire's parnassian rhetoric seem somewhat suspect. In fact, Ivanov appears to vacillate between apprehension and fascination when it comes to Baudelaire's style. While seemingly distancing himself from the French poet, his choice of words when talking about his "canonically correct and strict verse of marvelous precision" betrays unmitigated admiration. Was Ivanov perhaps con-demning in Baudelaire his own repressed parnassian and decadent leanings?

Unfortunately, Ivanov fails to explain how it could happen that two such an-tithetical tendencies, realism and idealism, appeared together in the same liter-ary text. Was Baudelaire himself torn between conflicting inclinations? Do his other poems and his prose writings show evidence of the same split? Ivanov does not elaborate on these points. One gets the impression, however, that the Russian symbolist indirectly takes a position against Baudelaire's enshrinement as a prophet of symbolism. He stresses the fact that Baudelaire, the "symbolist" and "decadent," appropriated the mystic content of the quatrains of "Corre-spondances" from the "realist" and "romantic" Balzac. He seems to suggest that this mysticism did not really express Baudelaire's own worldview. Perhaps also in an attempt to distance himself from Ellis, Ivanov shows a healthy dose of skepticism toward a text which, he acknowledges, was reputed to be the "fun-damental doctrine and symbol of faith" of the new poetic school.[78] (Ellis, not surprisingly, took issue with Ivanov's interpretation of "Correspondances," denying any discrepancy between the quatrains and the tercets of the sonnet.

The second half, according to Ellis, merely provides an illustration of the general principles pronounced in the first, and there is no poet more faithful to true being than Baudelaire.[79])

Ivanov's doubts about the validity of Baudelaire's metaphysical mysticism are shared by many twentieth-century critics (although, of course, not everybody would view the absence of a true "vertical" dimension as necessarily a negative feature). Ivanov's concept of "idealist symbolism" with its emphasis on subjective creation and willful transformation and distortion of reality bears a striking resemblance to the notion of "kreative Phantasie," which the German critic Hugo Friedrich has named in his influential study as one of Baudelaire's key contributions to the poetics of modernity.[80]

A remarkable feature of Ivanov's critique is his disregard for Baudelaire as a religious thinker. Unlike Ellis, and despite the fact that he himself converted to Catholicism in 1926, Ivanov did not pay any attention to the Catholic element in Baudelaire—a lack all the more remarkable because he was attentive to this issue in the life and work of Verlaine and Huysmans. In a long digression incorporated in his essay on the two elements in symbolism, he characterized both writers as "decadents" who developed the synaesthetic potential inherent in Baudelaire's "Correspondances." Later, motivated by a deep existential crisis, both writers turned to the Catholic faith. In this sense, Ivanov sees them as far superior to other modernists, although, because of their decadent background and "hypertrophied sensuality," their work "qualifies only partially and indirectly as a solution to the problem of true religious art in the future."[81] It becomes clear that in Ivanov's opinion, Baudelaire qualified even less for this task.

Even during the long years of exile in Rome, where Ivanov lived until his death in 1949, and despite his friendship with the religious writer and scholar Charles Du Bos, who advocated a Catholic reading of Baudelaire,[82] it did not occur to Ivanov to look for vestiges of a Christian faith in the French poet. We have direct evidence for this in the article "Simbolismo" which Ivanov wrote in 1936 for the *Enciclopedia Italiana*.[83] He essentially reiterates the thesis of the 1908 essay on the two elements in symbolism, with the only difference that "idealist symbolism" is now more appropriately called "subjectivist symbolism" (*simbolismo soggettivistico*). Baudelaire's name comes up more frequently than that of any other poet. Ivanov refers to him as the "true and acknowledged founder" of symbolism and to "Correspondances" as the "first stone in the building of the modern symbolist school"—a stone, however, with a fatal fissure.

The discrepancy between the quatrains and tercets of the poem foreshadowed the dichotomy between symbolism and decadence: "Symbolism, hardly born yet, turned into decadence (*decadentismo*)." The term *decadentismo*, which denotes decadence as a literary style, as opposed to the more general *decadenza*, played an important role in Italian criticism of the 1930s. Benedetto Croce used it to attack decadence in terms that seem similar to Ivanov's (for example, he called it a "sin"). Mario Praz gave a different evaluation of *decadentismo* in his classic *La carne, la morte e il diavolo* (1930), published in English as *The Romantic Agony* (1933).[84] In his *Enciclopedia Italiana* article, unlike the 1908 essay, Ivanov tried to give a rudimentary psychological and biographical explanation for the split between the quartets and tercets of "Correspondances," calling the sonnet "an unconscious and involuntary self-portrait of the poet subjected to an intimate split between the spiritual and the sensual man." It is due to this "original sin," according to Ivanov, that symbolism died as a literary school, although he prophesied that the immortal soul of "eternal symbolism" will eventually be resurrected.

It is unclear how familiar Ivanov really was with the total oeuvre of Baudelaire. In his 1908 essay, he does not make any reference to Baudelaire's writings except for "Correspondances" and "La Beauté." The *Enciclopedia Italiana* entry contains a truncated Italian translation of a passage from Baudelaire's article on Victor Hugo, stating that "the metaphors and epithets of excellent poets are drawn from the inexhaustable fund of the universal analogy. . . . Swedenborg already taught us that everything, form, movement, number, color, perfume, in the spiritual as well as in the natural, is significant, reciprocal, converse, correspondant."[85] Ivanov points out that Baudelaire abusively suggests this "universelle analogie" in the purely subjective tercets of "Correspondances." Otherwise, he never comments on any of Baudelaire's theoretical statements. This is regrettable, since one wishes to hear what Ivanov would have thought of a passage like the following, taken from "Puisque réalisme il y a": "Poetry is the most real thing, it is what is completely true only in *another world.*—This world here,—hieroglyphic dictionary."[86]

Baudelaire's statement sounds like a perfect endorsement of Ivanov's slogan "a realibus ad realiora" (from the real to the more real), which closes the essay on the two elements in symbolism. This is not to say, of course, that Baudelaire's scattered utterances of this sort add up to a coherent metaphysical or religious worldview. Baudelaire was a poet, not a philosopher. "Poésie" in itself was probably more important to him than the revelation of a "more real" world. It has to be said too that Baudelaire's Catholicism, if indeed he qualifies as a Catholic, significantly differed from Ivanov's. His preoccupation with Evil and Augustinian obsession with the sinfulness of the flesh were alien to the Russian poet, who joined the Catholic church mainly for ecumenical reasons, being attracted by the universalist claim of a unified Christian congregation,[87] but in his theological thinking remained very much rooted in the Eastern Orthodox tradition.

If there is any common ground between Baudelaire's aesthetics and the Ivanovian concept of theurgic art, it can perhaps be found in the notion of transfiguration. Although Baudelaire never used this term per se, it is perhaps implied in the closing verses of the planned epilogue to the 1861 edition of *Les Fleurs du Mal*:

> Anges revêtus d'or, de pourpre et d'hyacinthe,
> O vous! soyez témoins que j'ai fait mon devoir
> Comme un parfait chimiste et comme une âme sainte.
>   Car j'ai de chaque chose extrait la quintessence,
> Tu m'as donné ta boue et j'en ai fait de l'or.[88]

> Angels dressed in gold, purple and hyacinth,
> Oh you! be witnesses that I have done my duty
> Like a perfect chemist and like a saintly soul.
>   For I have extracted from every thing the quintessence,
> You have given me your dirt and I have turned it into gold.

To be sure, Baudelaire would have understood "turning dirt into gold" as a more narrowly poetic rather than a cosmological task. Nevertheless, his aesthetization of the unaesthetic by means of poetic language shares a common emphasis with Vladimir Solovyov's idea of salvation through beauty. Vyacheslav Ivanov, himself a genuine poet, was responsive to this transfigurative power of Baudelaire's poetic language, even though remaining skeptical, perhaps justifiably so, with regard to the ideological or theological content of his poetry.

Ivanov's fascination with Baudelaire becomes most tangible in his six translations from *Les Fleurs du Mal* ("Les Phares," "La Vie antérieure," "Bohémiens en voyage," "L'Homme et la mer," "Spleen [IV]," and "La Beauté"). He began translating Baudelaire while living in Geneva in 1905. On February 24, 1905, he wrote to Bryusov: "In the last few days I started working on Baudelaire. The impulse for that was the statement in a letter by Chulkov on the desirability of translations from Verhaeren and Baudelaire. Verhaeren is yours; as for Baudelaire, I love him, as you do. I am sending you my first attempts, they are dangerous, of course. Your judgment is appreciated and necessary."[89] In the same year, Ivanov published his translations in the religious journal *Voprosy zhizni* (Questions of Life), and later they were integrated, with some minor changes, in the volume *Cor ardens* (1911).

Ivanov's selection of texts may appear somewhat surprising. Strangely enough, he did not translate "Correspondances." (Was he put off by the spirit of "idealist symbolism" in the tercets?) On the other hand, he did translate the sonnet "La Beauté," although he referred to this text as a pure expression of Baudelaire's "parnassianism." The choice of "Spleen [VI]" with its representation of hopeless *taedium vitae* seems also rather unusual for Ivanov, although the text did perhaps attract him with its "aesthetic dignity" analyzed by Erich Auerbach.[90] "Les Phares," as will be shown, was perhaps the Baudelairean poem most congenial to Ivanov. "La Vie antérieure" also was bound to attract him with its sense of anamnesis and mystic unity in Nature, while Ivanov himself, as we will see, largely created the atmosphere of mysticism in his translation of "L'Homme et la mer." The gypsy theme of "Bohémiens en voyage," finally, could have been appealing to Ivanov because of his interest in Pushkin's "Tsygany."[91] His translation contains references to "old men" and "steppes" that do not exist in Baudelaire's text but figure in Pushkin's poema.

It is interesting to look at the order in which the poems appear in Ivanov's publication. In the text of *Les Fleurs du Mal* they form the sequence "Les Phares" (no. 6), "La Vie antérieure" (no. 12), "Bohémiens en voyage" (no. 13), "L'Homme et la mer" (no. 14), "La Beauté" (no. 17), "Spleen [IV]" (no. 78). Ivanov's sequence is "Spleen," "Les Phares," "L'Homme et la mer," "Bohémiens en voyage," "La Vie antérieure," "La Beauté." Since Ivanov, like Baudelaire, composed his books of poetry carefully, the transformation of Baudelaire's order cannot be simply the result of a random permutation. First of all, Baudelaire's three contiguous poems (no. 12, 13, 14) appear contiguously also in Ivanov's text, but *in reverse order.* This order starts to make more sense when we pay attention to the fact that the translations of Baudelaire's poems are included in a section of *Cor ardens* with the title "Speculum speculorum." Ivanov seems to offer a "mirror-image" of Baudelaire's texts rather than a simple translation. The "affective curve" of Baudelaire's sequence, leading from the proud expression of human dignity in "Les Phares" to the utter despair of "Spleen," is reversed in Ivanov's arrangement. His cycle starts with the taedium of Spleen and ends with the triumph of Beauty. Baudelaire's pessimism is reinterpreted to fit into Ivanov's message of transfiguration.

As a translator, Ivanov favored a free transposition rather than an exact literal rendering. As he declared himself, "The highest goal of poetic translation is to create a musical equivalent of the original."[92] The volume *Prozrachnost'* contains the rather whimsical sonnet "To a Translator" (*Perevodchiku*),[93] where Ivanov addresses aspiring translators as "birdcatchers" and exhorts them to "be Proteus with Proteus and echo each mask with [another] mask." Baudelaire makes two appearances in this sonnet: one of the birds to be caught is "Baudelaire's Albatross," and one of the epithets to the translator is "evil's botanist," which can be understood as an allusion to the Flowers of Evil. As several critics have noticed, Ivanov's concern as a translator consisted in creating a symbolist version of the original. Pamela Davidson's remark with regard to Ivanov's translation of Dante also applies to Baudelaire: "It was no longer enough simply to have a 'Russian Dante' . . . , it was necessary to have a new Russian *Symbolist* Dante who would reflect all the characteristics with which the Symbolists invested their image of the poet."[94]

Perhaps Ivanov's greatest achievement in this sense is his translation of "Les Phares." Baudelaire's poem was congenial to Ivanov for both its content and style. The presentation of the great masters of art as a beacon of light in the darkness of time (cf. the title of Ivanov's first collection of poetry, *Lodestars!*) and an affirmation of human dignity in the face of God's eternity must have pleased the Russian symbolist as much as the rich, solemn language of the poem. Baudelaire's series of hallucinatory, impressionistic medallions is attractively rendered in Ivanov's musical transposition, as a look at the first stanza will reveal:

> Rubens, fleuve d'oubli, jardin de la paresse,
> Oreiller de chair fraîche où l'on ne peut aimer,
> Mais où la vie afflue et s'agite sans cesse,
> Comme l'air dans le ciel et la mer dans la mer.

> Rubens, river of oblivion, garden of idleness,
> Pillow of fresh flesh where one cannot love,
> But where life is flowing and stirring incessantly,
> Like the air in the sky and the sea in the sea.

Река забвения, сад лени, плоть живая,—
О Рубенс,—страстная подушка бредных нег,
Где кровь, биясь, бежит, бессменно приливая,
Как воздух, как в морях морей подводных бег!

River of oblivion, garden of idleness, living fruit—
O Rubens—passionate pillow of delirious bliss,
Where blood, beating, runs, continuously rushing,
Like air, like in the seas the flow of underwater seas!

Ivanov's translation deserves high praise both for its semantic exactitude (even the strange "oreiller" is preserved!) and its ability to convey the forceful, dynamic flow of Baudelaire's text. If anything, Ivanov's series of [*b*]-alliterations in the third line (*Gde krov', biias', bezhit, bessmenno prilivaia*) creates an even more musical impression than the original. Ivanov does justice also to Baudelaire's ingenious and mysterious "mer dans la mer," which, with simple lexical means, manages to create a vertiginous sense of "l'infini dans le fini." In the last stanza of the poem, the rolling of the sea returns metaphorically transmuted and amplified:

Car c'est vraiment, Seigneur, le meilleur témoignage
Que nous puissions donner de notre dignité
Que cet ardent sanglot qui roule d'âge en âge
Et vient mourir au bord de votre éternité!

For this is really, o Lord, the best testimony
That we can give of our dignity,
This ardent sob which rolls from age to age
And comes to die at the verge of your eternity!

Поистине, Господь, вот за Твои созданья
Порука верная от царственных людей:
Сии горящие, немолчные рыданья
Веков, дробящихся у вечности Твоей![95]

Verily, oh Lord, this is for Your creation
The true guarantee of royal people:

These burning, incessant sobs
Of centuries, breaking against Your eternity!

Here we can observe a subtle distinction between Baudelaire and Ivanov. The French text does not postulate any direct connection between man and God. As Pierre Emmanuel has pointed out, God is perhaps evoked here only as "a pure hallucinatory expression so that a dignity, without Him relative or absurd, can be raised in His Face to the absolute."[96] Ivanov adds the observation that man is *created* by God. His *tsarstvennye liudy* (royal people) go beyond simple human "dignité." Ivanov seems to emphasize the idea that man is created in God's image and can become Godlike, a thought dear to Orthodox theological tradition but contrary to Baudelaire's anthropology of original sin.

Ivanov's translation of the sonnet "La Beauté" deserves special attention, since this text was translated not only by him but also by three other symbolist poets discussed—Bryusov, Balmont, and Ellis. Two of the Russian translators—Bryusov and Ivanov—explicitly criticized in their writings the parnassianism that the poem seems to embody. At the same time they both placed it at a privileged position in their Baudelaire cycle—Bryusov at the beginning and Ivanov at the end. A comparison of the different versions offers a unique glimpse of what can happen to a French parnassian text when it is seen through the eyes of a Russian symbolist. Each poet transformed the sonnet in a sort of manifesto of his own poetic credo.[97] Bryusov's and Balmont's translations have been discussed in the previous chapter. Here is Ellis's version:

Красота

Вся, как каменная греза, я бессмертна, я прекрасна,
Чтоб о каменные груди ты расшибся, человек;
Страсть, что я внушу поэту, как материя, безгласна
И ничем неистребима, как материя, во век.

Я, как сфинкс, царю в лазури, выше всякого познанья,
С лебединой белизною сочетаю холод льда;
Я недвижна, я отвергла беглых линий трепетанье,
Никогда не зная смеха и не плачу никогда!

Эти позы, эти жесты у надменных изваяаний
Мною созданы, чтоб душу вы, поэты, до конца
Расточили, изнемогши от упорных созерцаний;

Я колдую, я царую мне покорные сердца
Этим взором глаз широких, светом вечным и зеркальным,
Где предметы отразились очертаньем идеальным!⁹⁸

Beauty

All like a stony daydream, I am immortal, I am beautiful;
So that you hurt yourself against my stony breasts, man;
The passion which I inspire to the poet is silent like matter,
And indestructible, like matter, for ever.

Like a sphinx, I reign in the azure, higher than any cognition,
With swanlike whiteness I combine the cold of ice;
I am immobile, I spurned the trembling of fleeting lines,
Never knowing laughter, I also never cry!

These poses, these gestures of haughty statues
Are created by me, so that you, poets, to the end
Squander your soul, exhausted from the persistent contemplation;

I bewitch, I reign over hearts submissive to me
With this look of my wide eyes, an eternal and mirroring light,
Where objects are reflected in ideal form!

Unlike all other Russian translators, Ellis renders the alexandrines of "La Beauté" not with iambic hexameter but with the extremely rare trochaic octameter. The overly long meter conveys an impression of ponderous monumentality not unsuited to Baudelaire's text, but it also forces the translator, in order to fill his lines, to resort to expansions and additions of his own invention. Thus we encounter repetitions (*kak materiia*) that do not exist in the original, as well as lengthy paraphrases, such as the translation of "incompris" with *vysshe vsiakogo poznaniia* (higher than any cognition) or of "éternel" with *nichem neistrebima vo vek* (ineradicable by anything for ever). In his treatment of sound, Ellis is the

exact opposite of Balmont's mellifluousness. His translation starts off with a blatant cacophony with almost indecently comic overtones (*kak kamennaia*).[99]
Unlike all other translators of "La Beauté," Ellis renders "matière" not with the
Russian *veshchestvo* but the Latin *materiia*, thereby forfeiting the paronomasia
with *vechnyi*. He tries to preserve the abstract formulations of Baudelaire almost
literally: "J'unis un coeur de neige à la blancheur des cygnes" becomes *s lebedinoj
beliznoiu sochetaiu kholod l'da* (with swanlike whiteness I combine the cold of
ice). In his use of syntax, Ellis seems closer to Bryusov, representing as he does
the idea of immobility with a chiasm (*Nikogda—nikogda*). The concept of an
unattainable "Beauty" hostile to the world of common mortals was central to
Ellis's understanding of Baudelaire and of art in general, as we have seen. Some
details of his translation underline his platonic notion of Beauty as an abstract
ideal. He emphasizes that beauty is "higher than any cognition." The word *ideal'nyi* with which he ends his translation belongs to the vocabulary of philosophy rather than of lyric poetry.

Vyacheslav Ivanov's version of "La Beauté" is undoubtedly the most unusual
Russian translation of this text:

Красота

Я камень и мечта и я прекрасна, люди!
Немой, как вещество, и вечной, как оно,
Ко мне горит Поэт любовью. Но дано
Вам всем удариться в свой час об эти груди.

Как лебедь, белая,—и с сердцем изо льда,—
Я—Сфикс непонятый, царящий в тверди синей.
Претит движенье мне перестроеньем линий.
Гляди: я не смеюсь, не плачу—никогда.

Что величавая напечатлела древность
На памятниках слав,—мой лик соединил.
И будет изучать меня Поэтов ревность.

Мой талисман двойной рабов моих пленил:
Отображенный мир четой зеркал глубоких—
Бессмертной светлостью очей моих широких.[100]

Beauty

I am stone and dream; and I am beautiful, people!
With a love to me, mute and eternal like matter
Burns the Poet. But it is given to all of you
To hurt yourself against these breasts in your hour.

White like a swan, and with a heart of ice,
I am an incomprehensible Sphinx, reigning in the blue firmament.
Movement sickens me with its restructuring of lines.
Look: I do not laugh, do not cry—never.

What magnificent antiquity imprinted
On the monuments of glories—my face has reunited.
And the fervor of Poets will study me.

My double talisman has captivated my slaves:
The world reflected in a pair of deep mirrors—
The immortal clarity of my wide eyes.

The oracular language of the translation contains many features that have been
discussed before as typically "Ivanovian." Baudelaire's observation "où chacun
s'est meurtri tour à tour," stated in the past tense, turns with Ivanov into a
prophecy ("it is given to all of you in your [destined] hour to hurt yourselves
against these breasts"). Ivanov skillfully uses the polysemy of the verb *udarit'sia*, which can mean both "to hurt oneself by bumping against something"
and "to be moved to enthusiasm by something." In a nutshell, *udarit'sia* contains the entire ambivalence of Baudelaire's text. (In the first version of his
translation, published 1905 in *Voprosy zhizni*, Ivanov had *ushibit'sia*, which
does not allow this double reading.) Ivanov's predilection for allegory exceeds
even that of Baudelaire, who did not capitalize "poète." The abstract nouns
drevnost' (antiquity) and *revnost'* (jealousy, fervor) receive in Ivanov's text the
status of acting characters. The word *talisman* in the second tercet is entirely
Ivanov's invention and conveys to his translation an aura of pagan sorcery.
However, although Ivanov seems rather far from the original, in some instances he gives the most exact formal rendering of all the translators. He is the
only one to preserve the rhyme scheme of the original. And it is only in

Ivanov's text that Beauty *imitates* the "proud monuments," rather than being their "model," as in Bryusov, or even "creating" them, as in Ellis. (As for Balmont, the monuments are completely absent from his text!) Ivanov's formulation, it is true, sounds more Ivanovian than Baudelairean. His language is solemn and grave yet preserves its elegance. He signals "immobility" by a syntax that is fragmented into many subunits. As in Ellis's translation, the flow of verse is interrupted by frequent punctuation marks, but the effect is one of gravity rather than of clumsiness. As far as the sound instrumentation is concerned, Ivanov steers a middle course between Ellis's cacophonies and Balmont's obsession with euphony. Balmont's *Kak lebed' blednaia* is replaced by the correct *Kak lebed', belaia.*

Perhaps the most striking passage in Ivanov's translation is the beginning. The poem opens with the enigmatic words *Ia kamen' i mechta* (I am stone and dream). This is obviously rather different from Baudelaire's "Je suis belle . . . comme un rêve de pierre," where stone and dream are presented in a metonymic relation to each other and together they serve only as the term of comparison to qualify Beauty. Ivanov's laconic statement has a categorical and at the same time paradoxical quality: how can something be both stone and dream at the same time? An answer to this problem can perhaps be found in Ivanov's theory of *realiora*. The function of art, as we remember, is revealing the *ens realissimum* immanent in the material world. The objects of the world, understood as symbols, are both what they are and what they are not, simultaneously thing and idea. For a believer in Solovyov's pantheistic monism, everything, including stone and dream, ultimately is *one*. It is the function of poetic language to reveal this unity not yet realized in life. Baudelaire's idea of "Beauté" as a "rêve de pierre" is itself an oxymoron. The fantasy can come true only if we share the beliefs of Ivanov's mystic utopianism. As A. Meyer-Fraatz has observed, Ivanov's translation is on the whole more optimistic than Baudelaire's original. The poets are studying Beauty but not in vain as in Baudelaire's text, where they are "pining away their days." The reflection of the world in the "deep" mirroring eyes of Beauty is here not an embellishment, that is, a deceptive optical illusion, but a real or "more real" image of a transfigured reality.

Some of Ivanov's translations, while attractive Russian poems, perhaps overly "Ivanovize" Baudelaire's texts. As an example, we could point to "L'Homme et la mer," which turns into a sort of manifesto of mystic symbolism in Ivanov's rendering:

Человек и Море

Как зеркало своей заповедной тоски,
Свободный Человек, любить ты будешь Море,
Своей безбрежностью хмелеть в родном просторе,
Чьи бездны, как твой дух безудержный,—горьки;

Свой темный лик ловить под отсветом зыбей
Пустым объьятием и сердца ропот гневный
С весельем узнавать в их злобе моногозевной,
В неукротимости немолкнущих скорбей.

Вы оба замкнуты, и скрыты, и темны.
Кто тайное твое, о Человек, поведал?
Кто клады влажных недр исчислил и разведал,
О Море?... Жадные ревнивцы глубины!

Что ж долгие века без устали, скупцы,
Так в распре яростной так оба беспощадны,
Так алчно пагубны, так люто кровожадны,
О братья-вороги, о вечные борцы![101]

Man and Sea

Like a mirror of your intimate anguish,
Free Man, you will love the Sea,
Become intoxicated with your boundlessness in the familiar expanse,
Whose abysses, like your impetuous spirit, are bitter;

You will try to catch your dark face in the reflection of the ripples
In an empty embrace and recognize the angry murmur of the heart
Cheerfully in their much-shouting spite,
In the indomitableness of never silent grief.

You are both exclusive, and secret, and dark.
Who, o Man, has found out your secret?
Who has calculated and explored the treasure of your humid depths,
O Sea? . . . [You two are] avid and jealous of depth!

For long ages misers without tiring,
In furious striving both so merciless,
So avidly destructive, so ferociously blood-thirsty,
O brother-enemies, o eternal fighters!

In the original:

L'Homme et la mer

Home libre, toujours tu chérira la mer!
La mer est ton miroir; tu contemples ton âme
Dans le déroulement infini de sa lame,
Et ton esprit n'est pas un gouffre moins amer.

Tu te plais à plonger au sein de ton image;
Tu l'embrasses des yeux et des bras, et ton coeur
Se distrait quelquefois de sa propre rumeur
Au bruit de cette plainte indomptable et sauvage.

Vous êtes tous les deux ténébreux et discrets:
Homme, nul n'a sondé le fond de tes abîmes,
O mer, nul ne connaît tes richesses intimes,
Tant vous êtes jaloux de garder vos secrets!

Et cependant voilà des siècles innombrables
Que vous vous combattez sans pitié ni remord,
Tellement vous aimez le carnage et la mort,
O lutteurs éternels, ô frères implacables!

Man and Sea

Free man, you will always love the sea!
The sea is your mirror; you contemplate your soul
In the infinite unfolding of its waves,
And your spirit is an abyss no less bitter.

You enjoy plunging down into your image;
You embrace it with your eyes and arms, and your heart

Sometimes seeks relaxation from its own clamor
In the noise of this indomitable and savage moan.

You are both dark and discreet;
Man, nobody has sounded the bottom of your abysses,
O sea, nobody knows your intimate riches,
So jealous you are to guard your secrets!

And yet for innumerable centuries
You have fought each other without pity and remorse,
So much you love carnage and death,
O eternal fighters, o implacable brothers!

In Ivanov's transposition, Baudelaire's rather conventionally romantic poem appears basked in an aura of cryptic mystery. It opens not with the apostrophe to the "free man," but with the image of the mirror. Mirrors in general play an important role in Ivanov's work, as we have seen before with the mirroring eyes of Beauty. In his 1910 essay "Zavety simvolizma" (The Testament of Symbolism), Ivanov defined art as "mirroring" (*zerkal'nost'*)."[102] Unlike Plato, Ivanov did not see the work of the artist as a pale reflection of true reality: according to him, both the mirror image and the original constitute true being in their mutual interaction—hence the importance of the *double* mirror (*speculum speculorum*). In Ivanov's poetry, this image becomes frequently realized in the mutual reflection of sea and sky.[103] The sea is a key theme in Ivanov's early poetry, where it represents the dionysian element of primordial, dynamic chaos. A whole cycle in *Kormchie zvezdy,* entitled "Thalassia," is devoted to sea-scenes.[104] Ivanov outdoes Baudelaire in his predilection for allegory by capitalizing not only *Chelovek* (Man), but also *More* (Sea), trying to uplift these notions into the symbolic realm of *realiora.* Ivanov's declaration that "the name of Man, written with a capital letter, defines the content of all art" (in the essay "Mysli o simvolizme")[105] reads like a commentary to his translation of "L'Homme et la mer." The mirror theme is continued in the second stanza with the epiphany, in the "reflection of the ripples," of a mysterious "dark face" (*temnyi lik*). The Church Slavonic word *lik,* widespread in the poetry of mystic symbolism, is the iconographic term for the holy face appearing on an icon.[106] *Zamknuty, skryty i temny* (exclusive, secret, dark)—the adjectives Ivanov uses to describe the Man and the Sea—also provide an apt characterization for his own poetic style with his predilection for the archaic and the artificial. Words like *lik*, *raspria* (feud) and the old East Slavic *vorogi* (enemies), instead of the common *vragi*, clearly belong to a high, if not slightly overblown, rhetorical register. We also find "homeric" composite neologisms such as *mnogozevnyi* ("much-shouting") and a tendency to exploit various combinations of the same root with different prefixes (*povedal*—*razvedal* [communicate—ascertain]; the root *ved-* signifies "knowing"). The impression of gravity is reinforced by the long-winded, complex syntax, with the first two stanzas forming one single sentence.

All in all, Ivanov's translation could hardly qualify as a faithful rendering of Baudelaire's original but it certainly does have aesthetic appeal and the merit of internal coherence. For the sake of comparison, here is P. F. Yakubovich's version of the same poem:

Человек и Море

Свободный человек! не даром ты влюблен
В могучий океан: души твоей безбрежной
Он—зеркало; как ты, в движеньи вечном он,
Не меньше горечи в твоей груди мятежной.

Как по сердцу тебе в его волнах нырять,
На нем покоить взгляд! В его рыданьях гневных
И диких жалобах как любо узнавать
Родные отзвуки своих невзгод душевных!

Равно загадочны вы оба и темны,
Равно обвеяны молчаньем ледовитым.
Кто, море, знает ключ к твоим богатствам скрытым?
Твои, о человек, кто смерит глубины?

И что же? Без конца, не зная утомленья,
Войну вы меж собой ведете искони!
Так любите вы смерть и ужасы резни.
О, братья-близнецы, враги без примиренья![107]

Man and Sea

Free Man! not without reason are you in love
With the mighty ocean: of your boundless soul
It is a mirror; as you, it is eternally moving,
No less bitterness is in your rebellious soul.

How you like to dive into its waves,
To repose your eyes on it! In its angry sobs
And wild complaints how pleasant is it to recognize
Familiar echoes of your own mental misfortunes!

You are both equally mysterious and dark,
Equally suffused with icy silence.
Who, sea, knows the key to your hidden riches?
O man, who will measure your depths?

But what? Endlessly, without tiring,
You have waged war between you from time immemorial!
So much you love death and the horrors of slaughter.
O twin brothers, enemies without reconciliation!

Predictably, the terrorist and freedom-fighter Yakubovich gives his due to the "free man," who, like in Baudelaire's poem, appears at the beginning of the text and is honored with an exclamation mark. The agitated sea, as in Yakubovich's own poetry, seems to become a metaphor for struggle and revolution. Yakubovich adds to the text the adjective *miatezhnyi* (rebellious), which does not figure in Baudelaire's original. The mystical correspondence between man and sea is reduced to the common element of rebellious insurrection. With its conventional romantic imagery, Yakubovich's translation gives a rather successful rendering of Baudelaire's poem, which consists essentially of a skillful assemblage of romantic clichés. Yakubovich's derivative postromantic approach to poetry turns out to be an adequate method for reproducing Baudelaire's epigonous romantic text.

While Yakubovich's translation has the advantage of being more faithful to the original, it lacks the splendor of Ivanov's symbolist estrangement and "transfiguration" of Baudelaire. In a certain sense, Ivanov's modernist transposition is perhaps more Baudelairean than Baudelaire's original. Ivanov clearly

fell under the spell of Baudelaire's poetic power, even though he had reservations with regard to Baudelaire as a thinker and voiced doubts about his status
as a bona fide symbolist. His reaction seems to have been stronger on a purely
visceral and emotional basis than on an intellectual level, as we can see from his
declaration to Bryusov that he "loved" Baudelaire. This love prompted Ivanov
to assimilate Baudelaire's texts to his own aesthetic system and theurgic view of
art. In other words, he attempted to transform the "semi-idealist" Baudelaire,
whom he viewed with distrust, by means of poetic transfiguration into a true
Ivanonian "realist."

CHAPTER 4

Toward Modernity

One of the most widespread images of Baudelaire in twentieth-century criticism is that of the poet of modernity. Baudelaire himself made the "héroïsme de la vie moderne" a centerpiece of his critical discourse in his "Salon de 1846." Seventeen years later, in a famous essay that can be read as a sort of disguised self-portrait, he celebrated as the quintessential "peintre de la vie moderné" the artist Constantin Guys, who made a living by sketching current events for Parisian newspapers. Modernity for Baudelaire entailed more than a preoccupation with contemporary subject matter, such as the "fast life" in the urban metropolis—it also denoted a specific style of representation, characterized by a rapid pace and fragmentary, shifting approach to a reality that could no longer be leisurely taken in as a harmonious whole. The work of art, as Walter Benjamin has pointed out, was bound to lose its aura in this shattered world. Baudelaire, rather than trying to reestablish aura in his poetry, proceeded to rupture it consciously and provocatively.

Many critics have seen the logical conclusion of Baudelaire's modernity in the notion of art as a nonrepresentational artifact. Hugo Friedrich, in his bestselling study on the structure of the modern lyric, emphasized Baudelaire's seminal role as the founding father of a lineage that lead via Rimbaud and Mallarmé to surrealism and abstract art. This genealogy has become widely accepted even among critics who otherwise do not share Friedrich's approach (it has, however, been challenged by Paul de Man and, more recently, by Antoine Compagnon).[1] Friedrich himself acknowledged that Baudelaire's theoretical statements and his art criticism were sometimes bolder than his actual poetic practice. As a prime example of revolutionary modernism in Baudelaire's poetic oeuvre, Friedrich pointed to "Rêve parisien."[2] This poem provides an example of a literary text which, rather than describing an extratextual referent, creates its own highly constructed, dreamlike reality, reveling in the hallucinatory evocation of a lifeless urban landscape of shining rectilinear metallic surfaces, colonnades, and mirroring cascades. It is interesting to note that this vision, stretching for "millions of miles, to the confines of the universe," bears a striking resemblance to the imagery appearing in a central text of Russian modernist prose, Andrey Bely's *Petersburg*. One of the principal characters of this novel, the senator Apollon Apollonovich Ableukhov, fantasizes about intersecting networks of parallel prospects and houses, expanding "into the abysses of the universe in planes of squares and cubes. . . . All of Petersburg is an infinity of the prospect raised to the nth degree. Beyond Petersburg, there is nothing."[3]

The Russian avant-garde of the early twentieth century, with the abstract paintings of a Malevich or Kandinsky and the futurist experiments with "transsense language" (*zaum'*), was to play a key role in the liberation of art and literature from the function of representation. While it would be an exaggeration to name Baudelaire as a major influence in this process, the spiritual climate of the Russian avant-garde favored a new reading of Baudelaire which foregrounded certain features in his oeuvre that had been overlooked before. By 1910, "modernity" (*sovremennost'*) was used as a central term to describe Baudelaire's worldview by such diverse critics as Evgeny Anichkov and Valery Bryusov. The incipient "formalist" approach to Baudelaire by Andrey Bely, Nikolay Gumilyov, and Benedikt Livshits, to be discussed in this chapter, highlighted the "constructivist" side of the poet long before such a view became canonized in Hugo Friedrich's *Struktur der modernen Lyrik*.

To be sure, with the coming of our own postmodernist era, the modernist enterprise has lost some of its luster and the status of Baudelaire as a patron saint of modernism has been increasingly questioned. Baudelaire's complex attitude toward modernity, which also included nostalgic feelings for a lost aristocratic past and a distrust of progress and the notion of an artistic avant-garde, make him for some critics a forerunner of postmodernism rather than of modernism. In "Mon coeur mis à nu," Baudelaire rejected the notion of avant-garde literature, denouncing it as a hateful military metaphor: "These habits of military metaphors denote minds which are not militant but made for discipline, i.e., for conformity, minds born as lackeys, Belgian minds, which can think only in company with others."[4] There can be little doubt that Baudelaire would have despised the martial vocabulary of, for example, Mayakovsky's "Order of the Day to the Army of Art." Also, the belief in a "radiant future" was of course totally alien to him.

In any event, Baudelaire did not play the same role of patron saint for the postsymbolist avant-garde in Russia as he did for the symbolists. It did not occur to anyone to call him a "patriarch of futurism" (which would have been an oxymoron anyway). Characteristically, only the Francophiles among the acmeists and futurists still took an active interest in him, whereas in the symbolist period, even a Francophobe like Balmont had been drawn to Baudelaire. One wonders whether, rather than being a father of the Russian avant-garde movement, Baudelaire did not become in a certain sense its victim. The formalist approach to his oeuvre was ultimately as one-sided as had been the metaphysical appropriation of his poetry by the symbolists. Far from being the only "correct" approach, it would be better described as yet another creative misreading of Baudelaire.

BELY: FROM MYSTICISM TO FORMALISM

The name of Andrey Bely (i.e., Boris Nikolayevich Bugayev, 1880–1934) came up several times in chapter 3. In certain respects, Bely was almost an alter ego of his intimate friend and enemy Ellis, with whom he shares many common features: a flamboyant and eccentric personality prone to fanaticism, polemic attacks, and scandals; an unruly mind in constant search of the ultimate principle that would solve all contradictions; and an erratic spiritual development with changing allegiances and frequent and sudden conversions. The main difference, of course, lies in the scope of their artistic talent and impact: while Ellis's name has become no more than an obscure footnote in the history of Russian literature, Bely is increasingly recognized as one of the most important authors of this century and a "classic of modernity." Bely is frequently classified together with Ivanov and Blok as a mystic symbolist. This seems justified inasmuch as a rhetoric of metaphysics and mysticism indeed permeates many of his writings. However, there are significant differences between Bely's concept of symbolism and the theurgy of Vyacheslav Ivanov. As Steven Cassedy has shown, the assumption of a transcendent or supernatural realm is by no means necessary for Bely's theory of symbolism, which can be described entirely as a self-contained and self-generating system concerned with the formal principle of symbolization.[5]

Bely's interest in Baudelaire undoubtedly stems from the status of the French poet as a founding father or patriarch of symbolism. As the self-appointed theoretician of this movement, Bely could not afford to ignore a poet who was commonly believed to have laid the cornerstone of the new poetic creed. The apodictic statement with which Bely opens his 1909 article on Baudelaire comes with the ring of a truth universally acknowledged: "Two patriarchs of the 'symbolist movement' engraved with their whole life and work the postulates (*lozungi)* of the new art in the literature of the second half of the nineteenth century; these patriarchs are Baudelaire and Nietzsche."[6]

The juxtaposition of Baudelaire and Nietzsche does not mean that these two "patriarchs" enjoyed an equal status in Bely's symbolist pantheon. His involvement with the German philosopher certainly was deeper and more intense than that with Baudelaire. After 1904, Nietzsche becomes omnipresent in Bely's critical writing, superseding his earlier infatuation with Solovyov, Schopenhauer, and Kant.[7] Baudelaire's role is mainly that of a foil to Nietzsche: he appears as the *other* founder of symbolism and in many respects Nietzsche's opposite. Bely leaves little doubt to whom he gives the preference. In the article "Simvolizm" of 1907, he names as the founders of symbolism the triumvirate of Baudelaire, Nietzsche, and Ibsen. Whereas the two Germanic symbolists point to the future, Baudelaire, according to Bely, draws "pictures of death and destruction of the old life."[8] Subsequently, Bely even completely denied Baudelaire the status of a symbolist and located him in the decadent camp. To be sure, "decadence" did not have the same negative connotation for Bely as it had for Max Nordau. It was a step in the right direction on the road to symbolism. In fact, the decadents had to be defended from unfair attacks. In a draft to his 1933 memoirs *Nachalo veka* (The Beginning of the Century), Bely pointed out that the decadents were right to recognize the crisis of the old world: "The laughter of the philistines (*meshchan)* over Baudelaire reminds me of the laughter of a syphilitic father over a hereditary syphilitic, his son, who has the courage to show him his sores."[9] Still, the decadents were no true symbolists for Bely. Using an aviational metaphor, he compares the fate of decadence to that of the pioneer pilot Otto Lilienthal, who crashed in his flying machine before aviation got off the ground. A symbolist, in Bely's perception, is a pilot who manages to take off successfully without crashing. While Baudelaire is named as the chief example of a true decadent in *Nachalo veka*, Bryusov, according to Bely, belongs to an intermediate stage between decadence and symbolism, whereas Blok provides an example of a truly symbolist poet.[10] In a draft that, like the reference to the syphilitic father, remained unpublished in the original edition of the book (probably because Nietzsche had become a persona non grata under Stalin), Bely again juxtaposes Baudelaire and Nietzsche, presenting the first as a decadent and the second as a symbolist. The crucial difference for Bely lies in their understanding of the symbol: Baudelaire's symbol is defined as the "correspondence of two series" (*sootvetstvie dvukh riadov*), Nietzsche's symbol as the "intersection of series in a new quality" (*peresechenie riadov: v novom kachestve*).[11]

Remarkably, Baudelaire's famous correspondences (*sootvetstviia*), the cornerstone of symbolism, have thus become a sign of decadence. In order to understand better what Bely had in mind, it will be helpful to turn to the article "Smysl iskusstva" (The Meaning of Art, 1907). In this essay, Bely tries to grasp the essence of artistic symbolization by means of algebraic formulas. He distinguishes between eight possible styles, depending on the various ways in which b, the objects of the external world, and c, the inner experience of the artist, may be combined to form a, the symbol, which expresses the deeper unity of all phenomena. Baudelaire, together with Edgar Allan Poe and E. T. A. Hoffmann, falls into the category $cb(a)$. Artists of this type, according to Bely, start with emotions and find a correlative to them in the external world. The underlying unity that makes such a correlation possible is only indirectly implied, instead of being stated as a first principle. This is what distinguishes Baudelaire's poetry from true religious art: "There is no notion of unity; throwing himself into the chaos of contradictory emotions, the artist sees correspondences between them in colors, smells, and sounds; the artistic symbol (a) is the expression of this correspondence (not of unity), but the correspondence itself is only possible under the condition of this unity."[12]

The dichotomy of correspondence (implying difference and dualism) versus monistic unity is the main distinctive feature in Bely's confrontation of Baudelaire and Nietzsche. This idea is developed most fully in his article "Sharl' Bodler," which was published in the June issue of *Vesy* in 1909 and later reprinted in the collection *Arabeski* (1911). It remains the major statement of Bely's understanding of Baudelaire. Although written on the occasion of Ellis's 1908 translation of *Les Fleurs du Mal*, the article goes far beyond a simple book review and devotes considerably more space to Bely's own theories on Baudelaire than to the discussion of Ellis's translation.

The first section of the article, consisting entirely of a juxtaposition of Baudelaire and Nietzsche, is written in a style that is reminiscent of Ivanov's

"Dve stikhii v sovremennom simvolizme." We find the same rhetorical movement of a protracted, sweeping antithesis and a predilection for grandiose, "prophetic" imagery. Baudelaire and Nietzsche are presented as "colossal heroic figures" towering above the fog of being. One is introduced as the "lawgiver of the symbolism of the Latin race," the other as the "lawgiver of the symbolism of the Germanic race." While the first type of symbolism is characterized as a "new literary school," the second one "created a new attitude to reality." Among the differences outlined by Bely, the most essential one is that Baudelaire "proclaims the dualism of human existence" and Nietzsche the "monism of human creativity." This point is developed further in the second part of the article, where Bely switches from an "ornamental" to a "geometric" style. He tries to illustrate Baudelaire's and Nietzsche's symbolism and their common grounding in "Aryan" mythological thought by means of graphic schemes and algebraic formulas that appear rather baffling to the uninitiated reader. Baudelaire's theory of correspondences, according to Bely, postulates a correlation between the "acts of conscience" and the "acts of movement," or, more abstractly, between the elements of the psychological and the physical "series" (*riad*). With Nietzsche, the parallelism between the two series turns into a psychological monism. The series intersect and merge in the symbol of the "new man."

One striking feature of Bely's approach to Baudelaire has to be pointed out: unlike Vyacheslav Ivanov or Ellis, he does not pay attention to any "vertical" dimension in Baudelaire. His correspondence between the inner and outer world is a far cry from Ivanov's and Ellis's *ens realissimum*. The correspondences establish no connection with a "more real" transcendence. They only link physical and psychological phenomena of *this* world. The privileged agent of this linkage turns out to be the poetic word.

This impression is confirmed by the third and longest section of Bely's article, which is entirely devoted to Baudelaire's form. Bely offers a detailed analysis of Baudelaire's technique, versification, rhymes, rhythm, use of enjambement, and phonetic instrumentation, quoting extensively from Albert Cassagne's *Versification et métrique de Ch. Baudelaire* (1906). Baudelaire's mastery of form, which Ivanov had found suspiciously parnassian, becomes the main attraction for Bely. He uses Cassagne's findings to demonstrate what he considers the most important implication of Baudelaire's theory of correspondences: the intersection of content and form in poetic language. Bely shows how Baudelaire's ingenious use of rich rhymes allows him to establish links between seemingly incompatible semantic entities, and how his alliterations and assonances create correspondences between the content of an image and its verbal instrumentation. Baudelaire's unity of form and content, according to Bely, makes any translation impossible, since "more than of anyone else, one can say that the form of Baudelaire's lyric *is* Baudelaire himself."[13]

In the fourth and last section of his article, Bely shows how Ellis's translations fail to render Baudelaire's formal perfection. He sees this not so much as Ellis's fault as it is a consequence of Baudelaire's untranslatability (or, one could add, the general untranslatability of poetry). Bely's ideal of a perfect translation is indeed so utopian that it makes any attempt at rendering a poetic text in another language futile: he demands that all rhythmic and stylistic nuances of the original should be preserved at the exact same place in the verse line, together with an identical phonetic instrumentation, syntax, and punctuation. (No wonder that Bely himself never attempted to translate any poetry!) Not surprisingly, Bely asserts that even the Baudelaire translations by the "first stylist of our day," Stefan George, are inadequate. In Russia, according to Bely, the translation of Baudelaire is simply "not possible at the present time" for two reasons: since the Russian poets are still busy developing a rhythm and instrumentation for their own poetry, the Russian language is not yet flexible enough for such translations, and there is no "scientific-philological analysis of styles" which would provide a theoretical underpinning for the translational endeavor. Even the best translation of Baudelaire can only be the "prolegomenon to a future perfect translation."[14] It remains unclear when, or how, such a "perfect translation" would come into being.

The odd mixture of utopianism and attempts at scientific rigor is characteristic of Bely's thinking. However, his—at times—opaque and eccentric style should not deflect attention from the fact that his approach marks an important turning point in the modernist reception of Baudelaire. With his interest in the embodiment of correspondences in the horizontal, syntagmatic chain of the poetic text and his painstaking attention to questions of rhythm and sound repetition, Bely appears in many respects as a forerunner of the Russian formalists. To be sure, contrary to certain formalist pronouncements, Bely did not believe in the autonomy of art. Art and life were necessarily connected for him, and he admired in Baudelaire what he perceived as a correspondence between poetic theory and mode of existence. As he wrote in his essay: "Baudelaire's strange and dual style is a living embodiment of his strange and dual life; and this life is the embodied doctrine of correspondences; Baudelaire's symbol is the correspondence, and only the correspondence, between image and emotion; the basis of this correspondence is the relentless duality in the consciousness of himself and the world."[15]

Bely's emphasis on duality as Baudelaire's main characteristic feature (as opposed to Nietzsche's unity) could provide an additional explanation for his interest in Baudelaire. Bely's own thought is characterized by an eternal dilemma between two conflicting worldviews, one metaphysical and the other secular.[16] Vyacheslav Ivanov wrote that Bely "wishes for realism but cannot overcome idealism."[17] Bely's lack of a true religious feeling has also been noted by other Russian mystic philosophers such as Nikolay Berdyayev and Fyodor Stepun.[18] It is worth pointing out that if Bely has to be located halfway between realism and idealism, using Ivanov's terminology, he actually falls into the same category as Baudelaire himself. The French poet is Bely's "semblable" and "frère" in the perpetually frustrated quest for divine transcendence and the ultimate meaning.

One wonders, however, how much Bely really cared for Baudelaire, judging from the strangely abstract and secondhand nature of his approach. Bely's criticism seems to be prompted less by a direct confrontation with Baudelaire than by various intermediaries, notably Ellis and Cassagne. While casting Baudelaire's theory of correspondences into algebraic formulas, it never occurs to Bely actually to take a look at the concrete text of "Correspondances," or at any of Baudelaire's critical and theoretical writings. His starting point is the symbolist *image* of Baudelaire (the "patriarch of symbolism") rather than Baudelaire himself. By turning the French poet into Nietzsche's Siamese twin and eternal opposite, and by grounding Baudelaire's correspondences in Aryan mythology before giving them a formalist interpretation, Bely seems to play with the symbolist clichés of his day and at the same time to challenge and subvert them. His emphasis on the horizontal rather than vertical nature of the correspondences can be read as an indirect response to the theories of the mystical interpreters of Baudelaire. Although seemingly subscribing to the myth of Baudelaire as a patriarch of symbolism, Bely in fact undermines the foundations on which this transcendentalist interpretation was built.

GUMILYOV AND ACMEISM: THE "PURITY OF LINES"

After 1910, the otherworldliness and mysticism of Russian symbolism came under increasing fire from the emerging new poetic movement of acmeism.

Partially inspired by the French parnassians and the poetics of the late Innokenty Annensky, the acmeists rejected the symbolist quest for transcendence in
favor of a clearly delineated depiction of earthly reality. The doctrine of correspondences, the omnipresent catchword of the symbolists, became an argument to attack and ridicule symbolism. Interestingly enough, however, Baudelaire himself was not directly indicted in this process. Even those who professed
contempt for symbolism and its mystic tenets continued to treat him with respect. Some even tried to claim him for their cause by asserting implicitly that
Baudelaire had to be understood as a sort of pre-acmeist.

Several of the acmeist manifestoes took issue with the symbolist theory of
correspondences. Sergey Gorodetsky, in an essay on currents in contemporary
Russian poetry, accused the symbolists of turning the world into a mere phantom by filling it with "correspondences."[19] Perhaps the most telling and fun-
niest acmeist attack against correspondences is the one launched by Osip Mandelstam in his article "O prirode slova" (On the Nature of the Word, 1921–22):

> Everything that passes is only a symbol. Let's take, for example, a rose and
> the sun, a dove and a girl. For the symbolist, not one of these images is inter-
> esting in itself. The rose is a symbol of the sun, the sun—a symbol of a rose,
> the dove—a symbol of a girl, and the girl—a symbol of a dove. The images
> are disemboweled like stuffed animals, and filled with a different content. In-
> stead of the symbolist "forest of symbols"—a factory shop of stuffed ani-
> mals. This is where professional symbolism leads to. The perception is de-
> moralized. Nothing real, nothing authentic. A horrible quadrille of
> "correspondences" nodding to each other. Eternal winking. Not one clear
> word, only hints, unspoken allusions. The rose nods to the girl, the girl to the
> rose. Nobody wants to be himself.[20]

Although Baudelaire is indirectly quoted in this sweeping indictment of
symbolism, with references made to his "forêt de symboles" and "Correspondances," he is not named. Mandelstam's scorn seems directed rather against the
symbolist followers of Baudelaire than against Baudelaire himself. We know
indeed from other passages in Mandelstam's critical writings that he had great
respect for the French poet.[21] In his "Razgovor o Dante" (Conversation about
Dante, 1933), he praises Baudelaire, Verlaine, and Rimbaud for their closeness
to Dante's poetical method.[22] The essay "Deviatnadtsatyi vek" (Nineteenth

Century, 1922) opens with a quotation of the last line of "L'Albatros" ("Ses ailes de géant l'empêchent de marcher") given in Mandelstam's own verse translation, which wraps Baudelaire's simple statement into a double metaphor (*Shatrom gigantskikh kryl on prigvozhden k zemle* [With the tent of his gigantic wings he is nailed to the earth]). Mandelstam reads the "gigantic wings" of the Albatross as an allegory for the overdeveloped "cognitive forces" of the nineteenth century, which outgrew the development of will, character, and morality.[23] In the essay "Slovo i kul'tura" (Word and Culture, 1921) he suggests a Christian interpretation of Baudelaire, describing the poem "Une Charogne " as a "high example of Christian despair" and its author as a "selfless ascetic" (*podvizhnik*) and "martyr."[24]

Although Mandelstam treated Baudelaire with respect, there can be no doubt that he saw in him a figure of the past (evoking the nineteenth century and Christianity) rather than a symbol of modernity. For Mandelstam's own theory and practice of acmeism, Baudelaire proved to be of little consequence. The same can be said of Anna Akhmatova, who never translated Baudelaire or commented on him but certainly was aware of his work and seemed to have shared Mandelstam's interest in his "martyr"-like qualities. She used a quotation from "Une Martyre" ("Autant que toi sans doute il te sera fidèle, / Et constant jusqu'à la mort") as an epigraph to the poetic cycle "Cinque" (1946), which is devoted to the memory of her meetings with Isaiah Berlin.

Baudelaire was more important to the third great acmeist poet, Nikolay Stepanovich Gumilyov (1886–1921), Akhmatova's first husband and a graduate of the Lyceum in Tsarskoye Selo of which Annensky was the director. Gumilyov always harbored a special predilection for French culture. In 1907–8 he was enrolled in French literature studies at the Sorbonne. Later, he played an important role in the first and last attempt to publish a complete edition of Baudelaire's works in Russian. In 1919, the World Literature publishing house, directed by Gorky, appointed Gumilyov as the general editor of a planned complete Baudelaire edition. Gumilyov translated sixteen poems, wrote an introductory essay, and edited twenty-five more translations by V. Kolomiitsev, N. A. Otsup, V. A. Rozhdestvensky, and others. He also approached Aleksandr Blok with the request to translate Baudelaire's foreword to *Les Fleurs du Mal*, as we know from Blok's notebooks.[25] After Gumilyov's arrest and execution as a "counterrevolutionary" in 1921, the publisher abandoned the project. Unfortunately, all but four of Gumilyov's Baudelaire translations seem to have been lost.[26]

Gumilyov's six-page introductory essay on Baudelaire documents the anti-symbolist approach of the renegade symbolist and leading proponent of acmeism. In his attempt to free Baudelaire of the mystical ballast with which the symbolists had overloaded him, Gumilyov goes as far as to negate any mystical element in Baudelaire's work. As the only common feature between Baudelaire and the symbolists, he recognizes the "refined phonetics of verse." He can find in Baudelaire no "sense for the many-layeredness (*mnogoplannost'*) of being" or the "wish to give a feeling of the absolute behind the words." Gumilyov's approach resembles in many ways that of Bryusov (for whom Gumilyov had great respect). As Bryusov did ten years before, Gumilyov places Baudelaire in the context of the literary tradition of his time. He insists that Baudelaire does not belong to any literary school, although he was influenced by both the romantic and the parnassian movements. But for a romantic he lacks the "cult of feeling, theatrical pathos, and the characteristic verbosity," and for a parnassian he is "too nervous, too whimsical, and he speaks less about the things of the world than about the feelings they evoke in him."[27]

Gumilyov sees in Baudelaire the overlapping of two opposite influences: the Latin French tradition, "full of the clarity of the purity of lines and Latin harmony," and the Germanic English heritage, "over which the dark clouds of the Nibelungen are still wandering."[28] There can be no doubt that the sympathy of the acmeist belonged to the Latin rather than to the Germanic side. In a further attempt to find some common ground between Baudelaire and himself, Gumilyov points out that Baudelaire lived in an age of scientific and geographic discoveries, when "the forests and deserts of Africa, Asia, and America opened their age-old secrets to travelers and a handful of daredevils, as in the sixteenth century, conquered huge exotic kingdoms." In a similar fashion, Baudelaire, according to Gumilyov, "treated poetry like an explorer, and entered it like a conqueror."[29] With its martial macho imagery of the conquistador in exotic lands, the passage seems more inspired by Gumilyov's own poetry than by Baudelaire's.

More to the point are Gumilyov's remarks about Baudelaire's modernity. He quotes extensively from Baudelaire's various sketches for a foreword to *Les Fleurs du Mal*, once more stretching his nonmysticism with a provocative remark: "This book, essentially useless and absolutely innocent, was written with no other goal than to entertain myself and to exercise my passionate taste for obstacles."[30] Gumilyov also quotes the passage where Baudelaire describes poetry in a manner that seems to anticipate twentieth-century abstract art, asserting that the poetic phrase, similar to music and mathematics, is able to imitate a horizontal line, an ascending or descending curve, that it can describe a spiral or parabola or follow a zigzag course.[31] In modern poetry, Gumilyov asserts, the real face of the poet is always hidden behind a mask. In no way can we identify the feelings uttered in a poem with the real feelings of the poet. Lyric poetry turns into a "dramatic" poetry, where the poet appears as the speaker not for a real but for an imaginary, created self: "To the art of writing verse was added the art of creating one's poetic appearance, composed of the sum of masks that the poet puts on. Their number and variety indicates the importance of the poet, their neatness—his perfection. Baudelaire presents himself before us both important and perfect."[32]

The "mask" of the poet is the poetic word. Gumilyov describes how in Baudelaire's "mixed vocabulary" words belonging to different realms mingle in heretofore unseen combinations and acquire thereby "unexpectedness and corporeality." Baudelaire's preoccupation with negative, vicious, and repulsive subject matter seems to be no more than a compositional device for Gumilyov. He explains the absence of positive, "healthy" motifs, so irritating to Baudelaire's anti-decadent critics, as a necessary requirement of Baudelaire's specific poetic style. In an image that seems to anticipate the futurist enthusiasm for the machine age, Gumilyov reduces Baudelaire's oeuvre to a sort of grinding machine for which the whole world is only so much grist: "It is clear that the themes of love, goodness, and beauty, with their banal softness, would only have blunted the too sharp cogs of such a mill."[33] Gumilyov's machine imagery was perhaps inspired by Baudelaire himself, who wrote in his "Salon de 1846" that "there is no chance in art, no more than in mechanics. . . . A painting is a machine of which all systems are intelligible to a trained eye; where everything has its reason, if the painting is good; where a tone is always calculated to make the most of another; where an occasional fault of drawing is sometimes necessary in order not to sacrifice something more important."[34]

Gumilyov's anti-symbolist approach to Baudelaire becomes noticeable also in his translations. As an example, we can turn to his version of "La Mort des amants," a poem discussed earlier in Balmont's and Bryusov's translation.[35] It might seem surprising that Gumilyov would choose to translate a text known for its languorous musicality and mood of *décadence* so opposed to his own poetic ideals. We have to keep in mind, however, that Gumilyov was planning a complete edition of Baudelaire's works. He probably selected "La Mort des amants" as one of Baudelaire's most famous poems rather than because of a personal affinity to the text. Moreover, the fact that "La Mort des amants" had become a cult text of the symbolists made it a special challenge for someone like Gumilyov, who was out to prove that Baudelaire was *not* a symbolist.

Смерть любовников

Ложем будут нам, полные духами
Софы, глубоки, как могильный сон,
Этажерок ряд с редкими цветами,
Что для нас взрастил лучший небосклон.

И сердца у нас, их вдыхая пламя,
Станут, как двойной пламенник возжен
Пред очами душ, теми зеркалами,
Где их свет вдвойне ясно отражен.

Ветер налетит тихий, лебединий,
И зажжемся мы вспышкою единой,
Как прощанья стон, долог и тяжел;

Чтобы, приоткрыв двери золотые,
Верный серафим оживить вошел
Матовость зеркал и огни былые.[36]

The Death of the Lovers

Our bed will be full of perfumes
Couches, deep like the sleep of the grave,
A row of shelves with rare flowers,
Which a better horizon grew for us.

And our hearts, inhaling their flame,
Will become like a double torch lit
Before the eyes of the souls, those mirrors,
Where their light is twice as brightly reflected.

A quiet, swanlike wind will fly in,
And we will flare up in a single flash,
Like a moan of farewell, long and heavy;

So that, half opening the golden doors,
A faithful seraph will enter to revive
The dullness of the mirrors and the former fires.

In comparison with Balmont's and Bryusov's, Gumilyov's version is striking for its relative exactness and sobriety. Bryusov's exotic array of "magnolias, acacias and tulips" or Balmont's decadent "greedy coffins" are nowhere in sight. Gumilyov pays close attention to formal features. His two quatrains, like Baudelaire's, have identical rhymes. Perhaps the most striking feature of Gumilyov's translation is its unusual metric structure. His lines consist of two trochaic trimeters, with the first hemistich always ending on a stressed syllable. The collision of two stresses creates a strong caesura in the middle of each line. With this metrical innovation, Gumilyov achieves an exact Russian equivalent of Baudelaire's unusual form of *décasyllabes,* which are likewise interrupted by a caesura after five syllables (the customary distribution of syllables in the French *décasyllabe* is not 5 + 5, but 4 + 6, as one can see, for example, in Valéry's famous "Cimetière marin"). Bryusov's iambic pentameter does not achieve the same effect, since it misses the caesura and thereby the symmetry of Baudelaire's verses, which is reflected on the semantic level by mirrors and a whole series of paired objects. Balmont is even less exact: he renders Baudelaire's décasyllabes with iambic hexameters and thus throws "La Mort des amants" in the same bag with the large number of poems written in standard alexandrines.

The attempt to find an exact equivalent to the verse structure of the original is characteristic of Gumilyov's painstaking approach to translation, which he outlined in his 1919 article "O stikhotvornykh perevodakh" (On Verse Translations).[37] Gumilyov condems "free" renderings of a poem that focus on its meaning and neglect its formal features, since, as he makes clear, the meaning of a poem cannot be separated from its form. Among other things, he requires that at least one rhyme pair of the original has to be preserved (a principle he fails to follow in his rendering of "La Mort des amants"). As the basic "nine commandments of the translator," Gumilyov stipulates nine textual features that a translator should faithfully preserve: the number of lines, the meter, the alternation of feminine and masculine rhymes, the character of the enjambements, the rhyme structure, the vocabulary, the type of comparisons, "special effects" (*osobye priemy*), and transitions in tone. We might interpret all this as an attempt to create a specifically acmeist poetics of translation, which with its clarity and precision opposes symbolist fuzziness and fogginess.

Interestingly enough, however, Gumilyov failed to implement his principle of faithfulness in "La Mort des amants" for reasons that have more to do with ideology than with technical difficulties. Baudelaire's "étranges fleurs" become *rare* flowers in his version, probably because he found the word *strange* too decadent and unsuited for a poet of Latin purity. (Balmont, who was not inhibited by concerns of this sort, translated the passage correctly with "*strannye tsvety.*") An even more telling divergence from the original occurs in the line "Un soir fait de rose et de bleu mystique" (An evening made of pink and mystical blue). Instead of translating this verse, which must have appeared disturbingly symbolist to Gumilyov, he simply replaced it with a line of his own invention: "A quiet, swanlike wind will fly in." By substituting the pink and blue mysticism of the original with the quiet purity and whiteness of a swan, Gumilyov tried to salvage his acmeist reading of Baudelaire even at the price of a blatant violation of his own code of faithfulness to the original.

SEVERYANIN AND EGO-FUTURISM: FROM DECADENCE TO POP ART

Despite the fact that its name originated in Italy, Russian futurism as a literary movement was less cosmopolitan than were symbolism and acmeism. Some of its major figures, such as Velimir Khlebnikov, were even ignorant of foreign languages, and instead of turning toward Western Europe they propagated an antiurbanist, "Slavophile" ideology. However, there were exceptions to this rule. Ego-futurism, founded by Igor Severyanin (i.e., Igor Vasilyevich Lotaryov, 1887–1941), was the first literary movement in Russia to claim the futurist label. It displayed an ostentatiously modern, urban bent, flaunting an intense, if somewhat phony, cosmopolitanism. Unlike the exoticism of the genuine world traveler Balmont, Severyanin essentially was a middle-class armchair traveler toying with clichés of sophisticated modernity. As a poetic celebrity, Severyanin played a similar role after 1910 to that which Balmont had played a decade earlier. In his public lectures, he emerged as a sort of Elvis Presley of Russian poetry, delivering his verbal stunts in a peculiar singing voice to auditoriums packed with hysterical (largely female) crowds. Severyanin's verbal music exerted a galvanizing effect on the public and turned his volumes of poetry into instant best-sellers.

Severyanin was a declared Baudelairean. He stated that Baudelaire was his "favorite poet," alongside Mirra Lokhvitskaya and Konstantin Fofanov.[38] The fact that Severyanin placed Baudelaire in the company of two minor decadents of the 1890s is indicative of his taste. His approach to poetry could be described in many ways as a revival of decadence. To be sure, it was a decadence without skeletons, sadomasochism, and Satan. Instead, Severyanin celebrated the amenities of modern life, featuring shiny automobiles, lilac-flavored ice cream, and pineapples floating in champagne. With his focus on the reified objects of the high bourgeois lifestyle, he was a true "peintre de la vie moderne" in the Baudelairean sense, seeking the "beauté passagère, fugace, de la vie présente"[39] (although he was perhaps closer to Andy Warhol than to Constantin Guys). Severyanin's dandyism and desire to "épater le bourgeois" certainly had a Baudelairean tinge. In his poetry, he identified himself directly with his French model, declaring that he was "stigmatized like Baudelaire."[40] His masterful command of Russian verse with a predilection for bizarre expressions and unusual, innovative rhymes is also reminiscent of Baudelaire.

Severyanin translated five of Baudelaire's poems into Russian. "Réversibilité," "La Musique," "La Muse malade," and "Bohémiens en voyage" appeared in the volume *Poezoantrakt* (1915), and "A une dame créole" was published in *Zlatolira* (Goldlyre, 1916). All five translations are dated 1909 and bear the title "Pod Sharlia Bodlera" ("A la Charles Baudelaire"). They are some of the most bizarre Russian translations of Baudelaire ever written. Severyanin's approach to translation is one of estrangement. In several instances, he opts for solutions that seem entirely aberrant. Lines 7 and 8 of "A une dame créole," for example ("Grande et svelte en marchant comme une chasseresse, / Son sourire est tranquille et ses yeux assurés" [Tall and slender, walking like a huntress, her smile is tranquil and her eyes confident]), are rendered as:

Изящный бюст весь вылеплен удачей;
В улыбке—зыбь; в глазах ее—гранит.

The elegant bosom is all moulded with success;
In the smile—a ripple; in her eyes—granite.

The implicit erotic charm of Baudelaire's Creole lady becomes in Severyanin's version the proudly and ostentatiously displayed sex appeal of a pinup girl. The contrast between the suppleness of her movements and the calm of her facial expression is materialized in the strange images of "ripple" and "granite." Introducing strange words into his poems is a predilection Severyanin shares with

Baudelaire, but he goes farther than his French model, loading his translations with bizarre expressions even when there is no corresponding element in the original. Another striking example is provided by the first stanza of "Bohémiens en voyage:"

> La tribu prophétique aux prunelles ardentes
> Hier s'est mise en route, emportant ses petits
> Sur son dos, ou livrant à leurs fiers appétits
> Le trésor toujours prêt des mamelles pendantes.

> The prophetic tribe with the burning eyes
> Set out on the road yesterday, carrying their little ones
> On the back, or delivering to their proud appetite
> The always ready treasure of hanging breasts.

> Вчера опять пророческое племя
> Пустилось в путь, забрав своих детей;
> У матерей созрел дюшес грудей;
> Зрачки горят... (Не знойно ль было семя?...)

> Yesterday again the prophetic tribe
> Set out on the road, taking their children with them;
> The mothers' duchess pears of breasts ripened;
> The pupils are burning... (Was the seed not sultry?...)

While the first two lines render the content of the original almost literally (leaving out, however, "aux prunelles ardentes"), the third and fourth lines seem positively bizarre. The words *duchess pears* convey an air of appetizing sensual appeal and refined "Frenchness" to Baudelaire's rather coarsely naturalistic "mamelles pendantes." Unlike Baudelaire's de-erotized depiction of breasts, Severyanin's image appears provocatively erotic. The "sultry seed" seems generated by the semantic proximity of "sultry" with the "prunelles ardentes." Perhaps inspired by the futurist device of displacement, Severyanin transplanted this element from the first into the fourth line. Read *backwards*, the stanza could also suggest an image of human procreation, starting with the "seed" and "burning pupils," which lead via the "ripening of the mothers' breasts" to "children."[41]

Aside from his translations, Severyanin also devoted a poem of his own to

Baudelaire. Written in 1926, it appeared in the volume *Medal'ony* (Belgrad, 1934), a collection of one hundred sonnets devoted to various writers, artists, and musicians. Baudelaire's medallion reads as follows:

Бодлер

В туфле ли маленькой—«Les fleurs du mal»,
В большом ли сердце—те же результаты—
Не злом, а добродетелью объяты
Земнившие небесную эмаль.

В днях юности—семи грехов скрижаль
И одуряющие ароматы.
Благочестивые придут закаты,
И целомудрия до боли жаль.

Ты в комнаты вечерний пустишь воздух,
О ледяных задумаешься звездах,
Утоничишь дух, найдешь для тела тишь.

И выпрыгнут обиженно в окошки
Грехом наэлектриченные кошки,
Лишь пса раскаянья ты присвистишь . . .[42]

Baudelaire

Whether "Les fleurs du mal" are in a little shoe—
Or in a big heart—the results are the same:
Not with evil, but with virtue are embraced
Those who have earthened the heavenly enamel.

In the days of youth—the scroll of seven sins
And heavy scents.
The pious sunsets will come,
And you feel painfully sorry for chastity.

You will let the evening air into the rooms,
You will start thinking about icy stars,
You will sharpen the spirit and find silence for the body.

> And cats, electrified with sin,
> Will jump offended into the little windows,
> You will only whistle for the dog of repentance . . .

As in Baudelaire's own series of medallions devoted to illustrious artists (in the poem "Les Phares"), it would probably be a mistake to look for concrete intertexts in this poem. Rather than evoking specific works by Baudelaire, Severyanin conveys in his own style the general impression that Baudelaire's oeuvre left on him. As is frequently the case with Severyanin, one is not sure whether he is serious or parodic. By placing the *Fleurs du Mal* from the outset in a "little shoe," he certainly does not betray an overly reverential attitude toward Baudelaire's masterpiece. The text resembles vaguely the pattern of a life story with an account of youthful sins and later repentance. Most of the poem seems devoted to the decadent side of Baudelaire, with references to sins, heavy perfumes, and cats. It seems essentially a variation on Baudelairean clichés.

More important than the rather insignificant story is Severyanin's handling of the poetic form. The text is replete with rich rhymes (*mal—emal', skrizhal —zhal', vozdukh—zvezdakh, tish'—prisvistish' okoshki—koshki*). The strange effect of this device is that the shorter rhyme words are completely contained in the longer ones. The word *okoshki* (windows), for example, seems to be pregnant with *koshki* (cats). In some respects, the influence of Baudelaire's poetics becomes noticeable. The initial juxtaposition of the "little shoe" with the "big heart" seems to stand paradigmatically for the confrontation of low and high lexical material in Baudelaire's poetry. Severyanin's poem features clearly "unlyrical," prosaic words like *rezul'taty* and *naelektrichennye*, and neologisms like *zemnit'* (to "earthen"). A wide-reaching verbal palette, puns, and the formation of new words by combining existing roots and suffixes are procedures that Severyanin shares with other Russian futurists. He also shares Baudelaire's predilection for oxymora and the combination of semantically incompatible elements, such as "icy stars," or the "scroll of seven sins" (the word *skrizhal* is normally used for the ten commandments). The poem culminates with the daring metaphor "dog of repentance," which clearly goes beyond anything that one would find in Baudelaire, but evokes memories of Vladimir Solovyov's famous parodies of Bryusov's decadent poetry, which featured a "hyena of suspicion," "mice of anguish," "leopards of revenge," "owls of wisdom," "donkeys of patience," and "elephants of hesitation."[43]

In its formal experimentation, Severyanin's poetry intersects with that of the modernist avant-garde. Many of his techniques (semantic "shifts," play with roots and sound patterns, neologisms) go to the core of the futurist poetic revolution. What sets him apart from his futurist colleagues, however, is his apparent lack of seriousness in the pursuit of any societal or metaphysical agenda. We could perhaps interpret his self-irony and refusal to be part of a larger ideological "cause" as another Baudelairean feature of his personality. In reducing poetry to a self-conscious play with forms and clichés, Severyanin emerges, more than anyone else, as the first "postmodernist" in Russian poetry.

LIVSHITS AND CUBO-FUTURISM: POETRY AS CONSTRUCTION

While Severyanin's ego-futurism remained a rather marginal phenomenon in the history of Russian literature, the rival group of cubo-futurists left a much deeper mark, since it counted some of the most important Russian poets of this century among its members. There were some Baudelaireans in the ranks of the cubo-futurists, too. The best known Russian futurist poet, Vladimir Mayakovsky, was familiar with Baudelaire, although he could read him only in translation. As Mayakovsky acknowledges in his autobiography, he became acquainted with French poetry through David Burlyuk.[44] Baudelaire's name appears in the poem "Nashemu iunoshestvu" (To Our Youth, 1927):

И я
      Париж люблю сверх мер
(красивы бульвары ночью!).
Ну, мало ли что—
         Бодлер,
            Малларме
и эдакое прочее![45]

I too
      love Paris exuberantly
(the boulevards are beautiful at night!).
Well, what does it matter—
         Baudelaire,
            Mallarmé,
and other stuff like that!

To a certain extent, Mayakovsky's urbanist poetry with his predilection for provocative imagery certainly is reminiscent of Baudelaire, and despite its mocking tone, the passage can probably be understood as a sort of backhanded compliment.[46] The main Baudelairean among the cubo-futurists, however, was the poet and translator Benedikt Konstantinovich Livshits (1881–1939). With his memoirs *Polutoraglazyi strelets* (The One-and-a-Half-Eyed Archer, 1933), Livshits became the most important chronicler of Russian futurism. Like Bryusov, Annensky, and Gumilyov, Livshits was a Francophile with a strong interest in French modernism. Within the cubo-futurist group, he represented, rather paradoxically, the "classic" French tradition and at the same time the most radical theoretical stand, emphasizing the "liberation of the word" and propagating the notion of poetry as pure constructivity.[47]

According to his autobiography, Livshits became acquainted with Baudelaire's work at the tender age of seven, when he discovered the Russian translation of a Baudelairean prose poem called "*Oblaka*" (Clouds) in the journal *Zhivopisnoe obozrenie*. The text left a deep impression on him, which he only much later managed to define as a "feeling for the unrealness of the real world."[48] Inspired by Baudelaire's new genre as well as by the technique of cubism, Livshits later composed his own abstract prose poem "Liudi v peizazhe" (People in a Landscape), which was included in the important futurist manifesto *Poshchechina obshchestvennomu vkusu (A Slap in the Face of Public Taste)* (1912). Livshits also translated two poems by Baudelaire into Russian, "Correspondances" and "L'Idéal." They were first published in his 1934 collection *Ot romantikov do siurrealistov (From the Romantics to the Surrealists).* In his foreword (published only in 1989), Livshits explains that he did not include more poems by Baudelaire in his anthology because this poet was already well known to the Russian reader.[49]

Livshits's selection of poems proves that one does not need to be a symbolist in order to be fascinated by "Correspondances." His translation was perhaps prompted by a similar urge to what made Gumilyov translate "La Mort des amants"—to desymbolize a symbolist cult text (or rather, in the case of "Correspondances," *the* symbolist cult text). Obviously, Livshits understood the poem not as an expression of mystic faith but as an experiment in verbal art and rhetorical construction, a sort of *chreia*. This expression appears, rather surprisingly, in the second quatrain of Livshits's translation of "Correspondances:"

Как дальных отгулов прерывистая хрия
Нам предстоит порой в единстве звуковом,
Так в соответствии находятся прямом
Все краски, голоса и запахи земные.⁵⁰

In the same way as an intermittent chreia of distant rumbles
Is at hand for us in a unity of sounds,
So all colors, voices and earthly smells
Find themselves in a direct correpondence.

Chreia (χρεια, literally "usage") is the Greek term for a brief anecdote containing an example of practical wisdom and, more important, the rhetorical technique for constructing such an example. This technique was part of the curriculum in the classic and medieval propaedeutics of rhetoric.[51] The word provides a good example of Livshits's mixture of classical erudition and modernist provocation. It probably underlines his interest in poetry as construction, but it also exploits the futurist shock value of the unusual word completely unintelligible to the common reader (the expression is not listed in the Russian dictionaries or encyclopedias of the time). The word also appears in Livshits's poem "Fontanka" (1914), where this St. Petersburg river is described as "creeping away from the palaces like a *chreia* of perfidy."[52]

Livshits's reading of "Correspondances" seems entirely demystified. Baudelaire's enigmatic chiaroscuro, his subtle play with light and darkness, is eliminated in Livshits's translation: the "ténébreuse unité" as well as the paradoxical line "vaste comme la nuit et comme la clarté" have disappeared. The verb "se répondre" (in "Les parfums, les couleurs et les sons se répondent"), which suggests a sort of elusive "conversation" echoing the "confuses paroles" of the first quatrain, is replaced by an expression of almost mathematical dryness and precision ("find themselves in direct correspondence"), which sounds more like a quotation from a geometry textbook. Even Baudelaire's "parfums, couleurs et sons" seem more concrete and down to earth in Livshits's translation. *Kraska* is the word for paint (could it have something to do with the cubo-futurist interest in painting?); *golosa* are voices, that is, meaningful, concrete sounds coming from a person, rather than simply "sons"; and *zapakhi zemnye* ("earthly smells") are certainly different from "parfums."

Interestingly enough, this process of replacing an overly refined aesthetic system by one with full colors and earthly corporeality, which seems to be the hidden agenda of Livshits's translation of "Correspondances," appears as the explicit topic of the other Baudelairean poem translated by him—"L'Idéal."[53] In this sonnet, Baudelaire's lyrical persona rejects the "beautés de vignettes" and "pâles roses" of a "siècle vaurien" (worthless century) where he seeks in vain for "une fleur qui ressemble à mon rouge idéal." "Mon rouge idéal" could be interpreted in various ways—"my red-haired ideal" (talking about women), "my red ideal," "my ideal red color," or "the red color of my ideal." Livshits understood the text not as a commentary about the beauty of various women but as an aesthetic statement. One understands why he liked this poem: with its polemic condemnation of a past aesthetic and demand of a daring new color, "L'Idéal" sounds almost like a manifesto of cubo-futurism *avant la lettre.*

As we can see, the demise of symbolism in no way meant a disappearance of Baudelaire from the Russian literary scene. As a symbol of modernity, he was taken over by the following generations and adapted to their specific needs. Perhaps it was only at this time that the seeds of his poetic revolution really began to sprout. As a general tendency, the new, postsymbolist approach was more oriented toward form than content. This is not to say, of course, that the decadents and symbolists had paid no attention to Baudelaire's form. But for most of them, form remained ultimately always subordinated to a larger message—be it provocative amoralism or theurgic mysticism. Only Andrey Bely, who, as we remember, undertook an analysis of Baudelaire's verse structure and rhymes, stated that Baudelaire's form *was* his message. This approach was further developed by Gumilyov. His insight that the word in Baudelaire's poetry acquires a new "unexpectedness" and "corporeality" was only a step away from the futurist proclamation of the "liberated word." The notion of poetry as an abstract art, which Baudelaire had alluded to in some of his bolder theoretical writings (the passages quoted by Gumilyov) but hardly realized in his own poetry, had now become reality. With the Russian futurists and related avant-garde movements in the West pushing some implicit tenets of Baudelaire to the ultimate limits, it became possible to confer on the French poet retroactively the honorary title "father of twentieth-century poetry."

(Mis)reading "Baudelaireanness"

How can we assess Baudelaire's influence on Russian literature? As we have seen in the introduction to this study, Baudelaire is generally credited with a great impact on modern poetry. Inasmuch as Russian literature partakes of modernity, or even provided decisive impulses toward its development, logic seems to suggest that it must therefore contain a large dose of "Baudelaireanness." However, trying to pin down the exact nature of Russian Baudelaireanness is an enterprise fraught with difficulties. The very term *influence* has become problematic to the point of being elusive in contemporary literary theory. To be sure, if we understand influence as the passing on of concrete images and ideas from one creative artist to another, Baudelaire did indeed influence certain Russian poets, particularly the decadent generation of Bryusov and Balmont. It goes without saying, however, that this form of influence is not the most interesting one (in fact, inasmuch as Baudelaire's influence becomes clearly recognizable in the clichés of Russian decadent writing, it seems to have been frequently a rather negative influence). The issue becomes more complicated if we try to search for the general Baudelaireanness of modern Russian poetry (or, for that matter, modern poetry *tout court*). It becomes hard to distinguish between modernity in general, a concept Baudelaire was the first to develop, and the effect of a particular reading of Baudelaire on a particular poet. An assessment of this question would require insights into the workings of the creative mind of every single potentially Baudelairean Russian poet.

This difficulty has induced some critics to question the dogma of Baudelaire's influence on modern poetry altogether. In a provocative essay entitled

"Remarques sur le peu d'influence de Baudelaire" (Notes on Baudelaire's Little Influence), published in 1967 amidst a flurry of speeches, colloquiums, and articles commemorating the one-hundredth anniversary of Baudelaire's death, Henri Peyre made the startling assertion that, contrary to common perception, "the influence of *Les Fleurs du Mal* on twentieth-century poetry is almost nonexistent." While acknowledging Baudelaire's firmly grounded status as a classic of French poetry and favorite object of academic inquiry and oral examinations in French literature departments, Peyre pointed out that the admiration by nonacademic writers and poets for Baudelaire was on the whole rather lukewarm and frequently amounted to no more than lip service. In some instances it even turned into outright hostility, as in the case of Apollinaire, who wrote in 1917 about Baudelaire: "Son influence cesse à présent, ce n'est pas un mal."[1] Since the appearance of Harold Bloom's *The Anxiety of Influence* (1973), we are less likely to be amazed by the fact that the father of modern poetry would be repudiated by his own children. In fact, we might even be tempted to read Apollinaire's statement as indirect proof for Baudelaire's influence on him, in the same fashion as Baudelaire's own polemic attacks against Victor Hugo, according to Harold Bloom, belong to "one of the major modes of misprision, of that strong misreading of strong poets that permits other strong poets to be born."[2]

As far as Baudelaire's legacy in Russia is concerned, a similarly paradoxical picture emerges. It is a truth universally acknowleged that Baudelaire was a major influence on Russian symbolism, if not on all of modern, or at least modernist, Russian poetry. Georgette Donchin has taught us that Baudelaire "determined many of the moods which shaped the new sensibility of the Russian poets at the turn of the century."[3] The adjective *Baudelairean* has even turned into somewhat of a cliché which is applied to a multitude of Russian poetic texts. Georges Nivat, for example, describes Blok's poem "Neznakomka" (The Stranger) as "très baudelairien par son esthétique,"[4] and Peter France, in a book written for a nonspecialist audience on modern Russian poetry, mentions Baudelaire more frequently that any other Western poet. His name comes up in connection with Tyutchev, Blok (repeatedly), Annensky, Akhmatova, and Tsvetayeva. However, if we try to assess Baudelaire's influence in Russia more precisely, we run into trouble. For example, the question "Which Russian poets considered Baudelaire their favorite poet?" yields a surprising answer. Only two names come up: P. F. Yakubovich and Ellis—hardly luminaries of Russian poetry. Even if we allow for the fact that one's favorite poet is usually one that writes in one's own language, and reformulate the question as "Which Russian poets considered Baudelaire their favorite *foreign* poet?" the list does not become much longer. The only newcomer is the decadent ego-futurist Igor Severyanin, who, as we remember, named Baudelaire as his favorite poet alongside Konstantin Fofanov and Mirra Lokhvitskaya—hardly flattering company for a poetic genius. To be sure, Baudelaire was held in high esteem by such Francophiles as Valery Bryusov, Innokenty Annensky, Nikolay Gumilyov, and Benedikt Livshits but only as one of several influential French figures. Verlaine and Verhaeren for Bryusov, the parnassians and French decadents for Annensky, Théophile Gautier for Gumilyov, or Rimbaud for Livshits proved to be as important as Baudelaire, if not more so.

As Peyre did in his essay, it would be possible to build a case for Baudelaire's "peu d'influence" on Russian literature. One could point to a whole series of missed encounters. Dostoyevsky ignored Baudelaire, except as a translator of Poe. Turgenev, although he borrowed the genre of the prose poem from him, never mentioned Baudelaire's name. Tolstoy vilified and slandered him in *What Is Art?* We have no word about Baudelaire from such major nineteenth-century poets as Tyutchev, Fet, Nekrasov, Maykov, Polonsky, A. K. Tolstoy. The silence of Nekrasov, whom Bryusov baptized a Russian Baudelaire before the Soviets baptized Baudelaire a French Nekrasov, seems all the more astonishing as he was the editor in chief of *Otechestvennye zapiski* when the first Russian verse translations from *Les Fleurs du Mal* appeared there in 1869–72. One assumes that Nekrasov read it, although, if he knew Baudelaire only in N. S. Kurochkin's translation, it is hard to blame him for not noticing Baudelaire's genius. Baudelaire was discovered by the likes of N. S. Kurochkin, D. D. Minayev, S. A. Andreyevsky—hardly names associated with the greatness of Russian poetry. Even when we come to the symbolists, who are commonly regarded as the most Baudelairean of Russian poets, a strange paradox emerges: avowed enthusiasm for Baudelaire seems to stand in an inverse relationship to poetic greatness. Baudelaire's most fervent admirer, Ellis, was a poet of no importance; Bryusov and Balmont, who admired Baudelaire, although less fervently and exclusively than Ellis, were greater poets but still not the most important Russian symbolists; Ivanov and Bely, both with an ambivalent attitude toward Baudelaire, rank higher on the scale of poetic accomplishment; and Aleksandr Blok, the greatest Russian symbolist poet, hardly expressed any interest in Baudelaire at all. Do we have to conclude then that Baudelaire influenced mainly mediocre poets? Such a statement makes sense indeed if we recognize that mediocre writers are usually the most typical representatives of a literary school, and as "weak readers" (to use Harold Bloom's term) are the most likely to be influenced by a stronger talent.

Unfortunately, this scheme does not work so neatly in our case, since the most fervent (and mediocre) admirers of Baudelaire, Yakubovich and Ellis, both wrote poetry that hardly qualifies as Baudelairean. On the other hand, poets frequently characterized as Baudelairean, such as Fyodor Sologub or Aleksandr Blok, expressed no enthusiasm for Baudelaire. In other words, there seems to be a great discrepancy between the seeming Baudelaireanness of Russian poetry and the concrete "fortune" of Baudelaire as it appears in statements about him made by Russian poets.

It would be tempting to suggest a pattern shaping the relationship of the Russian poets to Baudelaire, which, in a formulaic way, could be expressed in the following fashion: the more overtly enthusiastic about Baudelaire, the more mediocre and the less Baudelairean. The formula is problematic, however, since not all of its elements can be asserted unequivocally. Enthusiasm, to be sure, is measurable inasmuch as it manifests itself in the quantity and intensity of written statements. As far as mediocrity is concerned, there is no absolute standard for gauging literary value, but we can at least refer to a consensus reached by the majority of members of an interpretive community. Thus, it is possible to state with a great degree of certainty that (a) Ellis was more enthusiastic about Baudelaire than Blok and (b) Ellis was more mediocre than Blok. But how can we state that Blok was more Baudelairean than Ellis?

The case of Blok deserves special attention, since the term *Baudelairean* has been applied to him perhaps more frequently than to any other Russian poet. His demonic portrayal of the urban landscape and of women, the presentation of the "poet-hero engaged on a tragic quest" and his "loathing and self-loathing" (P. France), the "épiphanie du musical dans l'antimusicalité hideuse de la vie contemporaine" (G. Nivat), the comparison of sexual love with a surgical operation and the lugubrious vision of contemporary life as a *dance macabre* (R. Poggioli) are some of Blok's Baudelairean features highlighted by literary critics. The parallels between Baudelaire and Blok have even been the object of two American doctoral theses of the 1970s. Milica Banjanin juxtaposed Baudelaire's "Tableaux parisiens" with Blok's cycles "Gorod" (City) and "Strashnyi mir" (Frightful World) as well as the poema "Dvenadtsat'" (The Twelve) and found numerous similarities in the presentation of the city and its inhabitants as well as in the general poetic sensitivity. Françoise Marie-Odile Beamish-Thiriet approached the oeuvre of Baudelaire and Blok from the viewpoint of

Jungian archetypal psychology and discovered many similarities in their symbolic portrait of the mother archetype. There are indeed some striking similarities between Baudelaire's and Blok's "family drama," although a Freudian approach might perhaps be more promising than a Jungian one. Both Baudelaire and Blok were exceedingly close to their mothers throughout their lives, each lost his father at an early age, and their mothers both remarried military men. Both poets were dominated by a sense of duty toward a wife-figure (Jeanne Duval, Lyubov Dmitrievna) who was working as an actress, yet both frequented prostitutes and contracted syphilis (a fact not mentioned by Beamish-Thiriet!). While Baudelaire has been "psychoanalyzed" rather extensively, the psychoanalysis of Blok remains to be done.

Neither Banjanin nor Beamish-Thiriet addressed the parallels between Baudelaire and Blok in terms of influence, reception, or intertextuality. Since this study is concerned with Russian readings of Baudelaire, the question of Blok's reading of Baudelaire has to be raised. There can be no doubt that Blok was familiar with Baudelaire from his early youth. Both Blok's mother and grandmother translated Baudelaire into Russian.[5] As we know from the memoirs of Blok's aunt, M. A. Beketova, Baudelaire was the favorite poet of Blok's mother, to whom Blok was close. According to Beketova, Blok's mother was attracted to Baudelaire because of his "striving toward the unknown and mysterious, his dark pessimism and negation of life." She even managed to convert her father, the botanist Andrey Beketov, to her Baudelairism. Although otherwise little inclined to modernist poetry, Beketov became interested in Baudelaire's prose poems.[6] In 1896, Blok's mother dedicated a sentimental poem to Baudelaire, inspired by the line "Comme tu es loin, paradis parfumé" in "Moesta et errabunda."[7] Blok himself, however, despite his early exposure to Baudelaire and all the alleged parallels between his poetry and Baudelaire's, was reticent about his relationship to the French poet. The only text directly inspired by Baudelaire is a parody, written at age eighteen, where Blok is lampooning the poem "L'Albatros" in a letter to his grandmother.[8] Unlike Yakubovich, Merezhkovsky, and Balmont, Blok was unimpressed by Baudelaire's allegory of the estranged poet. Perhaps inspired by the word *brûle-gueule*, he turned vulgarity into the guiding principle of his parody and featured an albatross smoking *papirosy* (cheap Russian cigarettes with cardboard mouthpiece). Eleven years later, in a letter to his mother, he dismissed Baudelaire's "L'Albatros" as a "sickly fable with a moral."[9] The only other statement about Baudelaire can be found in Blok's review of Balmont's *Gornye vershiny* (1904), where he approvingly quotes Balmont's description of Baudelaire as a "singer, destined by fate for torture, with a short, restrained, splendid, sharp and cold verse."[10] This hardly sounds like the grateful compliment of a Russian Baudelairean to the source of his poetic inspiration.

Of course, it would be tempting to ascribe Blok's coldness toward Baudelaire to "anxiety of influence." Was he afraid to confront a poet that he felt to be threateningly close to himself (similar perhaps to Balmont's rejection of Verlaine)? Blok's behavior toward Baudelaire and French symbolism in general was characterized indeed by a pattern of evasiveness. As Georgette Donchin has pointed out, "all Blok's undertakings regarding the French symbolists were abandoned half-way through."[11] He never wrote the article on French symbolism that he promised for the paper *Slovo* in 1905 and never translated Baudelaire's foreword to *Les Fleurs du Mal* as commissioned by Gumilyov in 1919.

Without denying the possible validity of a psychological explanation, such as the fear of confronting a "double" threatening the uniqueness of one's own poetic identity, I would like to suggest an additional argument for Blok's coldness, based on the general reception of Baudelaire as outlined in this study. Paradoxically, Baudelaire's immense popularity in the first decade of the twentieth century made it more difficult for a serious Russian poet such as Blok to voice his enthusiasm openly. The likes of Ellis or Georgy Chulkov touted the gospel of "Correspondances" as the quintessence of symbolism. Baudelaire's poems circulated in the translation of hacks like Panov or Alving. Yakubovich had made the poet palatable to readers of undistinguished taste and left-wing political circles with a utilitarian concept of poetry. Aikhenvald celebrated him as a "beautiful soul" and treasure of bourgeois culture. How could one praise Baudelaire without seeming trite?

The shock value of Baudelaire, as highlighted by Walter Benjamin and others, is difficult to reconcile with an officially sanctioned status as a classic. In his essay, Henri Peyre has suggested a correlation between Baudelaire's academic fortune in the twentieth century and a comparative lack of excitement for him among the creative literary minds of France. In order to make Baudelaire come alive once more, Peyre wished for more controversy. As a first step, he proceeded to point out some of the shortcomings of Baudelaire's poetry, pointing to overblown, melodramatic, or even clumsy passages. Vyacheslav Ivanov was perhaps propelled by a similar instinct when, despite his declared love for Baudelaire and his adherence to the doctrine of correspondences, he attacked the decadent and parnassian side of the French poet. Instead of celebrating

Baudelaire's sonnet "Correspondances" as the cornerstone of the symbolist creed, he demonstrated in fact the problematic status of this text as the gospel of any creed.

It seems to me that rather than as the proponent of a specific doctrine, be it symbolist, decadent, modernist, or otherwise, Baudelaire's significance lies in his capacity for challenging doctrines. His importance for Russian literature perhaps primarily lay in the negative potential of the *provocateur.* This negative potential was understood first of all politically by Baudelaire's populist discoverers, before it became in the decadent reception an aesthetic challenge to an outdated poetic system. In both cases, the figure of the *poète maudit* proved to be inspirational. A similar pattern applies also to the Soviet Union. There the creative response to Baudelaire developed in opposition to the official policy of the totalitarian government, which tried first to outlaw the French poet and later to co-opt him for its communist orthodoxy. Baudelaire's main appeal for the nonconformist reader lay in his status as an anti-establishment figure. In this sense, if we follow Henri Peyre's argument, Baudelaire was perhaps more alive in Stalin's Russia than in contemporary France, where he was enshrined as a national treasure.

We might wonder whether there is something typically Russian in the Russian reception of Baudelaire. One thing we have to stress is the Russian penchant for an "instrumental" reading of literature. Baudelaire's appropriation by left-wing political radicals in the nineteenth century is a case in point. With a few notable exceptions (among them the "parnassians" Bryusov and Gumilyov), Baudelaire's aesthetics of modernity never was understood as a value per se. It metamorphosed into various "calls for action"—from the social revolution of the populists to the religious myth building of the symbolists to the iconoclasm of the avant-garde. An additional "typically Russian" (although not uniquely Russian) feature in the reception of literature, probably connected with the reasons outlined above, is the romantic idea of the poet as a charismatic guru. Quasi-religious worship of poets is widespread in Russia, starting with the cult of the most venerated of all poetic icons, Aleksandr Pushkin, which began to become omnipresent in the late nineteenth century, the time of Baudelaire's appearance.[12] The influential concept of the poet as a prophet and martyr was applied to Baudelaire not only by his most fervent admirers but even by readers who otherwise showed no particular inclination toward him, such as Osip Mandelstam. If there exists such a thing as a typically Russian way of reading Baudelaire, one is tempted to evoke the terrorist Yakubovich, giving the "blood of his heart" to the translation of *Les Fleurs du Mal* in the coldness of his Siberian labor camp, or the fanatic Ellis preaching his doctrine of Baudelairism to a social democrat in the middle of the night in front of a portrait of Baudelaire dimly lit by candles—or are we indulging in stereotypes?

It seems that Baudelaire's significance lay perhaps ultimately less in his poetry, let alone his critical writings (which few Russians bothered to read), than in his *image*. He turned into a mythical presence, a poetic icon which could be upheld for veneration and derision. Blurring the boundaries among literature, art, and life, hero worship of the poet became a factor in the "semiotics of behavior." In extreme cases, the urge for identification (Balmont's "With you I want to fuse, oh magician and sorcerer!" [*S toboi dai slit'sia mne, o mag i charodei!*]) could go as far as trying to look like Baudelaire physically. Ellis, for example, consciously dressed to give himself a Baudelaire-like appearance, as we know from Bely's description of him: "The frock-coat, which struck me at the first meeting—tailored and dandy à la Charles Baudelaire, . . . the bowler hat gave Kobylinsky from afar the look of a Parisian."[13] An even more extreme case of *imitatio Baudelairii* is reported by Valentin Katayev, concerning the behavior of the poet Eduard Bagritsky (1895–1934): "Eduard Bagritsky was so captivated by Baudelaire's personality that his face and his entire attitude began to recall Baudelaire: the dark eyes, the lips pressed together bitterly and scornfully, the crossed arms, [were] an exact reproduction of the picture (*gravure*) of Baudelaire in the book that he had brought me."[14]

Ultimately, the poet was less venerated for what he wrote than for what he *represented,* and the existential injunction of his cult consisted not of writing like him but of bringing his picture to life. Art as "life-building" (*zhiznetvorchestvo*) is a widespread Russian attitude which transcends the factional boundaries between radicals and modernists, symbolists and Marxists. Baudelaire's influence, beyond its measurable dimension in terms of texts with Baudelairean features, became a powerful *mythical* presence in Russia, to the point that he could assume, in Andrey Bely's words, the position of a "patriarch." It was in this role of a charismatic icon that Baudelaire was able to radiate in Russia as an inspiration to modernists and anti-modernists alike.

However, the question of Baudelaire's status as a charismatic icon and provider of widely circulated catchwords has to be separated from that of his influence. Perhaps the time has come to withdraw the adjective *Baudelairean* from critical discourse. Like another shibboleth of modern literature talk,

Kafkaesque, it is a term that rather obfuscates than elucidates our understanding of a text. Like any great poet, Baudelaire was a phenomenon impossible to duplicate. *Les Fleurs du Mal* was not, as Ellis believed, a book that appears "once in a thousand years" but a book that appeared once. There can be no "Russian Baudelaires" but only Russian readers of Baudelaire, some "stronger" and some "weaker," *hypocrite lecteurs,* struggling, as we all do, to distill some meaning from the intricate provocation of Baudelaire's texts.

VALERY BRYUSOV'S UNPUBLISHED BAUDELAIRE TRANSLATIONS

The following translations are quoted from Bryusov's notebooks (*Zapisnye knizhki*) in the Manuscript Division of the Russian State Library, Moscow (Fond 386, kart. 14, ed. khran. 5/1, 5/7, and 5/14). The first two texts have recently appeared in print (see *Literaturnoe nasledstvo*, vol. 98, bk. 1 [1991], 636–37, and *Zarubezhnaia poeziia v perevodakh Valeriia Briusova*, ed. S.N. Gindin [Moscow: Raduga, 1994], 227–79). All other texts are published here for the first time. My reading of Bryusov's manuscript differs in two instances from Gindin's (see notes in the text).

1. La Mort des amants (Zapisnaia knizhka no. 1, p. 27)

Из Боделэра

Ласкающих кроватей аромат
Глубокие, как тайный склеп, диваны
Магнолии, акации, тюльпаны
Огни цветов и сладострастный яд.

Последний жар желаний и услад,—
Как факелы, проникшие в туманы,
Зажжет сердца—и этот свет багряный
Два зеркала—две мысли отразят.

Как долгий стон при трепетном прощании
Предстанет нам в мистическом сиянии
И голубой и розовою мгла.

Когда ж войдет архангел с ясным взглядом:
Два факела потухших будут рядом
И тусклые, как будка,* зеркала.

                    (November 28, 1894)

*Gindin reads бездна.

2. A une passante (Zapisnaia knizhka no. 1, p. 27)

Из Бодeлэра
Промелькнувшей

Бесновалась улица полная гула,
Восхитительной ручкой у шлейфа края
Подымая, качая*—и в трауре вся—
Высока и тонка незнакомка мелькнула.

Каку статуи была ее ножка стройна.
Я—безумец—я пил чару ласк в ее взоре,
В замолчавшем, но бурею дышащем море!
Эта чара манит—убивает она.

Проблеск молнии . . . ночь . . . ты! чей взор на мгновенья
Мне повеял забытым огнем возрожденья,
Неужели лишь в вечности встречу тебя?

Никогда? через годы? все тайной одето!
Не ищу я кто ты, ты не спросишь кто я,
Ты, кого я любил, ты, кто знала про это.

*Gindin reads нагая.

3. Le revenant (Zapisnaia knizhka no. 1, p. 46)

Le revenant

Как ангел проклятых снов
Я возвращаюсь в твой альков.
К тебе, храня тишину,
С тенями ночи скользну.

Уста мои холодны,
Лобзанье—ласки луны,
Мои объятья—змея,
Что вьется, жало тая.

И утро место мое
Пустым найдешь ты и все
Тебе покажется сном.

Но страх свиданий ночных
Верей, чем нежность других,
Хранится в сердце твоем.

(December 3, 1894)

4. Parfum exotique (Zapisnaia knizhka no. 7 (6), p. 3)

Parfum exotique

Когда, закрыв глаза, мечтаю я бессвязно,
Твоих живых грудей вдыхая аромат,—
Мои мечты плывут, мои мечты скользят,
Туда где солнце жжет, горит однообразно.

На дальнем острове я вижу сонный сад:
Там вечно спят ключи, застыв волной алмазной,
Там дремлют юности отдавшись неге праздной,
Там женщины в тени, усталые, лежат.

О дивно гордые, томительные страны! . . .
Но снова вижу я, как к призраку земли
Назад, в родимый порт, несутся корабли.

Они везут с собой весь юг благоуханный,
И странный аромат неведомых плодов
Сливается в душе с напевом моряков.

(February 28, 1896)

5. Sed non satiata (Zapisnaia knizhka no. 7 (6), p. 4)

Sed non satiata

Порока и земли божественная дочь!
Восточный опиум, гашиш благоуханный,
Ничто перед тобой, таинственной и странной,
Бесстыдной, как мечта, и измрачной, как ночь.

Кодга спешат к тебе желаний караваны
Ты холодна, как ключ,—я жадно пью всю ночь
В оазисе страстей—и брежжит день туманный
А я—я все с тобой, не удаляюсь прочь.

О демон! о палач! ты жжешь безмолвным взглядом . . .
Ты опьяняешь кровь всесильно тайным ядом . . .
О если бы, как Стикс, я девять раз обвил,

Как мрамор твервый, стань,—о если б над аидом
Алькова твоего я насладился видом
Тебя пресыщенной, тебя лишенной сил!

(March 1, 1896)

6. La Mort des amants (Zapisnaia knizhka no. 7 (6), p. 5)

La Mort des amants

Похожие на склеп глубокие кровати,
Диваны скрытые в тумане темноты,
Благоуханные и странные цветы,
Расцветшие для нас при солнечном закате.

И мы, вдвоем с тобой, в смертельном аромате:
Я—светоч истины, ты—факел красоты—

Два ярких зеркала,—две дерзкие мечты . . .
И этот гордый сон восторгов и объятий!

И будет ночь полна мистических мерцаний,
И будет долгий миг томится от прощаний
И будем мы с тобой—божественно одни.

А утром серафим с улыбкою смущенной
Войдет и оживит для жизни обновленной
Два тусклых зеркала и мертвые огни.

(February 27, 1896)

7. Le Mort joyeux (Zapisnaia knizhka no. 7(6), p. 6)

Le Mort joyeux

В сырой земле в отдаленном овраге
Себе могилу я вырую сам,
Чтоб было покойно усталым костям,
Как сонной акуле в безжизненной влаге.

Мне было бы скучно лежать в саркофаге,
Внимать моленьям и пошлым слезам.
Пусть вороны лучше по целым ночам
Клюют добычу и каркают саги.

Вы, черви, друзья без ушей и без глаз
Веселый мертвец лежит среди вас —
Терзайте свободно мой труп распростертый

И мне скажите в подземной тиши
Что значит телу страдать без души
И чем живой несчастней чем мертвый.

(March 2, 1896)

8. La Mort des amants (Zapisnaia knizhka no. 7 (6), p. 25)

И мы найдем с тобой глубокие диваны
Похожие на склеп широкие кровати
И расцветут для нас на солнечном закате
Цветы чужой страны и гордые тюльпаны.

Зажгутся в нас сердца при странном аромате
Последней вспышкою в предверии нирваны
Две мысли отразят их свет полубагряны,
Живые зеркала восторгов и объятий!

Склонившуюся ночь мистических мерцаний
Наполнит стон неслыханных прощаний
И будем мы с тобой единственно одни.

А утром серафим отворит дверь смущенно,
Войдет и принесет для жизни обновленной
Два тусклых зеркала и мертвые огни.

(March 21, 1896)

9. Les Yeux de Berthe (Zapisnaia kinizhka no. 7 (6), p. 26)

Глаза Берты

Прекрасные глаза—далекой но любимой—
Вы близ меня всегда, не удалитесь прочь,
Вы нежны, словно мрак, вы хороши, как ночь . . .
О лейте на меня свой мрак непобедимый.

Вы, тайны сладкие! вы, тепло голубые
Громадные глаза! вы—недоступный грот,
Магический приют, где властный дух живет,
А тени на часах застыли в летаргии.

Смотрю в глубокий взор, безмерный но прекрасный—
Его огни-любовь, Молитва и Мечта . . .
Откуда ж блещет мне иная красота,
О непонятный взор, невинно сладострастный!

(March 12, 1896)

10. Les Litanies de Satan (Zapisnaia knizhka no. 14, pp. 27–30)

Прекраснейший из всех представших человек,
Обманутый судьбой, лишенный славословий,

О Сатана, внемли мучительным мольбам.

О царь изгнания, еше никем не понят!
Кого не власть небес, а наша слабость гонит.

О Сатана, внемли мучительным мольбам.

Всеведущий и царь земле запретных знаний,
Единный знающий искусство врачеваний

О Сатана, внемли мучительным мольбам.

Ты прокоженным, всем, кто гибнет, изнывая,
Дающий виденье и предвкушенья рая,

О Сатана, внемли мучительным мольбам.

От Смерти, от своей бестрепетной подруги
Родивший дочь Мечту, убившую недуги,

О Сатана, внемли мучительным мольбам.

Даюший власть тому, кто распростерт во прахе,
Судяший весь народ, столкнувшийся у плахи,

О Сатана, внемли мучительным мольбам.

Ты знаюший в горах пристанища и залы,
Где скрыл ревнивый Бог блестящие металлы

О Сатана, внемли мучительным мольбам.

И ты, чей острый взор проник в те заточенья,
Где спят погребены всецветные каменья,

О Сатана, внемли мучительным мольбам.

О ты, лунатикам, бродящим ночью звездной,
Бросающий свой плашь над распростертой бездной

О Сатана, внемли мучительным мольбам.

В покой небытности передающий кости
И пьяниц и бродяг, забытых на погосте

О Сатана, внемли мучительным мольбам.

Для тех, чьи тяготы превысили бы меру,
Ты научивший нас мешать с селитрой серу

О Сатана, внемли мучительным мольбам.

Ты, не лишающий тех благостной печати,
Кто заслужил твой взор лишь яростью проклятий

О Сатана, внемли мучительным мольбам.

Влагающий в сердца властительницам оргий
Влеченье к гною ран и к рубищу восторги

О Сатана, внемли мучительным мольбам.

О посох изгнанных, о светоч всех бессонных
О сладкий духовник на петло осужденных

О Сатана, внемли мучительным мольбам.

Отец приемный всем кто в радости гордыне
Захочет позабыть о пригвожденном Сыне,

О Сатана, внемли мучительным мольбам.

тоже:

Отец приемный тех, кого для муки крестной
Из сада райского изгнал Отец Небесный.

Молитва

Слава тебе и хвала, Сатана, и в сияньи
Неба, где царствовал ты, и в глухой глубине
Ада, куда ниспровергнут, ты грезишь в молчаньи.
Рядом с тобою под Древом Познания мне
Некогда дай насладиться дыханьем свободы.
Ветви же нас осенят как церковные своды.

(October 6, 1900)

11. La Mort des amants (Zapisnaia knizhka no. 14, p. 30)

Смерть любовников

Кровати опьянят нас теплым ароматом,
Нас примут, как гроба, глубокие диваны,
И странные цветы задышат пред закатом . . .
(Растили их для нас неведомые страны).

И будем мы вдвоем на ложе сладко смятом,
Предчувствием конца невыразимо пьяны . . .
И взоры отразят сердец огонь багряный,
Как факел зеркало—каким-то резким златом.

И вечер спустится то розовый, то синний,
Вкушать мы будем смерть желаний, звуков, линий,
Замрет так радостно последний стон прощанья.

И ангел через миг войдет, посол безмолвный
И властно оживит для жизни лучшей, полной
Два тусклых зеркала и факелов сверканья.

(October, 1900)

12. Poem inspired by "Les Litanies de Satan" (*Zapisnaia knizhka* no. 14, p. 26)

> O Satan, prends pitié de ma longue misère
>
> Ch. Bodelaire [*sic*]

От жажды палящей воззвал я k тебе!
Ты властен в моей обреченной судьбе,
  О Дьявол, учитель великий!

Я ждал тебя годы—во мгле и в огне
Но ты проявлялся лишь в трепетном сне,
  Немой, неземной, многоликий!

Ребенком любил я уклончивый склон,
Там жадные маки качали мой сон,
  Там, смутно являлся ты детству.

И в ночи прельщений позора и слез,
Опутанный сумраком жгучих волос,
  Тебе я молился: ответствуй!

Как яды, впивал я вещанье наук
Чертил заклиная размеченный круг
  Лишь духи шныряли как мыши.

Изведал до глуби я таинства зла,
И муки росли без конца и числа
  Но ты не ответствовал свыше.

Проклятья тебе я принес на алтарь,
Взгляни—прихожу я, увенчан, как царь,
  Так будь благосклонен к упорству.

Я равен тебе, обреченный судьбой,
Лик с ликом могу упиваться тобой,
  О дьявол, владыка, покорствуй!
                    (October 5, 1900)

PREFACE

1. For the reception in England, see the books by Turquet-Milnes and Clements, for Germany, Sakell and Keck; for Spain, Aggeler. Book-length studies also exist on Baudelaire's reception in Holland and Hungary, written in Dutch and Hungarian (see Kopp and Pichois, Les Années Baudelaire, 180). For the French reception, see works by Stirnberg, Bandy, Carter, and Miller-Trottmann.

2. See in particular Donchin, *The Influence of French Symbolism on Russian Poetry*, which contains numerous references to Baudelaire.

3. *Les Années Baudelaire*, 181 (emphasis added). Unless otherwise indicated, all English translations of French, Russian, German, or Italian quotes are my own.

4. Trahard, *Essai critique sur Baudelaire poète*, 230–31.

5. Bodler, *Tsvety Zla*, per. (trans). P. Iakubovicha, 1.

INTRODUCTION

1. Valéry, *Oeuvres*, 1:598.

2. "Baudelaire" (1930), in Eliot, *Selected Essays*, 377.

3. Belyi, "Sharl' Bodler," 71.

4. Foreword to *Frantsuzskie liriki XIX veka* (1909), in Briusov, *Polnoe sobranie sochinenii*, 21:9.

5. See Valentinov, *Dva goda s simvolistami*, 154.

6. "Parmi les droits dont on a parlé dans ces dernier temps, il y en a un qu'on a oublié, à la démonstration duquel tout le monde est intéressé—le droit de se contredire." "Dans l'album de Philoxène Boyer." Baudelaire, *Oeuvres complètes*, 1:709.

7. See Friedrich, *Die Struktur der modernen Lyrik*; Benjamin, *Charles Baudelaire*, "Das Passagen-Werk"; Jameson, "Baudelaire as Modernist and Postmodernist."

8. For a useful survey of contemporary reader response theory, see Suleiman and Crosman, *The Reader in the Text*, and Tompkins, *Reader-Response Criticism*.

9. See the discussion of "reproduzierende Rezeption" and "produktive Rezeption" in Link, *Rezeptionsforschung*, 85 ff.

10. Bloom, *The Anxiety of Influence*, 95.

11. See Brunel, Pichois, and Rousseau, *Qu'est-ce que la littérature comparée?*, 51.

12. On the circumstances of this translation, see Belkina, *Skreshchenie sudeb*, 218–19, 233–35.

13. Briusov, "Fialki v tigele" (1905), *Sobranie sochinenii*, 6:104.

14. The parallels between Baudelaire and Dostoyevsky have been discussed in Ivask, "Bodler i Dostoevskii," and De Jonge, *Dostoevsky and the Age of Intensity*.

15. See Grossman, *Edgar Allan Poe in Russia*, 31–34.

16. See Valentinov, *Dva goda*, 155.

CHAPTER 1. SEARCHING FOR SOCIAL RELEVANCE

1. Terras, *A History of Russian Literature*, viii.

2. "Etre un homme utile m'a paru toujours quelque chose de bien hideux." "Mon coeur mis à nu," *Oeuvres complètes*, 1:679.

3. See "Pierre Dupont," ibid., 2:26.

4. Sharl' Bodeler, "Edgar Ellen Poe. Severo-amerikanskii poet," *Panteon* 4, no. 9 (1852), 1–34.

5. See Grossman, *Poe in Russia*, 29.

6. *Syn otechestva* 14, no. 21 (July 8, 1856), 33–36.

7. See the commentaries in Baudelaire, *Edgar Allan Poe, sa vie et ses ouvrages*.

8. For more details, see Grossman, *Poe in Russia*, 30.

9. For more details, see Wanner, "Le premier regard russe sur Baudelaire."

10. "Kain i Avel'," *Iskra*, no. 2 (1870), 57–58 (subtitle "S frantsuzskogo," author is not named). For a brief discussion of this translation, see Oragvelidze, "Pervye russkie perevody iz Bodlera."

11. On Minayev, see Iampol'skii, *Poety "Iskry*," 2:7–48.

12. *Delo*, no. 5 (1869). Quoted in Etkind, *Mastera russkogo stikhotvornogo perevoda*, 1:58.

13. Delo Gl. upr. po delam pechati, 1870, 16, 1–2. Quoted in Iampol'skii, *Poety "Iskry*," 2:942–43.

14. "Les Petites Vieilles" (no. 3, 1869), "Spleen [IV]" (no. 12, 1869), "La Fin de la journée" (no. 4, 1870), "Le Portrait," "Les Hiboux," "Spleen [I]" (no. 1, 1871), "Le Crépuscule du soir" (no. 8, 1872). The Soviet *Tsvety Zla* edition of 1970 names only three of these texts. "La Fin de la journée" is falsely called the "first Russian translation of Baudelaire" (445).

15. On N. S. Kurochkin, see Iampol'skii, *Poety "Iskry*," 2:573–78.

16. "Nocturno (iz Sharlia Bodlera)," *Otechestvennye zapiski*, no. 8 (1872), 507–9.

17. This text was to become the most widely translated poem by Baudelaire in the following years. Between 1872 and 1882, no fewer than four versions appeared: next to

Kurochkin's, a translation by O. Okhtenskaya (*Zhivopisnoe obozrenie*, no. 50 [1879], 498–99), P. Yakubovich (*Delo*, no. 5 [1881], 283–84), and D. Mikhalovsky (*Russkaia mysl'*, no. 1 [1882], 253–54).

18. "Unylo i temno den' tianetsia za dnem," *Otechestvennye zapiski*, no. 8 (1872), 510.

19. Okr[ei]ts, "O tom, kak I. Kurochkin perevodit iz Bodlera," 165–66.

20. On Likhachev, see A. I., *Novyi entsiklopedicheskii slovar'*, 24:715.

21. "Iz Bodlera" (ending of "Le Voyage"), *Biblioteka*, no. 6 (1871); "L'Homme et la mer," ibid., no. 9; "Le Vin de l'assassin," *Delo*, no. 5 (1880).

22. Quoted from *Tsvety Zla* (1970), 217.

23. P. F. Yakubovich, *Stikhotvoreniia* (1960). This edition contains twenty-seven of Yakubovich's Baudelaire translations. The editor, B. N. Dvinyaninov, is also the author of a monograph on Yakubovich (*Mech i lira*), which pays only scant attention to Yakubovich's significance for the Russian reception of Baudelaire. Other sources seem even more reticent: *Kratkaia literaturnaia entsiklopediia* points to "translations" by Yakubovich, but fails to mention *whom* he translated (see Mironov, "Iakubovich," 1071).

24. See Belyi, *Nachalo veka*, 20 and 53.

25. See on this Ulam, *In the Name of the People*, 390–91.

26. Wortman, *The Crisis of Russian Populism*, 184.

27. Letter to P. A. Grabovsky, September 22, 1896, published in *Russkoe bogatstvo*, no. 5 (1912), 53.

28. See Iakubovich, *Ocherki russkoi poezii*, 48.

29. B. Sadovskoi, *Vesy*, no. 8 (1905), 63.

30. Iakubovich, *Stikhotvoreniia* (1960), 245.

31. Sear, "Pis'ma iz Parizha. Poeziia i poety sovremennoi Frantsii," 31–45.

32. See Iakubovich, "V poiskakh sokrovennogo smysla," 87.

33. Bodler, *Tsvety Zla*. Per. P. Iakubovicha-Mel'shina (1909). Predislovie, 2.

34. The 1887 [Matvei Ramshev], *Stikhotvoreniia* contains 23 translations; the anonymous 1895 edition of Baudelaire's poems, *Stikhotvoreniia Bodlera*, contains 53 translations. The second volume of *Stikhotvoreniia*, published by Russkoe bogatstvo in 1901 and reissued in 1902 and 1906, contains 100 translations. A separate edition with the title *Tsvety Zla* appeared in 1909.

35. Balashov, "Legenda i pravda o Bodlere," 236.

36. Bodler, *Tsvety Zla* (1909), 3–4.

37. Ibid., 1.

38. See Friedrich, *Die Struktur der modernen Lyrik*, 47–49.

39. Iakubovich, *Stikhotvoreniia* (1960), 61–62.

40. See ibid., 325–26. Parts of the poem (stanzas 1–5 and 12) are quoted in the foreword to the 1909 edition of *Tsvety Zla*. Yakubovich originally planned to use it as a preface to his anonymous 1895 Baudelaire edition.

41. Wehrle, "Decadence in Russian Literature," 90.

42. On Gautier's essay and its influence on the French reception of Baudelaire, see Carter, *Baudelaire et la critique française*, 19–25, and Jauß, *Ästhetische Erfahrung und literarische Hermeneutik*, 848–51.

43. Iakubovich, "Sharl' Bodeler," 202.

44. See Gautier, "Charles Baudelaire," 14.

45. Iakubovich, "Sharl' Bodeler," 206.

46. Ibid., 208.

47. Gautier, "Charles Baudelaire," 23.

48. Iakubovich, *Stikhotvoreniia. Tom vtoroi* (1901), 274.

49. See "Balmont: The Music of Decadence" in chapter 2 for more details.

50. See Iakubovich, "Pis'ma K. D. Batiushkovu," 103.

51. Iakubovich, *Ocherki russkoi poezii*, 329.

52. See Iakubovich, "Bodler, ego zhizn' i poeziia," 143–44.

53. September 25, 1895. Quoted in Iakubovich, "Pis'ma K. D. Batiushkovu," 103.

54. Iakubovich, "Bodler, ego zhizn' i poeziia," 159.

55. *Severnyi vestnik*, no. 4 (1891), 110.

56. Iakubovich, "Bodler, ego zhizn' i poeziia," 167–68.

57. Andr-ich, "Dekadenty," 97–98.

58. *Vesy*, no. 7 (1907), 75.

59. See Iakubovich, "Zametki chitatelia."

60. Batiushkov, "Bodler i ego russkii perevodchik."

61. Iakubovich, "V poiskakh sokrovennogo smysla (otvet F. D. Batyushkovu)."

62. Batiushkov, "Eshche neskol'ko slov o Bodlere i ego russkom perevodchike (otvet g-nu P. Ia.)."

63. Fifteen of Yakubovich's letters to Batyushkov are preserved in the manuscript division of Pushkinskii Dom, St. Petersburg (IRLI, f. 20, no. 15273). Three of them were published by A. B. Muratov (see Iakubovich, "Pis'ma K. D. Batiushkovu").

64. In a footnote to the poem in the 1909 edition of *Tsvety Zla*, 248, Yakubovich wrote: "The use of the word 'sage' in connection with a woman usually has a special meaning: What do I care about your chastity? . . . The translation manages to express this idea only remotely." Starting with the 1902 edition of Yakubovich's poetry, the first line of the poem was changed to "May the proud world despise you" (*Pust' tebia gordyi svet preziraet*).

65. Batyushkov should not have given up so quickly. Modern French scholarship seems to side with his interpretation. See Claude Pichois's commentary ("Deux femmes sont ici en cause") in *Oeuvres complètes*, 1: 893.

66. Bodler, *Tsvety Zla* (1909), 5–6.

67. On the connection between romanticism and populist poetry, see Os'makov, *Poeziia revoliutsionnogo narodnichestva*, 162–92. However, Os'makov failed to take into account the decadent side of romanticism, highlighted by Mario Praz in his classic *La carne, la morte e il diavolo* (1930), published in English as *The Romantic Agony*. On Baudelaire, see in particular the chapter "The Shadow of the Divine Marquis," 95–186.

68. See, for example, "V buriu" (1881), "Fantaziia" (1882), or "Smert' orla" (1884) in *Stikhotvoreniia* (1960), 314, 100–3, 110–11.

69. "Bodler, ego zhizn' i poeziia," 169.

70. First published in P. Iakubovich, [M. Ramshev], *Stikhotvoreniia* (1887), 17. Yakubovich considered this translation as one of his best: "[The translator] regards this translation, free in details but exactly rendering the meaning, as one of his most successful works" (note to *Tsvety Zla* [1909], 245).

71. See, for example, Barbara Johnson's deconstructionist reading in *Défigurations du langage poétique.*

72. "Bodler, ego zhizn' i poeziia," 164.

73. *Severnyi vestnik*, no. 4 (1891), 110.

74. Iakubovich, *Stikhotvoreniia. Tom vtoroi*, 2-e izd. (1902), 186.

75. First published in *Severnyi vestnik*, no. 12 (1890), 217, as "Vino triapichnikov." For a brief discussion and comparison with Ellis's version of the same poem, see Etkind, "Baudelaire en langue russe," 254–57.

76. Iakubovich, *Stikhotvoreniia* (1960), 354–55.

77. "Baudelaire en langue russe," 255.

78. Cf. the poem "V Sibiri, okovannoi liutym morozom" (1907), *Stikhotvoreniia* (1960), 279.

79. Ibid., 59.

80. *Tsvety Zla* (1909), 7–8.

81. Avrelii [Briusov], "Novyi perevod Bodlera," 42. The number 200 is, of course, erroneous (Baudelaire himself did not write that many poems).

82. See *Literaturnoe nasledstvo. vol. 85: Valerii Briusov*, 732.

83. *Ocherki russkoi poezii*, 334

84. Gor'kii, *Sobranie sochinenii*, 23:128–29, 20:261.

85. *Obrazovanie*, no. 2 (1906), 154–55.

86. See on this Mary Louise Loe, "Gorky and Nietzsche: The Quest for a Russian Superman," and A. L. Tait, "Lunacharsky: A 'Nietzschean Marxist?'" in Rosenthal, *Nietzsche in Russia*, 251–92.

87. See "Zametki chitatelia," 154.

88. Quoted in Ruff, *Baudelaire*, 64.

89. Degen, "Noveishaia frantsuzskaia lirika," 95.

90. Mogilianskii, *Kriticheskie nabroski*, 44, 56.

91. Kogan, "Sharl' Bodler," 128, 124.

92. Friche, *Poeziia koshmarov i uzhasa*, 209. See also Friche's entry on Baudelaire in *Entsiklopedicheskii slovar' "Granat."*

93. Kogan, "Sharl' Bodler," 118.

94. For a discussion of this article with regard to Poe, see Grossman, *Poe in Russia*, 90–91.

95. "Bodler i Edgar Po," 97.

96. See Starobinski's influential *Portrait de l'artiste en saltimbanque*.

97. "Bodler i Edgar Po," 100.

98. Lunacharskii, "Bodler," 550.

99. See, for example, *ne plachu ia* ("Nad mogiloi druga," September 14, 1882), or *ne budem plakat'* ("Rasseian mrak...," July 24, 1882) in *Stikhotvoreniia* (1960), 70, 72.

100. Valentin Katayev made the same assertion in his speech at the 1967 Baudelaire colloquium in Belgium ("A cette époque, on considérait Baudelaire comme le 'Nekrassov français'"). "Mon Baudelaire," 203.

101. See Bryusov's "Anketa o Nekrasove" (1902), *Sobranie sochinenii*, 6:74.

102. See "Mon Baudelaire," 206.

103. Ironically enough, V. Aleksandrov had tried to make Baudelaire politically acceptable in 1941 by calling him a "liberal" ("Sharl' Bodler," 72). He added that liberalism in Baudelaire's time was not yet a "bad word" (as it became in Stalin's Russia and in Reagan's and Bush's America).

104. See "Balmont: The Music of Decadence" in chapter 2, this volume. Ilinskaya is also the author of the entry on Baudelaire in *Kratkaia literaturnaia entsiklopediia* 1:662–63 (1962), which ends with the same "Gorky" quote.

105. Oblomievskii, *Frantsuzskii simvolizm*, 129.

106. See Velikovskii, "Povorotnaia vekha."

107. Nol'man, *Sharl' Bodler*, 28–29.

108. Ibid., 157, 158.

109. Ibid., 165.

110. A rough draft of Shershenevich's translation is preserved in the Russian Archive for Literature and Art in Moscow (RGALI, f. 2145, op. 1, ed. khran. 12). In 1940, Shershenevich was able to present his translations at a public reading, as we know from an account in *Literaturnaia gazeta* ("Novye perevody Bodlera," no. 15 (866) [March 15, 1940], 6). Two poems, "Le Cygne" and "Abel et Caïn," appeared in *Krasnaia nov'*, no. 5–6 (1940), 128–130.

111. Aigi. *Zdes'*, 14. The poem was first published in *Stikhi 1954–1971* (Munich, 1975).

112. See Iakov Belinskii, "Bol'noi Bodler," *Iarmarka chudes* (Moscow: Sovetskii pisatel', 1975), 145; Vitalii Demchenko, "'Tsvety zla' Bodlera," *Kol'tsa zhizni* (Uzhgorod: Karpati, 1979), 70; Valerii Khatiushin, "Chitaia Bodlera," *Byt' chelovekom na zemle* (Moscow: Sovremennik, 1982), 43–44; Vladimir Koval'skii, "Pered maskoi Bodlera," *Prostor*, no. 6 (1977), 71; Novella Matveeva, "Moi Bodler," *Zakon pesen* (Moscow: Sovetskii pisatel', 1983), 78–79; Ekrem Melikhov, "Bodler," *Literaturnyi Azerbaidzhan*, no. 7 (1981), 96; Igor' Zhdanov, "Bodler," *Dvoinoi obgon* (Moscow: Sovetskii pisatel', 1978), 21.

CHAPTER 2. THE DECADENT RESPONSE

1. For an overview of the history of the term and its role in the literatures of France, Germany, England, and Italy, see Koppen, *Dekadenter Wagnerismus*, and Calinescu, *Five*

Faces of Modernity. A stimulating discussion of decadence in Russia can be found in Wehrle, "Decadence in Russian Literature." My inclusion of Annensky in this chapter follows Vladimir Markov's suggestion to extend the boundaries of Russian decadence beyond the 1890s. See his "K voprosu o granitsakh dekadansa v russkoi poezii."

2. Evelyn Bristol, "Decadence," in Terras, *Handbook of Russian Literature,* 94.

3. For an overview, see Calinescu, *Five Faces of Modernity,* 164–67; and Koppen, *Dekadenter Wagnerismus,* 25–32.

4. Quoted in Jameson, "Baudelaire as Modernist and Postmodernist," 247.

5. Quoted from Carter, *Baudelaire et la critique française,* 59.

6. Mirsky, *A History of Russian Literature,* 360.

7. On Andreyevsky, see Dolgopolov, *Poety 1880–1890-kh godov,* 262–67.

8. "Spleen [IV]," "Moesta et errabunda," "L'Amour et le crâne," no. 2 (1878), 690–92. "Réversibilité," "Recueillement," no. 3, 616–17. Three of these texts ("Spleen," "Moesta et errabunda," and "Recueillement") are included in *Tsvety Zla* (1970), and discussed in Oragvelidze, "Russkie perevodchiki Bodlera 80-kh godov XIX veka," 137–48.

9. *A History of Russian Literature,* 360. On the *Book of Death,* see also Baer, *Arthur Schopenhauer,* 30–44.

10. The image was perhaps suggested to Andreyevsky by his reading of other works by Baudelaire. In two of the poems condemned for obscenity by the French court in 1857 ("Les Bijoux," "Le Léthé"), the feminine addressee of the text is compared to a tiger.

11. Nadson, *Polnoe sobranie sochinenii,* t. I-II, kn. 3, 208.

12. See on this Schaarschuh, "Das Problem der Gattung 'Prosagedicht,'" and Levina, "'Stikhotvoreniia v proze' I. S. Turgeneva."

13. See "A Arsène Houssaye," *Oeuvres complètes,* 1:275.

14. "K Chitateliu." Turgenev, *Polnoe sobranie sochinenii,* 10:125.

15. In *Essais de psychologie contemporaine* and *Der Fall Wagner* (1888). See Koppen, *Dekadenter Wagnerismus,* 50, and Wehrle, "Decadence in Russian Literature," 85.

16. "Poemy v proze Bodelera. Perevod P. V. Ga-na." *Zhivopisnoe obozrenie,* no. 20 (1878) 406–7, no. 22, 444–45.

17. "Stikhotvoreniia v proze Sharlia Bodlera" ("L'Etranger," "Enivrez-vous," "Les Foules," "Chacun sa chimère," "Déjà!," "Le Vieux Saltimbanque," "Le Port," "Le Joujou du pauvre," "Le Fou et la Vénus," "Les Yeux des pauvres," "La Chambre double," "Any where out of the world"). *Iziashchnaia literatura* was a monthly journal which appeared from 1883 to 1885 in St. Petersburg under the editorship of P. I. Veinberg.

18. See *Russkii biograficheskii slovar',* 3:22–23.

19. Merezhkovsky's and Bibikov's prediction was wrong: unlike the French, the Russians never made the prose poem a major genre. See on this my paper "The Genre of the Prose Poem in Russian Literature."

20. First publications: *Vestnik Evropy,* no. 3, 1885 ("L'Invitation au voyage"); *Russkaia mysl',* no. 5, 1885 ("Chant d'automne"); *Stikhotvoreniia,* St. Petersburg, 1888 ("L'Invitation au voyage," "Chant d'automne," "L'Albatros"); *Sever,* no. 4, 1892 ("Spleen"). All ex-

cept "Spleen" are included in *Polnoe sobranie sochinenii*, vol. 22. "L'Invitation au voyage" and "L'Albatros" are also reprinted in *Tsvety Zla* (1970).

21. See the commentary in *Tsvety Zla*, 354.

22. Quoted in Iakubovich, *Stikhotvoreniia* (1960), 25.

23. First published in *Severnyi vestnik*, no. 12 (1890). Quoted from *Tsvety Zla* (1970), 18.

24. Ibid., 301–2.

25. As E. Vitkovskii has pointed out, this rhyme is used in 11 out of 12 Russian translations of "L'Albatros"! See "Ochen' krupnaia dich'," 171.

26. Etkind, "Baudelaire en langue russe," sees Merezhkovsky's Albatross as an "angel" and tries to explain the passage with Merezhkovsky's "spiritualistic Christianity" (260). In light of the early date of the translation, such an interpretation seems anachronistic.

27. See on this Rosenthal, *D. S. Merezhkovsky and the Silver Age*, 33.

28. *O prichinakh upadka*, 43, 48. Merezhkovsky seems to refer to the article "L'Art philosophique" (publ. 1868), where Baudelaire mentions "la valeur morale du poème, caractère satanique et byronien, caractère de désolation" (*Oeuvres complètes*, 2:600).

29. Merezhkovskii, *Polnoe sobranie sochinenii*, 23:256–57.

30. Vengerova, "Bodler" (1891), 214.

31. Vengerova, "Bodler" (1912), 139.

32. See Carter, *Baudelaire et la critique française*, 119–20. Interestingly enough, Brunetière found a common decadent element, a morbid "religion de la souffrance humaine," both in Baudelaire and the Russian novelists (ibid., 151). The dispute was also reported in *Severnyi vestnik* (see Robert de Cerisy, "Polemika po povodu statui Sharlia Bodlera").

33. Engel'gardt, "Smes'," 369–70.

34. Krasnov, "Pervye dekadenty," 188.

35. Bal'mont, "Kniaz' A. I. Urusov (stranitsy liubvi i pamiati)," *Gornye vershiny*, 105.

36. Quoted by Balmont from an unpublished manuscript (ibid., 106).

37. Ibid., 105. Balmont finds this remark "too categorical." His objection: "Some of Baudelaire's poems were successfully translated by Yakubovich"(!).

38. Published in *Kn. A. I Urusov, Stat'i ego, pis'ma ego i vospominaniia o nem*, 2:386–94.

39. This point is argued in Grossman, *Valery Bryusov and the Riddle of Russian Decadence*, 63–65.

40. *Gornye vershiny*, 105.

41. "Elementarnye slova o simvolicheskoi poezii," *Gornye vershiny*, 79.

42. Bal'mont, *Polnoe sobranie stikhov*, 1:37–38. Vladimir Markov has called this text "perhaps the first clearly Baudelairean poem." See his *Kommentar zu den Dichtungen von K. D. Bal'mont*, 1:34.

43. A. Hansen-Löve has described the "lunare Welt" as a central element in the poetic universe of early, "diabolic" Russian symbolism. See *Der russische Symbolismus*, 223–52.

44. Bodler, *Stikhotvoreniia* (1895), iv.

45. Ibid., vii–ix. Dated "1894. October 20. Moscow." As we have seen in the previous chapter, the last line of this poem later had an unexpected career in the Soviet Union, after Gorky plagiarized it in his essay "Pol' Verlen i dekadenty."

46. "O 'Tsvetakh zla,'" *Gornye vershiny,* 58 (Balmont's emphasis).

47. "K Bodleru." Quoted from Bal'mont, *Izbrannoe,* 114–15.

48. Markov tries to explain this rather puzzling passage as a reference to Baudelaire's "la terre polaire" in "De profundis clamavi." See *Kommentar,* 123. One wonders whether Balmont is not rather talking about his own cycle "V tsarstve l'dov" (see *Polnoe sobranie stikhov,* 1:229–32).

49. *Izbrannoe,* 66.

50. Ibid., 172.

51. "K Germesu Trismegistu," *Polnoe sobranie stikhov,* 2:121–22.

52. First publication: *Vestnik inostrannoi literatury,* no. 4, 1899 ("Le Gouffre," "La Mort des amants"); *Gornye vershiny* ("Les Litanies de Satan"); *Vestnik Inostrannoi literatury,* no. 1, 1908 ("Le Balcon"); ibid, no. 3, 1908 ("La Géante"); *Iz chuzhezemnykh poetov* ("La Beauté").

Balmont's alleged translation of "Correspondances," published in Etkind, *Frantsuzskie stikhi,* 389, was in reality written by P. F. Yakubovich (version of 1895). The same error can be observed as early as 1909, when the translation appeared under Balmont's name in *Antologiia sovremennoi poezii, chtets-deklamator,* vol. IV (Kiev), 83. Neither Balmont nor Yakubovich, who was still alive at that time, seems to have protested.

53. See Claude Pichois' commentary in Baudelaire, *Oeuvres complètes,* 1:1087. For a discussion of Nikolay Gumilyov's translation of the poem, see "Gumilyov and Acmeism" in chapter 4.

54. *Gornye vershiny,* 83.

55. Quoted from *Tsvety Zla* (1970), 206.

56. *Gornye vershiny,* 82 (Balmont's emphasis).

57. "Baudelaire as Modernist and Postmodernist," 263.

58. Jean Chuzeville in *Mercure de France,* 1913. Quoted in Donchin, *The Influence of French Symbolism on Russian Poetry,* 9.

59. Gofman, *Kniga o russkikh poetakh,* 63.

60. "Izmena" (1895), *Sobranie sochinenii,* 1:58.

61. See Chernov, "Modernizm v russkoi poezii," 122. The image occurs in Balmont's poetry too. See, for example, "Dva trupa" in "Budem kak solntse" (*Polnoe sobranie stikhov,* 3:140). For a general discussion of the role of necrophilia in the literature of decadence, see Koppen, "Luxuria und Tod," *Dekadenter Wagnerismus,* 177–83; and Hansen-Löve, "Thanatos und Eros: 'Liebestod' und 'Todesliebe,'" *Der russische Symbolismus,* 395–407.

62. See the examples collected in Donchin, *Influence,* 141–44.

63. *Russkie simvolisty* [vyp. 3], 33.

64. Dated July 8, 1898. Published in Briusov, *Neizdannye stikhotvoreniia,* 427.

65. Quoted from Bryusov's manuscript in the Russian State Library, Moscow, f. 386, kart. 14, ed. khran. 5/14. For the full text of the poem, see appendix.

66. For the full text of these translations, see appendix.

67. See in particular the article "O 'rechi rabskoi', v zashchitu poezii" (1910), directed against Ivanov and Blok (*Sobranie sochinenii*, 6:176–79).

68. In "Pierre Dupont" (1851), *Oeuvres complètes*, 2: 26.

69. *Sobranie sochinenii*, 6:92.

70. *Oeuvres complètes*, 1:430. The same idea is also expressed in Baudelaire's diaries. See ibid., 659: "Dans certains états de l'âme presque surnaturels, la profondeur de la vie se révèle tout entière dans le spectacle, si ordinaire qu'il soit, qu'on a sous les yeux. Il en devient le symbole."

71. *Sobranie sochinenii*, 1:447.

72. *Polnoe sobranie sochinenii*, 21:224.

73. Ibid., 253–54.

74. *Sobranie sochinenii*, 1: 331, 412.

75. Ibid., 2:21.

76. Ibid., 2:91.

77. Bodler, *Tsvety Zla*. Per. Ellisa, 1.

78. First publications in *Utro svobody*, no. 17 and no. 20 (1907) ("Le Rebelle" and "Abel et Caïn") and *Frantsuzskie liriki XIX veka* ("La Beauté" and "Crépuscule du soir," together with the former two poems). "Parfum exotique" and "Le Revenant" were added to the second edition of this book, printed as volume 21 of *Polnoe sobranie sochinenii i perevodov*. They have almost nothing in common with the version in the 1890s notebooks.

79. Published in *Vesy*, no. 7 (1908), 42–44.

80. See in particular "Fialki v tigele" (1905), *Sobranie sochinenii*, 6:103–9.

81. See "First Encounters and Translations," in chapter 1.

82. Quoted from *Tsvety Zla* (1970), 158. One wonders whether *prostitutsiia* is not a misprint and should be capitalized, as it is in Baudelaire's text. After all, Bryusov did capitalize *Razvrat*.

83. Interestingly enough, the rendering of "catins" with *kamelii* had already occurred in the first Russian translation of "Le Crépuscule du soir" (O. Okhtenskaia, *Zhivopisnoe obozrenie*, no. 50 [1879], 499).

84. See Zapisnaia knizhka no. 1, p. 22. Russian State Library, Fond 386, kart. 14, ed. khran. 5/1.

85. *Sobranie sochinenii*, 6:86.

86. For an overview of the discussion, see Claude Pichois's commentary in *Oeuvres complètes*, 1:870–72.

87. See Ryan, "More Seductive than Phryne," 1133–34.

88. Quoted from *Tsvety Zla* (1970), 35.

89. Solodub and Khrapovitskaia, in "Perevod 'Krasoty' Bodlera," attempted to prove

that Bryusov's version is "warmer, more human and more emotional" than the original. Their arguments do not seem overly convincing, however: (1) Bryusov's Beauty addresses the "mortal" first, before talking about herself; (2) a singular mortal is addressed, rather than a plurality of mortals; (3) Bryusov's first verse has two exclamation marks, Baudelaire's only one; (4) of Baudelaire's "coeur de neige," Bryusov renders only the snow and omits the inhuman "cold heart"; (5) Bryusov's Beauty *loves* immobility, Baudelaire's *hates* movement; (6) the eyes of Bryusov's Beauty are "sleepless," conveying to the image a human touch absent from Baudelaire's.

90. Bal'mont, *Iz chuzhezemnykh poetov*, 101.

91. See the poem "Sfinks" in "Tishina," 1897 (*Izbrannoe*, 67–68). I have discussed this image in "Schwarze Dekadenz," 68.

92. Briusov, *Sobranie sochinenii*, 3:187.

93. The term is V. Setchkarev's. See his *Studies in the Life and Work of Innokentij Annenskij*, 54.

94. Foreword to "Kniga otrazhenii" (1905). Annenskii, *Izbrannye proizvedeniia*, 374.

95. "Bal'mont-lirik," ibid., 486–522.

96. Renato Poggioli even claimed that Annensky was "the only poet of his nation and time whose temper and vision could be compared . . . to those of Baudelaire." *The Poets of Russia*, 172.

97. *Oeuvres complètes*, 2:418 (emphasis added). The similarities between Annensky's and Baudelaire's concept of criticism have been noticed also by B. Conrad in *I. F. Annenskijs poetische Reflexionen*, 62.

98. "Chto takoe poeziia?," 54.

99. Annenskii, *Lirika*, 58.

100. See Etkind, *Frantsuzskie stikhi v perevode russkikh poetov*, 37.

101. Annenskii, *Izbrannye proizvedeniia*, 198.

102. The poem was translated more faithfully by Bryusov (see *Polnoe sobranie sochinenii i perevodov*, 21:72) and by Gumilyov (see *Vestnik russkogo khristianskogo dvizheniia* 144 [1985], 160).

103. Annenskii, *Izbrannye proizvedeniia*, 200.

104. For a more detailed discussion of this translation, see Tittler, "Annenskij as Translator of French Symbolism," 80–83.

105. *Tsvety Zla* (1970), 115.

106. Ibid., 111.

107. Ibid., 408.

108. Chernov, "Modernizm v russkoi poezii," 108.

109. Mikhailovskii, "Russkoe otrazhenie frantsuzskogo simvolizma," 57. To my knowledge, Mikhailovsky never commented specifically on Baudelaire.

110. SPb. k-t tsens. inostr., raporty za 1859 g., no. 448, January 24, 1859. Quoted in Aizenshtok, "Frantsuzskie pisateli v otsenkakh tsarskoi tsenzury," 821.

111. See ibid., 823.

112. D-ev [P. D. Boborykin], "Priznaniia literaturnykh ottsov," 530, 533.

113. See Nordau, *Entartung*, 2:81–95.

114. See Vengerov, *Russkaia literatura XX veka*, 1:30.

115. See Belyi, *Chetyre simfonii*, 178, 184–85, 193–94, 196.

116. See *Mezhdu dvukh revoliutsii*, 215–16. Bazhenov also served as the prototype for the character Pepesh-Dovliash in Bely's novel *Maski* (see A. V. Lavrov's commentary, ibid., 508).

117. Bazhenov, *Psikhiatricheskie besedy*, 47–48.

118. Tolstoi, *Polnoe sobranie sochinenii*, 52: 84.

119. Ibid., 30:100.

120. Ibid., 94.

121. Ibid., 519.

122. Ibid., 107.

123. Ibid., 99.

124. Ibid., 519.

125. K. Lomunov, "Predislovie," ibid., xxv.

126. *Vesy*, no. 6 (1908), 71.

127. Shebnev, "K. Bal'mont okolo imeni A. I. Urusova," 2.

CHAPTER 3. THE "YOUNGER SYMBOLISTS"

1. For an overview of the discussion from a proreligious standpoint, see Emmanuel, *Baudelaire: The Paradox of Redemptive Satanism*, 15–23.

2. *L'univers poétique de Baudelaire*, 130.

3. "Anthropomorphism and Trope in the Lyric," 129.

4. "Itogi simvolizma," *Vesy*, no. 7 (1909), 68.

5. "Svetleiut dali," ibid., no. 3 (1904), 13.

6. "Correspondances" was translated into Russian at least eleven times: by P. Yakubovich, E. Beketova (see conclusion, this volume), N. Bazhenov, A. Panov, A. Alving, Ellis, N. Gumilyov, B. Livshits (see "Livshits and Cubo-Futurism" in chapter 4), A. Lamblé, V. Shershenevich, and the Soviet translator V. Levik.

7. See *Oeuvres complètes*, 1:844.

8. Petrovskaia, "Iz 'Vospominanii'," 778.

9. See on this Carter, *Baudelaire et la critique française*, 183–84.

10. "Having a street" in Paris was tantamount to official glory. Baudelaire's street is located in the 12th arrondissement, between rue de Prague and faubourg saint-Antoine (see Carter, 184).

11. Aikhenval'd, *Etiudy o zapadnykh pisateliakh*, 246–47.

12. *Vesy*, no. 7 (1907), 76.

13. Ibid., no. 6 (1908), 70.

14. Kachorovskaia, *Zametki o modernizme*, 13.

15. "Nashi epigony. O stile, L. Andreeve, Borise Zaitseve i mnogo drugom," *Vesy,* no. 2 (1908), 68.

16. See Ellis's review of Ivanov's *Po zvezdam* in Vesy, no. 8 (1909), 59.

17. See in particular the chapters "Student Kobylinskii" and "Ellis" in Belyi, *Nachalo veka,* 39–64; "Briusov i Ellis" in Valentinov, *Dva goda s simvolistami,* 139–71, and A. Tsvetaeva, *Vospominaniia,* 258–59, 283–89, 302–7. "N. Valentinov" was the pseudonym of the Menshevik Social Democrat N. V. Volsky (1878–1964).

18. "Plennyi dukh," *Sochineniia,* 2:257.

19. See Karlinsky, *Marina Tsvetaeva,* 28–31.

20. *Dva goda,* 151.

21. This incident is reported by Valentinov, who heard it from Ozerov (ibid., 151).

22. On the Argonauts, see Lavrov, "Mifotvorchestvo 'argonavtov.'"

23. See *Nachalo veka,* 127.

24. "V zashchitu dekadentstva," *Vesy,* no. 8 (1907), 66.

25. "Valerii Briusov. *Puti i pereput'ia,*" ibid., no. 1 (1908), 84.

26. "*Frantsuzskie liriki XIX veka,*" ibid., no. 7 (1909), 92.

27. Russian State Library, fond 167, kart. 7, ed. khran. 6.

28. "Ellisu" (1914), Briusov, *Sobranie sochinenii,* 3:332.

29. *Vesy,* no. 8 (1909), 53–62.

30. Ibid., no. 10–11 (1909), 168.

31. *Russkie simvolisty,* 336 (Ellis's emphasis).

32. Quoted in Grechishkin and Lavrov, "Ellis—Poet-simvolist, teoretik i kritik," 61.

33. Sh. Bodler, *Moe obnazhennoe serdtse,* xiii; "Nashi epigony," *Vesy,* no. 2 (1908), 68.

34. *Stigmata,* 48.

35. See *Gedichte W. Solowjews* (Mainz, 1926), *Monarchia St. Petri* (Mainz, 1929), *Der hl. Wladimir und der christliche Staat* (Paderborn, 1930).

36. See Leo Kobilinski-Ellis, *Alexander Puschkin. Der religiöse Genius Russlands,* 195.

37. *Nachalo veka,* 42.

38. *Dva goda,* 152.

39. In recent years, some poems by Ellis have been published in Soviet anthologies of Russian sonnets. See Sovalina, *Russkii sonet XVIII-nachalo XX veka,* 359–64 ("Liubov' i smert'," "Sonety-gobeleny," "K Bodleru," "K chitateliu"); and Fedotov, *Sonet serebrianogo veka* 310–13 ("Iz tsykla 'Gobeleny'").

40. West, *Russian Symbolism,* 110.

41. "Itogi simvolizma," *Vesy,* no. 7 (1909), 74. The same statement is repeated verbatim in *Russkie simvolisty,* 29.

42. See "Chto takoe teatr?," *Vesy,* no. 4 (1908), 86.

43. "Chto takoe literatura? (O knige S. Vengerova: *Ocherki po istorii russkoi literatury),*" ibid., no. 10 (1907), 54–57.

44. *Russkie simvolisty,* 171.

45. "Ob aforizmakh," *Vesy*, no. 9 (1907), 50–52.

46. The article was promised for the coming year in the November issue of *Vesy* (1908), 91. A book with the title "Frantsuzskie simvolisty" is announced under "Knigi Ellisa" in *Russkie simvolisty*. Ellis's plan for a book on European symbolism is preserved in RGALI, fond 575, op. 1, ed. khran. 12.

47. See the letters quoted in Bartlett, "Wagner and Russia," 213, 218, 221.

48. French orthography and grammar seem not to have been Ellis's forte. He also misspelled the title of Baudelaire's prose poems as "Petites poèmes en prose" ("Nashi epigony," *Vesy*, no. 2 [1908], 64).

49. "Chto takoe teatr?," ibid., no. 4 (1908), 89–90.

50. *Dva goda*, 157.

51. *Immorteli*, vyp.I-i. See the poems "K chitateliu" (9), "Bodleru" (31) and "K Bodleru" (139).

52. Bodler, *Moe obnazhennoe serdtse*, xi.

53. "Sharl' Bodler. *Tsvety Zla*," *Vesy*, no. 7 (1907), 75 (Ellis's emphasis).

54. "O sovremennom simvolizme, o 'chorte' i o 'deistve,'" ibid., no. 1 (1909), 82.

55. *Russkie simvolisty*, 329–30.

56. *Vigilemus!*, 57–58.

57. Eliot, *Selected Essays*, 374.

58. See the chapter on Yakubovich. A brief comparison of Ellis's and Yakubovich's versions of "Le Vin des chiffonniers" can be found also in Etkind, "Baudelaire en langue russe," 257.

59. Quoted from *Tsvety Zla* (1970), 177.

60. *Immorteli*, 41. This version was republished in the collection *Chtets-Deklamator*, t. 3, izd. 2-e (Kiev, n. d.), 250.

61. *Stikhotvoreniia Bodlera* (1895), 20.

62. *Tsvety Zla*, Per. Ellisa, 78.

63. For the French text, see "The Triumph of 'Correspondances'" in chapter 3.

64. Avrelii [Briusov], "Novyi perevod Bodlera," 48.

65. See *Nachalo veka*, 453.

66. Blok and Belyi, *Perepiska*, 82. Belyi never wrote a review.

67. See "Bely: From Mysticism to Formalism" in chapter 4.

68. B. Bugaev [A. Belyi], *Pereval*, no. 6 (1907), 54–55.

69. September 23, 1909. Russian State Library, fond 167, kart. 2, ed. khran. 7. Despite Belyi's vituperations, Ellis's edition of Baudelaire's prose poems was published by Musaget in 1910.

70. "Sharl' Bodler. *Tsvety Zla*," *Vesy*, no. 7 (1907), 75.

71. "Mon coeur mis à nu," *Oeuvres complètes*, 1:684 and 693.

72. See Ivanov's essay "O veselom remesle i umnom veselii," *Po zvezdam*, 237.

73. Ivanov, *Sobranie sochinenii*, 2:611–12. It is true that toward the end of his life,

Ivanov saw Mallarmé in a more positive light. In his Italian article "Simbolismo" (1936), he presented him as an "emulatore poetico del panlogista Hegel" (ibid., 658).

74. Ibid., 1:537.

75. Ibid., 1:606.

76. *Po zvezdam,* 266.

77. Ibid., 271.

78. *Po zvezdam,* 266. In a later rejoinder to Andrey Bely's critique of his article, Ivanov emphasized once more Baudelaire's status between "realism" and "idealism," whereas Verlaine and Huysmans, according to him, belong to the "realist" camp (see "B. N. Bugaev i 'Realiora,'" *Vesy,* no. 7 [1908], 77).

79. See Ellis's review of *Po zvezdam, Vesy,* no. 8 [1909], 58.

80. See Friedrich, *Die Struktur der modernen Lyrik,* 53–55.

81. *Po zvezdam,* 296.

82. See Du Bos's "Méditations sur la vie de Baudelaire" and his introduction to "Mon coeur mis à nu" in *Approximations,* 183–237, 977–1036.

83. The article is reprinted in *Sobranie sochinenii,* 2:653–59.

84. For a survey of the Italian debate on *decadentismo,* see Calinescu, *Five Faces of Modernity,* 211–21.

85. *Oeuvres complètes,* 2:133.

86. "La Poésie est ce qu'il y a de plus réel, c'est ce qui n'est complètement vrai que dans *un autre monde.*—Ce monde-ci,—dictionnaire hiéroglyphique." Ibid., 59. In fairness to Ivanov, it has to be said that he could not have known this text in 1908, or even 1936, since it was published for the first time only in 1938.

87. Ivanov discusses the reasons for his conversion in his "Lettre à Charles Du Bos," *Sobranie sochinenii,* 3:418–30.

88. *Oeuvres complètes,* 1:192.

89. Quoted in *Sobranie sochinenii,* 2:739. Unfortunately, Bryusov's answer is not preserved.

90. See Auerbach, "Baudelaires *Fleurs du Mal* und das Erhabene," 275–79. For a comparison of Ivanov's translation of this poem with Annensky's, see "Annensky: The Aesthetics of Pessimism" in chapter 2, this volume.

91. See Ivanov's article "O 'Tsyganakh' Pushkina," *Po zvezdam,* 143–88. Robert Füglister has discussed Pushkin's "Tsygany" (translated into French by Mérimée) as a possible source for "Bohémiens en voyage" (see "Baudelaire et le thème des bohémiens," 126–28).

92. Quoted in Ivanov, *Stikhotvoreniia i poemy,* 505.

93. *Sobranie sochinenii,* 1:788–89.

94. Davidson, *The Poetic Imagination of Vyacheslav Ivanov,* 231. On Ivanov as a translator, see also Lowry Nelson, Jr., "*Translatio Lauri:* Ivanov's Translations of Petrarch," in Jackson and Nelson, *Vyacheslav Ivanov,* 162–89.

95. Quoted from *Sobranie sochinenii*, 2:344–45. In the Soviet editions of this text, *Gospod'* and *Tvoi* are misspelled as *gospod'* and *tvoi*.

96. Baudelaire. *The Paradox of Redemptive Satanism*, 132.

97. For a more detailed comparative analysis of Ivanov's, Balmont's, and Bryusov's translations of "La Beauté," see also Meyer-Fraatz, "Die 'Schönheit' des Symbolismus."

98. *Tsvety Zla*, Per. Ellisa, 94.

99. For a sampling of other cacophonies in Ellis's translations of Baudelaire, see the review of L. V. in *Mir Bozhii*, no. 7 (1904), 61–62 (e.g., *Ia vse zh otmshchu emu, ia tak otmshchu, chtob plod*).

100. Quoted from *Tsvety Zla* (1970), 321.

101. *Sobranie sochinenii*, 2:346.

102. See ibid., 601.

103. See on this Mints and Obatnin, "Simvolika zerkala v rannei poezii Viach. Ivanova."

104. See on this the chapter "Meer und Himmel" in Tschöpl, *Vjačeslav Ivanov*, 109–15.

105. *Sobranie sochinenii*, 2:614.

106. By a strange coincidence, *Temnyi lik* is also the title of an anti-Christian book by the religious philosopher Vasily Rozanov, published in 1911 (i.e., after Ivanov's translation).

107. Quoted from *Tsvety Zla* (1970), 317–18.

CHAPTER 4. TOWARD MODERNITY

1. See Paul de Man's "Lyric and Modernity" in *Blindness and Insight*, 166–86, and the chapter "La religion du futur: avant-gardes et récits orthodoxes" in Compagnon, *Les cinq paradoxes de la modernité*, 47–78.

2. *Die Struktur der modernen Lyrik*, 55.

3. Bely, *Petersburg*, 11–12.

4. *Oeuvres complètes*, 1:691.

5. See "Bely's Theory of Symbolism" in Malmstad, *Andrey Bely*, 285–312.

6. "Sharl' Bodler," 71.

7. On Bely's reception of Nietzsche, see Virginia Bennett, "Esthetic Theories from *The Birth of Tragedy* in Andrei Bely's Critical Articles, 1904–1908," in Rosenthal, *Nietzsche in Russia*, 161–79; and Clowes, "Belyi and the Crucified Dionysus," in *The Revolution of Moral Consciousness*, 152–72.

8. *Arabeski*, 247.

9. *Nachalo veka*, Prilozhenie, 536.

10. Ibid., 128.

11. Ibid., 535.

12. *Simvolizm*, 216.

13. "Sharl' Bodler," 76.

14. Ibid., 77.

15. Ibid., 76.

16. See on this Steven Cassedy, "Bely the Thinker," in Malmstad, *Andrey Bely*, 313–35.

17. *Vesy*, no. 7 (1908), 77.

18. See Elsworth, "Andrei Bely's Theory of Symbolism," 332–33.

19. "Nekotorye techeniia v sovremennoi russkoi poezii," *Apollon*, no. 1 (1913). See Jane G. Harris, "Acmeism," in Terras, *Handbook of Russian Literature*, 6.

20. Mandel'shtam, *Sochineniia*, 2:182–83.

21. For a survey of Mandelstam's opinion of Baudelaire, see Dutli, *Ossip Mandelstam*, 98–102.

22. *Sochineniia*, 2:231.

23. Ibid., 195.

24. Ibid., 170.

25. See Blok, *Zapisnye knizhki*, 471.

26. I. F. Martynov established a bibliography of Gumilyov's translations for "Vsemirnaia literatura," based on the publisher's record book of honoraria (see "Gumilevskie chteniia," vyp. 2, 87–91). According to this list, Gumilyov translated the following poems by Baudelaire: "Bénédiction," "Correspondances," "L'Ennemi," "Don Juan aux Enfers," "Le Vampire," "Le Chat ("Dans ma cervelle . . .)," "Le Chat (Viens, mon beau chat . . .)," "Invitation au voyage," "Le Revenant," "Spleen [IV]," "Horreur sympathique," "Madrigal triste," "Les Plaintes d'un Icare," "Une Martyre," "Abel et Caïn," "La Mort des amants."

Four manuscripts were preserved in various archives (RGALI, IRLI, Russian State Library) and have been published over the last decade. The translation of "La Mort des amants" appeared first in "Gumilevskie chteniia," vyp. 1; "Une Martyre" ibid., vyp. 2; "Le Revenant," together with Gumilyov's essay on Baudelaire, in *Vestnik russkogo khristianskogo dvizheniia*, no. 144 (1985); and "Abel et Caïn" in Gumilev, *Stikhotvoreniia i poemy*.

27. Gumilev, "Poeziia Bodlera," 158.

28. Ibid., 155. Baudelaire himself, in "La Fanfarlo," described his alter ego Samuel Cramer as "the contradictory product of a pale German and a dark Chilean" (Oeuvres complètes, 1: 553).

29. "Poeziia Bodlera," 156.

30. "Ce livre, essentiellement inutile et absolument innocent, n'a pas été fait dans un autre but que de me divertir et d'exercer mon goût passionné de l'obstacle." *Oeuvres complètes*, 1:181.

31. See ibid., 183: "La phrase poétique peut imiter (et par là elle touche à l'art musical et à la science mathématique) la ligne horizontale, la ligne droite ascendante, la ligne droite descendante . . . elle peut suivre la spirale, décrire la parabole, ou le zigzag."

32. "Poeziia Bodlera," 158.

33. Ibid., 157.

34. *Oeuvres complètes*, 2:432

35. See chapter 2.

36. Quoted from *Vestnik russkogo khristianskogo dvizheniia,* no. 144 (1985), 161.

37. Gumilev, *Sobranie sochinenii,* 4:190–96.

38. "Avtobiograficheskaia spravka," in *Kritika o tvorchestve Igoria Severianina.*

39. *Oeuvres complètes,* 2:724.

40. "*Ia zakleimen, kak nekogda Bodler.*" Gumilyov quotes this line disapprovingly in his review of Severyanin's poetry, published 1911 in *Apollon.* See Gumilev, *Pis'ma o russkoi poezii,* 118.

41. I am indebted to Irina Reyfman for this suggestion.

42. Quoted from Severianin, *Stikhotvoreniia i poemy,* 184.

43. See the poem "Na nebesakh goriat panikadila . . ." (1895), quoted in Sokolov, *Russkaia poeziia,* 250.

44. "Burlyuk made me a poet. He read the French and the Germans to me." "Ia sam," Maiakovskii, *Izbrannye sochineniia,* 1:44.

45. Ibid., 328.

46. For a discussion of Baudelaire's influence on Mayakovsky, see Khardzhiev and Trenin, "Poetika rannego Maiakovskogo," in *Poetichsekaia kul'tura Maiakovskogo,* 50–72, especially 61–62. For a comparison of Baudelaire and Mayakovsky, see also Potter, *Finding a City to Live in.*

47. See J.-C. Lanne, "Le futurisme russe," in Etkind, *Histoire de la littérature russe,* 584.

48. Livshits, "Avtobiografiia" (1928), in *Polutoraglazyi strelets,* 548. The text referred to is "L'Etranger," which, together with four other prose poems, was published in *Zhivopisnoe obozrenie,* no. 18 (1894) in the translation of O. Vilova.

49. *Polutoraglazyi strelets,* 583.

50. Ibid., 201.

51. See Lausberg, *Handbuch der literarischen Rhetorik,* 536–40.

52. *Polutoragalzyi strelets,* 68.

53. For a more detailed discussion of this translation, see Etkind, "Master poeticheskoi kompozitsii, 206–9.

CONCLUSION: (MIS)READING
"BAUDELAIREANNESS"

1. Peyre, "Remarques sur le peu d'influence de Baudelaire," 430.

2. Bloom, "Introduction," *Charles Baudelaire. Modern Critical Views,* 3.

3. Donchin, *Influence,* 163.

4. "Alexandre Blok," in Etkind, *Histoire de la littérature russe,* 145.

5. A. A. Kublitskaya-Piottukh, Blok's mother, published her translation of five poems by Baudelaire in *Vestnik inostrannoi literatury* ("Chant d'automne," no. 12, 1894; "Le Revenant," "Harmonie du soir," no. 4, 1895; "De profundis, no. 12, 1895; "Le Portrait," no.

8, 1896). Blok's grandmother, E. G. Beketova, translated two poems by Baudelaire included in tales by Maupassant. See Mopasan, *Sobranie sochinenii* (St. Petersburg, 1894), 3:71 ("Les Chats"); 4:14 ("Correspondances").

6. See Beketova, *Al. Blok i ego mat'*, 132–33.

7. "Pamiati Bodlera," quoted ibid., 132.

8. "Iz Bodlera," *Sobranie sochinenii*, 1:554.

9. April 10, 1909. *Pis'ma k rodnym*, 1:225.

10. *Sobranie sochinenii*, 5:537.

11. Donchin, *Influence*, 29.

12. A good survey of the "Pushkin myth" can be found in Catherine Theimer Nepomnyashchy's introduction to Tertz, *Strolls with Pushkin*, 26–41.

13. Belyi, *Nachalo veka*, 47.

14. Kataev, "Mon Baudelaire," 205.

BIBLIOGRAPHY

For a complete bibliography of Russian Baudelaire translations and Russian criticism of Baudelaire in chronological order, see my Ph.D. thesis "Metamorphoses of Modernity: Russian Readings of Baudelaire," Columbia University, 1992, 278–301. The entries under Bodler, Sharl', are Russian editions of Baudelaire's works.

Aggeler, William F. *Baudelaire Judged by Spanish Critics 1857–1957.* Athens: University of Georgia Press, 1971.

Aigi, Gennadii. *Zdes'. Izbrannye stikhotvoreniia 1954–1988* (Here. Selected poems). Moscow: Sovremennik, 1991.

Aikhenval'd, Iulii. *Etiudy o zapadnykh pisateliakh* (Studies on Western writers). Moscow: Nauchnoe slovo, 1910.

Aizenshtok, I. "Frantsuzskie pisateli v otsenkakh tsarskoi tsenzury" (French writers evaluated by tsarist censorship). *Literaturnoe nasledstvo 33–34.* Moscow: Izd-vo AN SSSR, 1939, 769–858.

Aleksandrov, V. [Keller, V. B.] "Sharl' Bodler" (Charles Baudelaire). *Literaturnoe obozrenie,* no. 6 (1941), 71–74.

Andr-ich [Solov'ev, Evgenii]. "Dekadenty" (Decadents). *Nauchnoe obozrenie,* no. 8 (1901), 76–99.

Anichkov, Evgenii. "Bodler i Edgar Po" (Baudelaire and Edgar Poe). *Sovremennyi mir,* no. 2, vyp. 1 (1909), 75–98. Republished in *Predtechi i sovremenniki. I. Na Zapade.* St. Petersburg: Osvobozhdenie, 1910, 213–71.

Annenskii, I. F. "Chto takoe poeziia?" (What is poetry?). *Apollon,* no. 6 (1911), 51–57.

———. *Izbrannye proizvedeniia* (Selected works). Leningrad: Khudozhestvennaia literatura, 1988.

———. *Lirika* (Lyric poetry). Sost., vstup. stat'ia i primech. A. V. Fedorova. Leningrad: Sovetskii pisatel', 1959.

Auerbach, Erich. "Baudelaires Fleurs du Mal und das Erhabene" (Baudelaire's *Fleurs du Mal* and the sublime). *Gesammelte Aufsätze zur Romanischen Philologie.* Bern-Munich: Francke Verlag, 1967, 275–90.

Austin, L. J. *L'univers poétique de Baudelaire, symbolisme et symbolique* (The poetic universe of Baudelaire). Paris: Mercure de France, 1965.

Baer, Joachim T. *Arthur Schopenhauer und die russische Literatur des späten 19. und frühen 20. Jahrhunderts* (Arthur Schopenhauer and Russian literature of the late 19th and early 20th centuries). Munich: Otto Sagner, 1980.

Balashov, N. I. "Legenda i pravda o Bodlere" (Legend and truth about Baudelaire). In Bodler, *Tsvety Zla* (Moscow: Nauka, 1970), 233–87. Republished in German as "Legende und Wahrheit über Baudelaire." *Beiträge zur romanischen Philologie*, Heft 2 (1976), 217–36.

Bal'mont, K. D. *Gornye vershiny. Sbornik statei* (Mountain peaks. Collected essays). Moscow: Grif, 1904.

———. *Izbrannoe. Stikhotvoreniia, perevody, stat'i* (Selections. Poems, translations, essays). Moscow: Khudozhestvennaia literatura, 1983.

———. *Iz chuzhezemnykh poetov* (From foreign poets). St. Petersburg: Prosveshchenie, 1909.

———. *Polnoe sobranie stikhotvorenii* (Complete poetry). 10 vols. Moscow: Skorpion, 1908–13.

Bandy, W. T. *Baudelaire Judged by his Contemporaries (1845–1867)*. New York: Columbia University, 1933.

Bandy, W. T., and Claude Pichois. *Baudelaire devant ses contemporains* (Baudelaire before his contemporaries). Monaco: Editions du Rocher, 1957.

Banjanin, Milica E. "The City Poetry of Baudelaire and Blok." Ph.D. thesis, Washington University, St. Louis, Missouri, 1970.

Bartlett, R. A. "Wagner and Russia: A Study of the Influence of the Music of Richard Wagner on the Artistic and Cultural Life of Russia and the Soviet Union 1841–1941." Ph.D. thesis, University of Oxford, 1990.

Batiushkov, F. D. "Bodler i ego russkii perevodchik" (Baudelaire and his Russian translator). *Mir Bozhii*, no. 8 (1901), 11–19.

———. "Eshche neskol'ko slov o Bodlere i ego russkom perevodchike (otvet g-nu P. Ia.)" (Some more words on Baudelaire and his Russian translator [an answer to Mr. P. Ya.]). *Mir Bozhii*, no. 10 (1901), 8–15.

Baudelaire, Charles. *Edgar Allan Poe, sa vie et ses ouvrages*. Edited by W. T. Bandy. Toronto-Buffalo: University of Toronto Press, 1973.

———. *Oeuvres complètes* (Complete works). Texte établi, présenté et annoté par Claude Pichois. 2 vols. Paris: Gallimard, 1975.

Bodler, Sharl'. *Edgar Po, zhizn' i tvorchestvo* (Edgar Poe, his life and work). Per. L'va Kogana. Odessa: Tip. N. Gal'perina, 1910.

———. *Iskaniia raia* (Les Paradis artificiels). Per. V. Likhtenshtadt. Moscow: Zapad, 1908.

———. *Lirika*. Perevody s frantsuzskogo. Sost. E. Etkind. Predislovie P. Antokol'skogo. Moscow: Khudozhestvennaia literatura, 1966.

———. *Malen'kie poemy v proze* (Prose poems). Perevod A. Aleksandrovicha. Moscow: F. I. Bulgakov, 1902.

————. *Malen'kie poemy v proze*. Perevod M. Volkova. St. Petersburg: Vseob-shchaia biblioteka, 1909 (second edition: 1911).

————. *Moe obnazhennoe serdtse* (Mon Coeur mis à nu). Per. Elis [sic]. Moscow: Diletant, 1907.

————. *Ob iskusstve* (Art criticism). Sost. Iu. I. Stefanova i A. I. Chegodaeva. Vstup. stat'ia V. V. Levika. Posleslovie V. A. Mil'chinoi. Moscow: Iskusstvo, 1986.

————. *Poezii* [Ukrainian translation]. Kiev: Dnipro, 1989.

————. *Stikhotvoreniia Bodlera*. Moscow: Izdanie Petrovskoi biblioteki, 1895 [53 poems translated by P. F. Yakubovich. Foreword by K. D. Balmont].

————. *Stikhotvoreniia v proze* (Prose poems). Perevod pod redaktsiei L. Gure-vicha i S. Parnoka. St. Petersburg: Posev, 1909.

————. *Stikhotvoreniia v proze*. Perevod Ellisa. Moscow: Musaget, 1910.

————. *Tsvety Zla* (Les Fleurs du Mal). Polnyi perevod s frantsuzskogo A. A. Panova. 2 vols. St. Petersburg: F. I. Bulgakov, 1907.

————. *Tsvety Zla*. Perevod Arseniia Al'vinga. St. Petersburg: Gelios, 1908.

————. *Tsvety Zla*. Perevod Ellisa. So vstupitel'noi stat'ei Teofilia Got'e i pre-disloviem Valeriia Briusova. Moscow: Zaratustra, 1908.

————. *Tsvety Zla*. Perevod P. Iakubovicha-Mel'shina. St. Petersburg: Obshch-estvennaia pol'za, 1909.

————. *Tsvety Zla*. *Izbrannye stikhotvoreniia v perevodakh russkikh poetov*. St. Pe-tersburg: Vseobshchaia biblioteka, 1912.

————. *Tsvety Zla*. Perevod Adriana Lamble. Paris: Imprimerie de Navarre, 1929.

————. *Tsvety Zla*. Po avtorskomu proektu tret'ego izdaniia. Sost. I. I. Balashov i I. S. Postupal'skii. Moscow: Nauka, 1970 (Akademiia nauk SSSR: Literaturnye pamiatniki).

————. *Tsvety Zla*. Rostov-na-Donu: Rostovskoe knizhnoe izdatel'stvo, 1991.

Bazhenov, N. N. *Psikhiatricheskie besedy na literaturnye i obshchestvennye temy* (Psychiatric conversations on literary and social themes). Moscow: A. I. Ma-montov, 1903.

Beamish-Thiriet, F. M. "The Myth of Woman in Baudelaire and Blok." Ph.D. thesis, University of Washington, 1973.

Beketova, M. A. *Al[eksandr] Blok i ego mat'. Vospominaniia i zametki* (Alexander Blok and his mother. Memories and notes). Leningrad-Moscow: Izd-vo "Petro-grad," 1925.

Belkina, Mariia. *Skreshchenie sudeb. Popytka Tsvetaevoi dvukh poslednikh let ee zhizni. Popytka vremeni, liudei, obstoiatel'stv* (The intersection of fates. Tsvetaeva in the last two years of her life. Times, people, circumstances). Izd.-vtoroe, dopoln. Moscow: Blagovest', Rudomino, 1992.

Belyi, Andrei. *Arabeski* (Arabesques). Moscow: Musaget, 1911. Repr. Munich: Wil-helm Fink Verlag, 1969.

————. *Chetyre simfonii* (Four symphonies). Munich: Wilhelm Fink Verlag, 1971.

————. *Na rubezhe dvukh stoletii. Nachalo veka. Mezhdu dvukh revoliutsii* (At the turn of the century. The beginning of the century. Between two revolutions [first publ. 1930–34]). Podg. teksta i kommentarii A. V. Lavrova. Moscow: Khudozhestvennaia literatura, 1989–90.

————. *Petersburg.* Translated, annotated, and introduced by R. A. Maguire and J. E. Malmstad. Bloomington: Indiana University Press, 1978.

————. "Sharl' Bodler" (Charles Baudelaire). *Vesy,* no. 6 (1909), 71–80. Republished in *Arabeski,* 248–55.

————. *Simvolizm* (Symbolism). Moscow: Musaget, 1910. Repr. Munich: Wilhelm Fink Verlag, 1969.

Benjamin, Walter. *Charles Baudelaire: Ein Lyriker im Zeitalter des Hochkapitalismus. Zwei Fragmente.* Frankfurt a. M.: Suhrkamp Verlag, 1969. Available in English as *Charles Baudelaire, a Lyric Poet in the Era of High Capitalism.* London: Verso, 1983.

————. "Das Passagen-Werk" (The arcades project). *Gesammelte Schriften,* vol V. Frankfurt a. M.: Suhrkamp Verlag, 1982.

Bibikov, V. I. *Tri portreta. Stendal'-Flober-Bodler* (Three portraits. Stendhal, Flaubert, Baudelaire). St. Petersburg: Tip. L. Bermana i G. Rabinovicha, 1890.

Blok, A. A. *Pis'ma Aleksandra Bloka k rodnym* (Alexander Blok's letters to his relatives). 2 vols. Leningrad: Academia, 1927.

————. *Sobranie sochinenii* (Collected works). 8 vols. Moscow: Gos. izd-vo khudozh. lit-ry, 1960–63.

————. *Zapisnye knizhki 1901–1920* (Notebooks). Moscow: Khudozhestvennaia literatura, 1965.

Blok, A. A., and A. Belyi. *Perepiska* (Correspondence). Moscow: Izd-vo Gos. literaturnogo muzeia, 1940.

Bloom, Harold, ed. *Charles Baudelaire. Modern Critical Views.* New York: Chelsea House Publishers, 1987.

————. *The Anxiety of Influence: A Theory of Poetry.* New York: Oxford University Press, 1973.

Briusov, V. Ia. *Neizdannye stikhotvoreniia* (Unpublished poems). Moscow: Khudozhestvennaia literatura, 1935.

————. *Polnoe sobranie sochinenii i perevodov* (Complete works and translations). Vols. 1–4, 12–13, 15, 21 [of 25 projected]. St. Petersburg: Sirin, 1913–14.

————. *Russkie simvolisty* (Russian symbolists). Vyp. 3. Moscow: V. A. Maslov, 1895.

————. *Sobranie sochinenii.* (Collected works). 7 vols. Moscow: Khudozhestvennaia literatura, 1973–75.

————. "Novyi perevod Bodlera" [review of Ellis's Immorteli]. *Vesy,* no. 4 (1904), 42–48.

Brunel, Pierre, Claude Pichois, and A.-M Rousseau. *Qu'est-ce que la littérature comparée?* (What is comparative literature?). Paris: Armand Colin, 1983.

Burzhe, Pol' [Bourget, Paul]. *Ocherki sovremennoi psikhologii* (Sketches of modern psychology). Per. E. K. Vatsona. St. Petersburg: Zhurnal "Panteon literatury," 1888.

Calinescu, Matei. *Five Faces of Modernity. Modernism, Avant-Garde, Decadence, Kitsch, Postmodernism.* Durham, N. C.: Duke University Press, 1987.

Carter, A. E. *Baudelaire et la critique française 1868–1917* (Baudelaire and French criticism). Columbia: University of South Carolina Press, 1963.

Cassagne, Albert. *Versification et métrique de Ch. Baudelaire* (Versification and metrics of Ch. Baudelaire). Paris: Hachette, 1906.

Cerisy, Robert de. "Polemika po povodu statui Sharlia Bodlera" (Polemics on the occasion of Baudelaire's statue). *Severnyi vestnik,* no. 11 (1892), 77–80.

Chernov, Viktor. "Mezhdu Bodlerom i Verkharnom (Modernizm v russkoi poezii)" (Between Baudelaire and Verhaeren [Modernism in Russian poetry]). *Vestnik Evropy,* no. 12 (1910), 107–35.

Clements, Patricia. *Baudelaire and the English Tradition.* Princeton: Princeton University Press, 1985.

Clowes, Edith W. *The Revolution of Moral Consciousness. Nietzsche in Russian Literature, 1890–1914.* De Kalb: Northern Illinois University Press, 1988.

Compagnon, Antoine. *Les cinq paradoxes de la modernité* (The five paradoxes of modernity). Paris: Editions du Seuil, 1990.

Conrad, Barbara. *I. F. Annenskijs poetische Reflectionen* (I. F. Annenskii's poetic reflections). Munich: Otto Sagner, 1976.

Davidson, Pamela. *The Poetic Imagination of Vyacheslav Ivanov. A Russian Symbolist's Perception of Dante.* Cambridge–New York: Cambridge University Press, 1989.

Degen, Evgenii. "Noveishaia frantsuzskaia lirika. I. Reaktsiia protiv Romantizma. Bodeler" (The latest French poetry. I. The reaction against romanticism. Baudelaire). *Novoe slovo,* no. 9 (1896), 90–117.

De Jonge, Alex. *Dostoevsky and the Age of Intensity.* New York: St. Martin's Press, 1975.

De Man, Paul. *Blindness and Insight: Essays in the Rhetoric of Contemporary Criticism.* 2nd ed. Minneapolis: University of Minnesota Press, 1983.

D-ev [Boborykin, P. D.]. "Priznaniia literaturnykh ottsov" (Confessions of literary fathers). *Vestnik Evropy,* no. 2 (1875), 519–58.

Dolgopolov, L. K., ed. *Poety 1880–1890-kh godov* (Poets of the 1888s and 1890s). Leningrad: Sovetskii pisatel', 1972.

Donchin, Georgette. *The Influence of French Symbolism on Russian Poetry.* The Hague: Mouton, 1958.

Du Bos, Charles. *Approximations.* Paris: Fayard, 1965.

Dutli, Ralph. *Ossip Mandelstam: "Als riefe man mich bei meinem Namen."* (Ossip Mandelstam: "As if I were called by my name.") Zurich: Ammann Verlag, 1985.

Dvinianinov, B. N. *Mech i lira. Ocherk zhizni i tvorchestva P. F. Iakubovicha* (Sword and lyre. A sketch of the life and work of P. F. Yakubovich). Moscow: Nauka, 1969.

Eliot, T. S. *Selected Essays.* New York: Harcourt, Brace, 1950.

Ellis [Kobylinskii, L. L.]. *Alexander Puschkin. Der religiöse Genius Russlands* (Alexander Pushkin. The religious genius of Russia). Olten: O. Walter Verlag, 1948.

———. *Argo. Dve knigi stikhov i poema* (Argo. Two books of poetry and a *poema*). Moscow: Musaget, 1914.

———. *Immorteli. Vyp.1-yi: Sharl' Bodler* (Immortelles. First installment: Charles Baudelaire). Moscow: Tip. Mosk. gor. Arnol'do-Tret'iakovsk. uchil. glukhone-mykh, 1904.

———. *Russkie simvolisty. Konstantin Bal'mont, Valerii Briusov, Andrei Belyi* (Russian symbolists). Moscow: Musaget, 1910.

———. *Stigmata. Kniga stikhov* (Stigmata. A book of poems). Moscow: Musaget, 1911.

———. *Vigilemus! Traktat* (Let's be vigilant! A treatise). Moscow: Musaget, 1914.

———. *W. A. Joukowski. Seine Persönlichkeit, sein Leben und sein Werk* (V. A. Zhukovsky. His personality, life and work). Paderborn: F. Schöningh Verlag, 1933.

Elsworth, John. "Andrei Bely's Theory of Symbolism." *Forum for Modern Language Studies* 11, no. 4 (1975), 305–33.

Emmanuel, Pierre. *Baudelaire. The Paradox of Redemptive Satanism.* Transl. Robert T. Cargo. University: University of Alabama Press, 1970.

Engel'gardt, A. N. "Smes'. Iz obshchestvennoi i literaturnoi khroniki Zapada" (Miscellany. From the social and literary chronicle of the West). *Vestnik inostrannoi literatury,* no. 11 (1892), 357–84.

Etkind, Efim. "Baudelaire en langue russe" (Baudelaire in Russian). *Europe* 456–57 (April–May 1967), 252–61.

———. "Master poeticheskoi kompozitsii (opyt tvorcheskogo portreta Benedikta Livshitsa)" (A master of poetic composition [a creative portrait of Benedikt Livshits]). *Masterstvo perevoda.* Vol. 8 (1971), 187–230.

———, ed. *Frantsuzskie stikhi v perevode russkikh poetov XIX-XX vv.* (French poems translated by Russian poets of the 19th and 20th centuries). Moscow: Progress, 1969. 2nd ed. 1973.

———, ed. *Mastera russkogo stikhotvornogo perevoda* (Masters of Russian verse translation). 2 vols. Leningrad: Sovetskii pisatel', 1968

———, et al., eds. *Histoire de la littérature russe. Le XXe siècle: L'Age d'argent* (History of Russian literature. 20th century: The Silver Age). Paris: Fayard, 1987.

Fedotov, O. I., ed. *Sonet serebrennogo veka* (The sonnet of the Silver Age). Moscow: Pravda, 1990.

France, Peter. *Poets of Modern Russia.* Cambridge–New York: Cambridge University Press, 1982.

Friche, V. F. "Bodler" (Baudelaire). *Entsiklopedicheskii slovar' "Granat."* St. Petersburg, 1911, 6:127–28. Repr. Tokio: Nauka Reprint, 1982.

———. *Poeziia koshmarov i uzhasa. Neskol'ko glav iz istorii literatury i iskusstva na zapade* (The poetry of nightmares and horror. Some chapters from the history of literature and art in the West). Moscow: Sfinks, 1912.

Friedrich, Hugo. *Die Struktur der modernen Lyrik.* Revised edition. Hamburg: Rowohlt Verlag, 1985. Available in English as *The Structure of Modern Poetry: From the Mid-Nineteenth to the Mid-Twentieth Century.* Evanston, Ill.: Northwestern University Press, 1974.

Füglister, Robert. "Baudelaire et le thème des bohémiens" (Baudelaire and the gypsy theme). *Etudes Baudelairiennes II.* Neuchâtel: A la Baconnière, 1971, 99–143.

Gautier, Théophile. "Charles Baudelaire" (1868). In *Oeuvres complètes de Ch. Baudelaire,* Paris: Alphonse Lemerre, n. d., 1–90. Russian translation: Got'e, *Sharl' Bodler. Biografiia-kharakteristika.* Per. s frants. V. Izrastsova. St. Petersburg: Akts. obshch. tipogr. dela, 1910 (second edition 1915).

Gofman, M. L., ed. *Kniga o russkikh poetakh poslednego desiatiletiia; ocherki, stikhotvoreniia, avtografy* (A book of Russian poets of the last decade; sketches, poems, autographs). St. Petersburg: M. O. Vol'f, 1909.

Gor'kii, Maksim. *Sobranie sochinenii* (Collected works). 30 vols. Moscow: Gos. izd-vo khudozh. lit-ry, 1949–56.

Grechishkin, S., and A. Lavrov. "Ellis—Poet-simvolist, teoretik i kritik (1900–1910-e gg.)" (Ellis, a symbolist poet, theoretician and critic). *Gertsenovskie chteniia,* vol. 25, Literaturoveden'e. Leningrad, 1972, 59–62.

Grossman, Joan Delaney. *Edgar Allan Poe in Russia. A Study in Legend and Literary Influence.* Würzburg: Jal-Verlag, 1973.

———. *Valery Bryusov and the Riddle of Russian Decadence.* Berkeley: University of California Press, 1985.

Gumilev, N. S. "Poeziia Bodlera" (Baudelaire's poetry [written 1919–1921]). *Vestnik russkogo khristianskogo dvizheniia,* no. 144 (1985), 154–59.

———. *Pis'ma o russkoi poezii* (Letters about Russian poetry). Moscow: Sovremennik, 1990.

———. *Sobranie sochinenii* (Collected works). 4 vols. Washington, D. C.: Viktor Kamkin, 1962–68.

Haldas, Georges. "Tolstoï juge de Baudelaire. A propos d'une différence" (Tolstoy as a judge of Baudelaire. Concerning a difference). *Europe* 456–57 (April–May 1967), 246–52.

Hansen-Löve, Aage. *Der russische Symbolismus. System und Entfaltung der poeti-schen Motive. I. Band: Diabolischer Symbolismus* (Russian Symbolism. System and development of poetic motifs. Vol. 1: Diabolic symbolism). Vienna: Verlag der Österreichischen Akademie der Wissenschaften, 1989.

Iakubovich, P. F. "Bodler, ego zhizn' i poeziia" (Baudelaire, his life and poetry). *Russkoe bogatstvo*, no. 4 (1896), 142–73. Republished in *Stikhotvoreniia*, t. II, 237–74; izd. 2-e, 1902, 245–85; izd. 3-e, 1906, 271–308; Sh. Bodler, *Tsvety Zla*. Per I. Iakubovicha, 9–58.

———. [L. Mel'shin–P. F. Grinevich]. *Ocherki russkoi poezii* (Sketches of Russian poetry). St. Petersburg: Russkoe bogatstvo, 1904.

———. "Pis'ma K. D. Batiushkovu" (Letters to K. D. Batyushkov). Publ. A. B. Mu-ratova. *Ezhegodnik rukopisnogo otdela Pushkinskogo Doma na 1972 g.* Leningrad: Nauka, 1974, 101–11.

———. [anonymous]. "Sharl' Bodeler" (Charles Baudelaire). *Severnyi vestnik*, no. 12 (1890), 201–10.

———. [Matvei Ramshev]. *Stikhotvoreniia* (Poems). St. Petersburg: Tip. I. N. Sko-rokhodova, 1887.

———. *Stikhotvoreniia. Tom vtoroi (1898–1901).* St. Petersburg: Izdanie redaktsii zhurnala Russkoe bogatstvo, 1901.

———. *Stikhotvoreniia. Tom vtoroi (1898–1902).* 2-e izdanie. St. Petersburg: Russkoe bogatstvo, 1902.

———. *Stikhotvoreniia.* Vstup. stat'ia, podgotovka teksta i primech. B. N. Dvinian-inova. Leningrad: Sovetskii pisatel', 1960.

———. "V poiskakh sokrovennogo smysla (otvet F. D. Batiushkovu)" (Searching for a hidden meaning [an answer to F. D. Batyushkov]). *Russkoe bogatstvo*, no. 8 (1901), 77–87.

———. "Zametki chitatelia" (Notes of a reader). *Russkoe bogatstvo*, no. 4 (1900), 140–60. Republished in *Ocherki russkoi poezii*, 391–404.

Iampol'skii, I. G., ed. *Poety "Iskry."* (The poets of *Iskra*). 2 vols. Leningrad: Sovetskii pisatel', 1955.

Il'inskaia, O. "Bodler" (Baudelaire). *Kratkaia literaturnaia entsiklopediia.* Moscow, 1962, 1:662–63.

———. "Bodler." *Bol'shaia sovetskaia entsiklopediia*, 3-e izd. Moscow, 1970, 3:454. Republished in English as "Baudelaire." *Great Soviet Encyclopedia*, New York and London: Macmillan, 3:78.

Ivanov, V. V. *Po zvezdam. Stat'i i aforizmy* (By the stars. Essays and aphorisms). St. Petersburg: Izd-vo "Ory," 1909. Repr. Letchworth: Bradda Books, 1971.

———. *Stikhotvoreniia i poemy* (Poems). 3-e izd. Leningrad: Sovetskii pisatel', 1978.

———. *Sobranie sochinenii* (Collected works). 4 vols. Brussels: Foyer Oriental Chrétien, 1971–87.

Ivask, Iurii. "Bodler i Dostoevskii" (Baudelaire and Dostoevsky), *Novyi zhurnal* 60 (1960), 138–52.

Jackson, Robert Louis, and Lowry Nelson, Jr., eds. *Vyacheslav Ivanov: Poet, Critic and Philosopher.* New Haven, Conn.: Yale Center for International and Area Studies, 1986.

Jameson, Fredric. "Baudelaire as Modernist and Postmodernist: The Dissolution of the Referent and the Artificial 'Sublime.'" In Chaviva Hosek and Patricia Parker, eds. *Lyric Poetry Beyond New Criticism.* Ithaca and London: Cornell University Press, 1985, 247–63.

Jauß, Hans Robert. *Ästhetische Erfahrung und literarische Hermeneutik* (Aesthetic experience and literary hermeneutics). Frankfurt a. M.: Suhrkamp Verlag, 1982.

Johnson, Barbara. *Défigurations du langage poétique. La seconde révolution baudelairienne* (Defigurations of poetic language. The second Baudelairean revolution). Paris: Flammarion, 1979.

Kachorovskaia, A. S. *Zametki o modernizme. Sharl' Bodler* (Notes on modernism. Charles Baudelaire). Tomsk: Tipo-lit. Sib. t-va pech. dela, 1910.

Karlinsky, Simon. *Marina Tsvetaeva. The Woman, Her World and Her Poetry.* Cambridge-New York: Cambridge University Press, 1986.

Kataev, Valentin. "Mon Baudelaire" (My Baudelaire). *Journées Baudelaire. Actes du colloque Namur-Bruxelles 1967.* Brussels: Académie royale de langue et littérature française, 1968, 203–7. Republished in Russian as "Moi Bodler," *Sobranie sochinenii v 9-i tt..* Moscow: Khudozhestvennaia literatura, 1968–72, 8:459–62.

Keck, Thomas. *Der deutsche "Baudelaire"* (The German "Baudelaire"). Heidelberg: Carl Winter Verlag, 1991.

Khardziev, N. I., and V Trenin. *Poeticheskaia kul'tura Maiakovskogo* (The poetic culture of Mayakovsky). Moscow: Iskusstvo, 1970.

Kogan, P. S. "Sharl' Bodler" (Charles Baudelaire). *Russkaia mysl'*, no. 10 (1904), 114–34. Republished in *Ocherki po istorii zapadno-evropeiskoi literatury,* t. II. Moscow: M. S. Skirmunt, 1905.

———. "Bodler" (Baudelaire). *Bol'shaia sovetskaia entsiklopediia,* Moscow, 1927, 6:637–38.

Kopp, Robert, and Claude Pichois. *Les Années Baudelaire* (The Baudelaire years). Etudes Baudelairiennes 1. Neuchâtel: A la Baconnière, 1969.

Koppen, Erwin. *Dekadenter Wagnerismus. Studien zur europäischen Literatur des Fin de siècle* (Decadent Wagnerism. Studies on European literature of the fin de siècle). Berlin–New York: W. de Gruyter Verlag, 1973.

Krasnov, P. "Pervye dekadenty [First decadents]. Charles Baudelaire. *Les Fleurs du Mal.*–Paul Verlaine. *Choix de poésies.*" *Knizhki "Nedeli,"* no. 8 (1894), 182–99.

Lausberg, Heinrich. *Handbuch der literarischen Rhetorik; eine Grundlegung der Literaturwissenschaft* (Handbook of literary rhetoric, a foundation of literary criticism). Munich: M. Hueber Verlag, 1960.

Lavrov, A. V. "Mifotvorchestvo 'argonavtov'" (The myth-building of the "Argonauts"). *Mif-Folklor-Literatura*, Leningrad: Nauka, 1978, 137–70.

Levina, N. "Stikhotvoreniia v proze I. S. Turgeneva i proizvedeniia etogo zhanra Aloiziia Bertrana i Sharlia Bodlera" (Turgenev's prose poems and the works of this genre by Aloysius Bertrand and Charles Baudelaire). *Gertsenovskie chteniia*, vol. 22, Filologicheskie nauki. Leningrad, 1969, 117–19.

Link, Hannelore. *Rezeptionsforschung. Eine Einführung in Methoden und Probleme* (Reception research. An introduction to methods and problems). Stuttgart: Kohlhammer, 1976.

Literaturnoe nasledstvo (Literary heritage). Edited by A. N. Dubovikov and N. A. Trifonov et al. Vol. 85. Valerii Briusov. Moscow: Nauka, 1976.

Livshits, Benedikt. *Polutoraglazyi strelets. Stikhotvoreniia, perevody, vospominaniia* (The One-and-a-half-eyed Archer. Poems, translations, memoirs). Leningrad: Sovetskii pisatel', 1989.

Lunacharskii, A. N. "Bodler" (Baudelaire). *Literaturnaia entsiklopediia*, Moscow, 1929, 1:547–51.

Maiakovskii, V. V. *Izbrannye sochineniia* (Selected works). 2 vols. Moscow: Khudozhestvennaia literatura, 1981.

Malmstad, John E., ed. *Andrey Bely. Spirit of Symbolism*. Ithaca-London: Cornell University Press, 1987.

Mandel'shtam, Osip. *Sochineniia* (Works). 2 vols. Moscow: Khudozhestvennaia literatura, 1990.

Markov, Vladimir. *Kommentar zu den Dichtungen von K. D. Bal'mont* (Commentary to the poetry of K. D. Balmont). 2 vols. Cologne-Vienna: Böhlau Verlag, 1988–1992.

———. "K voprosu o granitsakh dekadansa v russkoi poezii (i o liricheskoi poeme)" (On the question of the boundaries of decadence in Russian literature [and on the lyrical *poema*]). In V. Terras, ed. *American Contributions to the Eight International Congress of Slavists*. Vol. 2: Literature. Columbus, Ohio: Slavica Publishers, 1978, 485–98.

Martynov, I. F., ed. "Gumilevskie chteniia" (Gumilyov lectures). Vyp. 1-yi. *Wiener Slavistischer Almanach*, no. 9 (1982), 377–492. Vyp. 2-oi. Ibid., Sonderband 15, 1984.

Merezhkovskii, D. S. *O prichinakh upadka i o novykh techeniiakh sovremennoi russkoi literatury* (On the causes of the decline and on the new trends of contemporary Russian literature). St. Petersburg: Tip. B. M. Vol'fa, 1893.

———. *Polnoe sobranie sochinenii* (Complete works). 24 vols. Moscow: Izd-vo M. O. Vol'f, 1911–14.

———. "Stikhotvoreniia v proze Sharlia Bodlera" (Charles Baudelaire's prose poems). *Iziashchnaia literatura*, no. 10 (1884), 141–42.

Meyer-Fraatz, A. "Die 'Schönheit' des Symbolismus: Baudelaires Sonett 'La Beauté' in russischer Übersetzung" (The "beauty" of symbolism: Baudelaire's sonnet 'La Beauté' in Russian translation). *Zeitschrift für Slawistik* 38, no. 4 (1993), 584–603.

Mikhailovskii, N. K. "Russkoe otrazhenie frantsuzskogo simvolizma" (A Russian reflection of French symbolism). *Russkoe bogatstvo*, no. 2 (1893), 45–68.

Miller-Trottmann, Paul. "French Criticism of Charles Baudelaire: Themes and Ideas (1918–1940)." Ph.D. thesis, University of Georgia, 1973.

Mints, Z. G., and G. B. Obatnin. "Simvolika zerkala v rannei poezii Viach. Ivanova (sborniki 'Kormchie zvezdy' i 'Prozrachnost')" (The symbolism of the mirror in the early poetry of Vyacheslav Ivanov). *Uchenye Zapiski Tartuskogo gosudarstvennogo universiteta*, vol. 831, Zerkalo: Semiotika zerkal'nosti. Trudy po znakovym sistemam, no. 22. Tartu, 1988, 59–65.

Mironov, G. M. "Iakubovich." *Kratkaia literaturnaia entsiklopediia*. Moscow, 1975, 8:1070–71

Mirsky, D. S. *A History of Russian Literature*. New York: Vintage Books, 1960.

Mogilianskii, M. *Kriticheskie nabroski* (Critical sketches). St. Petersburg: Tip. A. A. Porokhovshchikova, 1898 ("Poeziia Sh. Bodlera," 33–56).

Nadson, S. Ia. *Polnoe sobranie sochinenii* (Complete works). 2 vols. Petrograd: A. F. Marks, 1917.

Nol'man, M. L. *Sharl' Bodler. Sud'ba, estetika, stil'* (Charles Baudelaire. Fate, aesthetics, style). Moscow: Khudozhestvennaia literatura, 1979.

Nordau, Max. *Entartung*. 2nd edition. 2 vols. Berlin: C. Duncker, 1893. Russian translation: *Vyrozhdenie*. Per. s nem. R. I. Sementkovskogo. St. Petersburg: Tip. P. P. Soikina, 1894. Available in English as *Degeneration*. Lincoln: University of Nebraska Press, 1993.

Oblomievskii, D. D. *Frantsuzskii simvolizm* (French symbolism). Moscow: Nauka, 1973 (Chapter "Sharl' Bodler," 89–143).

Okreits, S. "O tom, kak N. Kurochkin perevodit iz Bodlera" (How N. Kurochkin translates Baudelaire). *Biblioteka*, no. 6 (1871), 165–66.

Oragvelidze, G. G. "Pervye russkie perevody iz Bodlera" (The first Russian translations from Baudelaire). *Sbornik nauchnykh trudov Tashkentskogo Universiteta* 512 (1975), 104–13.

———. "Russkie perevodchiki Bodlera 80-kh godov XIX veka" (Russian Baudelaire translators of the 1880s). *Sbornik nauchnykh trudov Tashkentskogo Universiteta* 545 (1977), 137–56.

Os'makov, N. V. *Poeziia revoliutsionnogo narodnichestva* (The poetry of revolutionary populism). Moscow: Izd-vo Akademii nauk SSSR, 1961.

Petrovskaia, N. I. "Iz 'Vospominanii'" (Memoirs). Publ. Iu. A. Krasovskogo. *Literaturnoe nasledstvo*. Edited by A. N. Dubovikov and N. A. Trifonov et al. Vol. 85: Valerii Briusov. Moscow: Nauka, 1976, 773–88.

Peyre, Henri. "Remarques sur le peu d'influence de Baudelaire" (Notes on Baudelaire's little influence). *Revue d'histoire littéraire de la France* 67 (1967), 424–36.

Plekhanov, G. V. "Evangelie ot dekadansa" (The gospel of decadence). *Sovremennyi mir*, no. 12 (1909), 167–202.

Poggioli, Renato. *The Poets of Russia 1890–1930*. Cambridge, Mass.: Harvard University Press, 1960.

Pommier, Jean. *La Mystique de Baudelaire* (The mysticism of Baudelaire). Paris: Les Belles Lettres, 1932. Repr. Geneva: Slatkine Reprints, 1967.

Potter, Daniel L. *Finding a City to Live in: Metaphor and Urban Subjectivity in Baudelaire and Mayakovsky*. Stanford, Calif.: Humanities Honors Program, Stanford University, 1986.

Praz, Mario. *The Romantic Agony*. Transl. Angus Davidson. London: Oxford University Press, 1933.

Protsenko, N. "Pushkin i Bodler" (Pushkin and Baudelaire). *Trudy Voronezhskogo Universiteta*, t. 14, vyp. 1 (1946), 137–56.

Rapoport, L. "Sharl' Bodler v russkikh perevodakh" (Charles Baudelaire in Russian translations). *Knizhnye novosti*, no. 12 (1936), 65–67.

Robinson, Douglas. *The Translator's Turn*. Baltimore-London: Johns Hopkins University Press, 1991.

Rosenthal, Bernice G. *D. S. Merezhkovsky and the Silver Age: The Development of a Revolutionary Mentality*. The Hague: Martinus Nijhoff, 1975.

———, ed. *Nietzsche in Russia*. Princeton: Princeton University Press, 1986.

Ruff, Marcel A. *Baudelaire. L'homme et l'oeuvre* (Baudelaire. The man and his work). Paris: Haitier, 1955.

———. *L'esprit du mal et l'esthétique baudelairienne* (The spirit of evil and the Baudelairean aesthetics). Paris: Armand Colin, 1955.

Russkii biograficheskii slovar' (Russian biographical dictionary). 25 vols. (St. Petersburg, 1908). New York: Kraus Reprint Corporation, 1962.

Ryan, Judith. "More Seductive than Phryne: Baudelaire, Gérôme, Rilke, and the Problem of Autonomous Art." *PMLA* 108, no. 5 (October 1993), 1128–41.

Sakell, V. P. "Baudelaire in Germany: The Critical Reception, 1900–1957," Ph.D. thesis, University of North Carolina at Chapel Hill, 1964.

Schaarschuh, F.-J. "Das Problem der Gattung 'Prosagedicht' in Turgenevs Стихотворения в прозе" (The problem of the genre "prose poem" in Turgenev's *Stikhotvoreniia v proze*). *Zeitschrift für Slawistik* 10, no. 4 (1965), 500–18.

Sear, Anri [Céard, Henri]. "Pis'ma iz Parizha. Poeziia i poety sovremennoi Frantsii" (Letters from Paris. Poetry and poets of contemporary France). *Slovo*, no. 5 (1879), 29–62. Republished in P. Iakubovich [Matvei Ramshev]. *Stikhotvoreniia*, 1887, ix-xxxii.

Setchkarev, Vsevolod. *Studies in the Life and Work of Innokentij Annenskij.* The Hague: Mouton, 1963.

[Severianin, Igor'.] *Kritika o tvorchestve Igoria Severianina* (Critical essays on Igor Severyanin's work). Moscow: Izd-vo V. V. Pashukanisa, 1916.

————. *Stikhotvoreniia i poemy 1918–1941* (Poems). Moscow: Sovremennik, 1990.

Shebnev, N. "K. Balmont okolo imeni A. I. Urusova" (K. Balmont about the name of A. I. Urusov). *Russkoe slovo,* no. 69 (March 11, 1903), 2.

Shtakhel', Karl' [Stachel, Karl]. "Noveishaia poeziia vo Frantsii, v Italii i v Anglii (pis'ma k redaktoru 'Otechestvennikh zapisok')" (The latest poetry in France, Italy, and England [letters to the editor of *Otechestvennye zapiski*]). Pis'mo pervoe (Parizh, 30-go dekabria 1855). *Otechestvennye zapiski,* no. 2 (1856), 1–26.

Sokolov, A. G., ed. *Russkaia poeziia kontsa XIX-nachalo XX veka* (Russian poetry of the end of the 19th and beginning of the 20th centuries). Moscow: Izdatel'stvo Moskovskogo Universiteta, 1979.

Solodub, Iu., and G. Khrapovitskaia. "Perevod 'Krasoty' Bodlera kak otrazhenie novogo etapa v tvorchestvom razvitii V. Briusova" (The translation of Baudelaire's "Beauté" as a reflection of a new phase in V. Bryusov's creative development). *Briusovskie chteniia 1983 g.* Erevan: Sovetakan grokh, 1985, 352–63.

Sovalina, V. S., ed. *Russkii sonet. XVIII-nachalo XX veka* (The Russian sonnet. 18th to early 20th centuries). Moscow: Moskovskii rabochii, 1983.

Starobinski, Jean. *Portrait de l'artiste en saltimbanque* (Portrait of the artist as a comedian). Geneva: Albert Skira, 1970.

Stirnberg, Hildegard. *Baudelaire im Urteil der Mit- und Nachwelt* (Baudelaire judged by his contemporaries and by posterity). Münster: H. Pöppinghaus, 1935.

Suleiman, S. R., and I. Crosman, eds. *The Reader in the Text. Essays on Audience and Interpretation.* Princeton: Princeton University Press, 1980.

Sychkov, V. "Iazychno-stilisticheskoe vyrazhenie kategorii vremeni v tvorchestve Sh. Bodlera" (The linguistic-stylistic expression of the category of time in the work of Ch. Baudelaire). Avtoreferat dissertatsii. Leningrad: LGU, 1977.

Terras, Victor. *A History of Russian Literature.* New Haven–London: Yale University Press, 1991.

————, ed. *Handbook of Russian Literature.* New Haven–London: Yale University Press, 1985.

Tertz, Abram (Andrei Sinyavsky). *Strolls with Pushkin.* Transl. by Catharine Theimer Nepomnyashchy and Slava I. Yastremsky. New Haven–London: Yale University Press, 1993.

Timasheva, O. "Bodler-kritik" (Baudelaire as a critic). Avtoreferat dissertatsii. Moscow: MGU, 1973.

Tittler, Nancy J. "Annenskij as Translator of French Symbolism." In Marilyn Gaddis

Rose, ed. *Translation Perspectives II.* Selected Papers, 1984–85. Binghamton: State University of New York, 1985, 79–85.

Tolstoi, L. N. *Polnoe sobranie sochinenii* (Complete works). 90 vols. Moscow-Leningrad: Khudozhestvennaia literatura, 1928–58.

Tompkins, Jane P., ed. *Reader-Response Criticism. From Formalism to Post-Structuralism.* Baltimore-London: Johns Hopkins University Press, 1980.

Trahard, Pierre. *Essai critique sur Baudelaire poète* (Critical essay on Baudelaire the poet). Paris: A.-G. Nizet, 1973.

Tschöpl, Carin. *Vjačeslav Ivanov. Dichtung und Dichtungstheorie* (Vyacheslav Ivanov. Poetry and poetic theory). Munich: Otto Sagner, 1968.

Tsvetaeva, Anastasiia. *Vospominaniia* (Memoirs). Izd. 3-e. Moscow: Sovetskii pisatel', 1984.

Tsvetaeva, Marina. *Sochineniia* (Works). 2 vols. Moscow: Khudozhestvennaia literatura, 1980.

Turgenev, I. S. *Polnoe sobranie sochinenii i pisem* (Complete works and letters). 30 vols. Moscow: Nauka, 1978–.

Turquet-Milnes, Gladys. *The Influence of Baudelaire in France and England.* New York: Dutton, 1913.

Ueland, Carol. "From Bohémiens to Gypsies: Vyacheslav Ivanov's Translations of Baudelaire." Paper presented at the 1991 AATSEEL Conference, San Francisco (unpublished).

Ulam, Adam. *In the Name of the People: Prophets and Conspirators in Prerevolutionary Russia.* New York: Viking Press, 1977.

[Urusov, A. I.] Alexandre Ourousof. "Etude sur les textes des 'Fleurs du Mal.' Commentaire et variantes" (Study on the texts of *Les Fleurs du Mal.* Commentary and variants). In *Le Tombeau de Charles Baudelaire.* Ouvrage publié avec la collaboration de Stéphane Mallarmé. Paris: Bibliothèque artistique et littéraire, 1896, 7–37. Repr. New York: AMS Press, 1979.

———. *Kniaz' A. I. Urusov, stat'i ego o teatre, o literature i ob iskusstve. Pis'ma ego. Vospominaniia o nem A. A. Andreevoi i dr.* (Prince A. I. Urusov. Essays on theatre, literature, and art. Letters. Memoirs about him by A. A. Andreeva and others). 3 vols. Moscow: I. N. Kholchev, 1907.

Valentinov, N. [Volskii, N. V.]. *Dva goda s simvolistami* (Two years with the symbolists). Stanford, Calif.: Hoover Institution, 1969.

Valéry, Paul. *Oeuvres* (Works). 2 vols. Paris: Gallimard, 1957.

Velikovskii, S. "Povorotnaia vekha" (A turning point). *Voprosy literatury,* no. 6 (1979), 287–95.

Vengerov, S. A. *Russkaia literatura XX veka* (Russian literature of the 20th century). 3 vols. Moscow: Izd-vo t-va "Mir," 1914–16.

Vengerova, Z. "Bodler" (Baudelaire). *Entsiklopedicheskii slovar' Brokgauz-Efron,* St. Petersburg, 1891, 7:214–15.

———. "Bodler." *Novyi entsiklopedicheskii slovar'*, St. Petersburg, 1912, 7:139–43.

———. "Poety simvolisty vo Frantsii. Verlen, Mallarme, Rimbo, Moreas" (Symbolist poets in France. Verlaine, Mallarmé, Rimbaud, Moréas). *Vestnik Evropy*, no. 10 (1892), 115–43.

———. "Zhizn' Bodlera" (Baudelaire's life). *Literaturnye kharakteristiki*, kn. III. St. Petersburg: Tipo-lit. A. E. Vineke, 1910, 165–87.

Vitkovskii, Evgenii. "Ochen' krupnaia dich', ili rekviem po odnoi ptitse (zametki o tom, kak 'Al'batros' Sharlia Bodlera okolo sta let kovylial po palube russkoi poezii i chto on preterpel za eto vremia) (Very large game, or a requiem to a bird [notes on how Baudelaire's "Albatross" has hobbled for about a century over the deck of Russian poetry and what it suffered during that time]). *Literaturnaia ucheba*, no. 5 (1989), 169–75.

Wanner, Adrian. "Bodler v russkoi kul'ture kontsa XIX–nachala XX veka" (Baudelaire in late 19th- and early 20th-century Russian culture). In B. Averin and E. Neatrour, eds. *Russkaia literatura XX veka: Issledovaniia amerikanskikh uchenykh*. St. Petersburg: Petro Rif, 1994, 24–45.

———. "Le premier regard russe sur Baudelaire et la publication du 'Flacon'" (The first Russian look at Baudelaire and the publication of "Le Flacon"). *Bulletin Baudelairien* 26, no. 2 (December 1991), 43–50.

———. "Metamorphoses of Modernity: Russian Readings of Baudelaire." Ph.D. thesis, Columbia University, 1992.

———. "Populism and Romantic Agony: A Russian Terrorist's Discovery of Baudelaire." *Slavic Review* 52, no. 2 (Summer 1993), 298–317.

———. "Schwarze Dekadenz. Zum Pessimismus in der russischen Lyrik der Jahrhundertwende" (Black decadence. On the pessimism in Russian poetry of the turn of the century). *Neue Zürcher Zeitung*, no. 21 (January 26–27, 1991), 68.

———. "The Genre of the Prose Poem in Russian Literature." Paper presented at the 1991 Ivy League Graduate Student Conference in Russian and Soviet Affairs, Harvard University (unpublished).

Wehrle, I. "Decadence in Russian Literature." *The Modern Encyclopedia of Russian and Soviet Literatures*, ed. Harry B. Weber. Gulf Breeze, Fla.: Academic International Press, 1981, 5:81–99.

West, James. *Russian Symbolism. A Study of Vyacheslav Ivanov and the Russian Symbolist Aesthetic*. London: Methuen, 1970.

Wortman, Richard. *The Crisis of Russian Populism*. Cambridge: Cambridge University Press, 1967.

Zhdanov, Igor'. *Dvoinoi obgon. Stikhi* (Double passing. Poems). Moscow: Sovetskii pisatel', 1978.